Jim W. tells a very compelling story of his own journey from addiction to alcohol followed by more than five decades of recovery in Alcoholics Anonymous. Woven quite masterfully within his story are stories of others he met along the way – some who also found the help they needed and some who didn't. Jim offers great insight and hope to anyone who dares to wonder, "Could my problem be alcoholism?" This book is truly a great read, educational and extremely hopeful.

—Karen Casey, PhD, retired vice president of publications, Hazelden Foundation, and author of *Each Day a New Beginning* (published in 1982), the seminal recovery book for women.
www.womens-spirituality.com

I have thoroughly enjoyed reading *The Bar That Wasn't* by Jim W. A powerful anti-stigma tool, it is an eloquent story that captures the core of the A.A. experience, the mechanisms of change within A.A., and fulfillment of the A.A. promises. Much has been written about A.A.'s Twelve Steps, but I don't think I have ever read a more detailed account of the meaning of "Step Work" on a day-to-day basis and across the stages of long-term recovery. That in itself will make it a valuable resource for those seeking recovery and a worthy contribution to the literature on addiction. It will draw many appreciative readers.

—William L. White, author of *Slaying the Dragon: A History of Addiction Treatment and Recovery in America*, and *Recovery Rising*. bwhite@chestnut.org

After a few pages, *The Bar That Wasn't* had me hooked. I found it to be a truly great story. Jim W. strikes a unique balance between the very personal and the scientific. His personal lived experiences in dealing with alcohol are engaging and enlightening. What is different with this book is blending in the science to make it more than the typical personal narrative to educate the reader to broader issues and facts about addictions. This makes the book suitable not only for those who might be dealing with their own struggles, but also for students and aspiring clinicians to understand addictions and recovery from the perspective of one affected by the conditions.

—Norman G. Hoffmann, PhD, has been an internationally acclaimed expert on the design of assessment tools and the evaluation of treatment services for over forty years. He is the founder of Evince Diagnostics, an online clinical assessment service. norman@evincediagnostics.com

*The Bar That Wasn't* has been written with the help of thousands who have gone before. Jim W.'s story lays out an approach to the Twelve Steps that is at once complex, yet practical. And while no two people are exactly alike, these basic fundamentals will apply to both the newly sober and those with years of sobriety. In the end, this book is about helping people live happier, more satisfying lives by providing them with the tools to establish and maintain long-term sobriety.

—George Watkins, founder of Performance Resource Press and founder of The Employee Assistance Society of North America

# THE
# BAR THAT
# WASN'T

## JOURNEY OF A SOUL IN
## LONG-TERM RECOVERY

JIM W.

**The Bar That Wasn't: Journey Of A Soul In Long-Term Recovery**
Published by Jim W. Publications, LLC
Madison, WI

ISBN: 978-0-578-80135-3
SELF-HELP / Substance Abuse & Addictions / Alcohol

Cover and Interior design by Victoria Wolf, wolfdesignandmarketing.com

QUANTITY PURCHASES: Professional groups, clubs, and other
organizations may qualify for special terms when ordering quantities of
this title. For information, email jimw010666@gmail.com.

*To my sponsors and my wife.*

# CONTENTS

# FORWARD

Jim W's *The Bar That Wasn't* is a beautifully written memoir that chronicles in such amazing detail one man's journey into a life of recovery.

This book follows his pain and quiet desperation with heartfelt honesty. In particular, he captures the destructive power and emotional turmoil caused by his alcoholism.

This is a story of recovery from seemingly hopeless addiction to a life in balance, and a wonderfully detailed and grace-filled journey home to a full, meaningful and productive life. Jim beautifully illustrates the important relationships in his life that carried him through an amazing transformation to wellness, peace and serenity. He makes the 12-step program come alive as the foundation of a life well lived. His message is one of hope and healing that will touch anyone who has suffered from alcoholism or drug dependency and is seeking the grace of a whole life in recovery.

Whether you're new to recovery or an old timer, or seeking recovery for yourself or someone you love, this book is a reminder that we are not alone, and that our stories are not so unique after-all. Jim walks the reader through the process of *taking the Steps* that ultimately lead to a deep spiritual connection to self, family, community and the God of our understanding. It is a journey from acceptance to surrender, self examination to willingness to change, from reconciliation to forgiveness, from daily inventory to the power of prayer and meditation and it culminates with a heartfelt commitment to practice principles and carry the message of hope and recovery to others who still suffer.

Jim describes that moment that all of us who eventually found our way into the rooms of Alcoholics Anonymous has experienced: when we knew we belonged. That move from isolation to connection, from self-centeredness to other-centeredness, from "me" to "we." We were no longer alone on this journey.

This book provides its reader with a fascinating view of what the world of AA and treatment looked like in Minnesota in the 1960s and 70s. For those of us who found our sobriety during these times, it is a nostalgic look at the simplicity and hope filled excitement of those times.

As a pioneer of Employee Assistance Programs (EAP's) in the United States and one of the principle architects of the Minnesota Department of Human Services' Chemical Health Division, it's difficult to calculate the lives that have been saved by one man's journey into recovery. Thank you Jim for being such a fine example of a life well-lived in our community of Twelve Step recovery.

**John H. Curtiss, M.A.**
*President/CEO and co-founder of The Retreat, a chemical dependency recovery center in Wayzata, Minnesota and former Hazelden Foundation executive for 20 years.*

# INTRODUCTION

Sometime in 2012 while sitting at my computer, I started writing about a night in the dead of winter in Minnesota that had changed my life forty-six years earlier. I had no intention of writing a book. I just wanted to see what that night might look like on paper. Once I got started, I kept writing off and on, sometimes leaving it for months. Then the mood would strike, and I'd write some more.

It grew. The first several pages ended up being about how I got to my first A.A. meeting. Then how I took the steps. Nearly eight years passed before I finished Step 12. My sponsor, Mac, read it. He liked it and suggested I send a copy to a mutual friend, Bill White, a great researcher and author of several books on addiction and recovery. I also sent it to Karen Casey, who had served for several years as vice president of publications at Hazelden, and George Watkins, a friend and EAP colleague of many years and a former publisher. Norm Hoffman, PhD, one of the great researchers and designers of addiction diagnostic tools, also looked it over. They and others encouraged me to talk to publishers.

It had no target audience when I started writing; it was just a personal memoir. But those who have read it believe it could fill a gap in the current literature and be of interest to those already in recovery as well as those starting out. They thought sponsors, therapists, and treatment organizations might find it helpful. Personally, I'm not sure about all of that. My purpose in getting this published, and my fervent hope, is that it can help others who are afflicted with alcoholism or any other substance use disorder, whether they are new to recovery or blessed with many years of sobriety.

This work isn't a prescription. As Bill Wilson, co-founder of A.A., often said, there are many paths to recovery both within and outside of A.A. But like any story of struggle, it is full of joy and sorrow, success and failure, isolation and fellowship. Happily, as I come down the homestretch of my life, it looks like it will end well — one day at a time. And just like my life and this memoir, my recovery began unintentionally.

So here it is for you to take what you need and leave the rest: the story of one flawed man's recovery from addiction.

# DEPRESSION

The year 1937 was not a good one for either the economy or a seventeen-year-old Irish Catholic girl in Brownsville, Minnesota. Both were in a state of deep depression. After the stock market crash of 1929, FDR's New Deal had stimulated the economy enough to prevent the disaster from getting worse. But recovery had been snail-slow. Then, in 1937, the Treasury Department, fearing higher inflation, retarded the money growth by suddenly sterilizing gold: it didn't turn out as planned, and the country experienced the third worst recession in its history. It was referred to as the "Recession within the Depression." Correcting its mistake in 1938, Treasury reversed course and the recovery resumed, albeit still slowly, until the United States entered World War II four years later.

That July, in 1937, Catherine O'Hara went on a date with a young man from a neighboring farm, and her evening didn't turn out as she had planned, either. They were intimate and she became pregnant. Not only were the times hard economically, but the O'Hara family had experienced hardships beyond what most families endured.

Driven from South Dakota's parched plains of economic despair in December of 1931, they ended up in Lansing, Iowa, just across the Minnesota-Iowa border from Brownsville. The social pecking order had Scandinavian Lutherans at the top, followed by German Lutherans. German Catholics were third, and at the bottom were the few Irish Catholics who had migrated to the area. The O'Hara's were hard-working share-crop farmers who, after many years of toil, bought the Brownsville farm only to be swindled out of it later. Catherine was an excellent student with a wonderful spirit, the family's shining star, its brightest hope. She had intended to be a teacher.

The O'Haras were devoutly Catholic and lovingly supportive of Catherine when she broke the news. But the times did not embrace an unmarried, pregnant teenager. As loving as it was, the family had no money. Help came from a relative in North Dakota, Jerry O'Hara, who sent $500 — a significant amount for an O'Hara at the time — so Catherine could travel to the Twin Cities and get the assistance she needed through Catholic Charities. She quietly had her baby on April 27, 1938. It was a boy. She christened him Raymond O'Hara. She deeply loved the child, nursed him, and cared for him, but just couldn't see her way clear to raising him alone. Wanting to give him the best chance possible for a good life, she sorrowfully signed the papers a few months later at the courthouse in Caledonia and gave him up for adoption. He ended up in the care of Catholic Charities in St. Paul and was placed in foster homes for nearly two years. Catherine prayed for him every day of her life. Fifty-eight years later, her prayers were answered when he and his wife knocked on her door, commencing a reunion that lasted the rest of her life. It gave him two half-sisters and ultimately a half-brother on his birth-father's side, a birth-father he never met but who by all accounts was a good and decent man and one with whom he felt a visceral connection. His birth-father's obituary stated that he had been an active member of Alcoholics Anonymous for eighteen years when he died on March 13, 1993.

On August 10, 1935, Margaret Bell married Stanley W. She was one of twelve children and the daughter of a coal yard laborer who drank too much. He was the youngest of eleven, the son of an often-violent, alcoholic father who had lost both legs to gangrene. The mothers of both had died while they were young — he at age eleven, she at sixteen. Stanley worked in the sandpaper ovens of Minnesota Mining and Manufacturing Co., earning twenty-two dollars per week; Margaret was a housewife. They looked forward to having a family of their own but found they were unable to conceive. The orphanages and foster homes were teeming with children of all ages, some of whom had been left on the doorstep of a rectory, hospital, or orphanage. But stigma and the economy militated against people adopting someone else's children. Many, in desperation, were giving away their own.

After supper on December 22, 1939, Margaret and Stanley went to a foster home to see "the little boy who danced." They fell in love with him and took him home. He wailed in protest at yet another attachment being torn away, while Stanley steered their 1937 Chrysler Royal up Maryland Avenue to their modest single-bedroom East Side bungalow, and Margaret cried tears of joy. They were thrilled. They would have a child and the Christmas present of a lifetime. Shortly thereafter, they rebaptized him and renamed him James Thomas W. A year later, after numerous home visits by the Catholic Charities social worker, which filled Margaret with anxiety, the adoption was finalized. At last, they really had their child. They had me.

That was how I got started on the path of life: one with many twists and turns, peaks and valleys.

## THE EARLY YEARS

School was difficult for me all the way through. In grade school, it manifested itself in disciplinary problems. These subsided somewhat in a high school that did not require homework or final exams unless a student was absent ten or more days. But this all caught up with me in college. Years later, we were able to figure out that ADHD and mild dyslexia — unknown disorders in the 1950s — were at the heart of my problems. Following the advice of my high school guidance counselor, I disavowed any notion that I could succeed in college and instead took up a trade at St. Paul Boys Vocational School. I would not have even attempted college except a local Catholic priest thought I might have a vocation to the priesthood. He didn't believe the questions I was asking would ever be answered at the trade school. So, in the fall of 1958, I was allowed to enroll at St. John's University, the great Benedictine institution and monastery in Collegeville, Minnesota. Suddenly, I was in competition with students from good Catholic high schools who had had lots of homework and exams and had studied history and the classics. I nearly flunked out in my freshman year and dropped out of the seminary. But the Benedictines, who had been educating young men since the sixth century, saw something I myself couldn't see.

They not only took me back for my sophomore year, but they also secured grant money and a campus job so I could get through. Hardly able to read, I scored in the 22nd percentile in literature on my sophomore comprehensive tests and 90 percent in mathematics. Fascinated by the great writers, poets, and philosophers, I thought, *I don't want to leave this place as dumb as I was when I came in.* So, I majored in English literature, minored in philosophy and sociology, and never took a math or accounting course. I wanted to teach high school. I graduated in 1962 in the lower fourth of my class, and throughout my life I have had anxiety dreams about ascending the commencement exercise stage without enough credits to graduate and having to walk away in empty-handed humiliation without a diploma. Academics aside, there was one thing I could really do well both in high school and college. I could really drink.

In my senior year, I was going to become a father, and I got married. Upon graduation, I was short on teaching credits so I went to work for a Fortune 500 company, Gould National Batteries, as the assistant government contracts administrator. The position afforded exposure to top management. I was number three in a five-person department, with my boss and the department head both approaching retirement age. While the drinking kept me in the good graces of company executives who also drank to excess, it was taking its toll on my personal life.

I am not sure exactly when, but early on I crossed the line from social drinking into alcoholism. From my first drink as a small child, I liked it. By age twenty-seven, I had a drinking problem that was obvious to those close to me, most of whom knew little or nothing about alcoholism.

# LOOKING FOR SOMETHING THAT WASN'T THERE

Late one December night between Christmas and New Year's in 1965, I staggered out of Mitch's Downtowner bar on Robert Street in St. Paul. Instead of turning left to walk the three blocks to the bus stop on 7th Street as I had always done, I turned right.

It had gotten later than usual that night. As had happened hundreds of times before, when walking out onto the sidewalk in front of Mitch's, it hit me how very alone I was. Most of the other regulars who drank there late had long downed their last. A few diehards lingered with me for a while but, as their suppers and the hearts of their waiting loved ones cooled, one by one they headed out. I imagined that, like me, they were probably trying to figure out what they would tell their families this time. That is, those who still had families.

Desolation wafted over me whenever the little money I had at the start of an evening disappeared along with my fellow drinkers. Normally I would have left earlier, but this night I had cashed a five-dollar check. It was supposed to cover one drink, bus fare, and a couple of lunches to finish out the week. Mixed drinks were fifty-five cents, and a bottle of beer, thirty-five cents at Mitch's. In that day, it was cheap enough to get a good buzz on for a lot less than five bucks.

As the night wore on, Mitch's changed. Boisterous gaiety faded into a subdued, drab quiet. By 11 p.m., the bartenders were no longer cracking jokes or even engaging in conversation. Tired and looking forward to getting home, they started cleaning up. All that was in front of me on the bar was an empty glass and bus fare to get home. Somehow, I'd need to scrounge up enough the next morning to get to work, searching the apartment for loose change. I'd have to skip lunch the next two days. I'd need to cash another check the next day, one for seven dollars, to cover a few drinks with enough left over to make a deposit in the checking account to cover the five-dollar check I had written earlier at Mitch's. The day after that, I'd write a ten-dollar check to cover the one for seven. By then it would be Friday, which was payday. Getting down to bus fare was becoming the end line for me many evenings. At that point, with no options, I would finally leave and go home. But not this night.

As my drinking problem deepened over the years, more and more I looked for something in the bars that wasn't there. Not finding it added to the dejection that had steadily grown over time. I began to wonder if my life was going anywhere. It hadn't always been that way. In the beginning, drinking gave me a wonderful feeling of euphoria and command of myself. As intoxication approached, I could usually stop, enjoy the high, and avoid doing anything that I would regret later.

From my early teens through my mid-twenties, alcohol had been my best, most faithful friend. When scared, it gave me courage. When shy, it bolstered my confidence. When sad, it lightened my heart. If I was discouraged, it injected a jolt of optimism. As a teenager, it made me feel like a man. As an adult, it helped me feel like a success, sitting in places like Mitch's with important people from my company, holding forth on any and all subjects. All my insecurities vanished when I drank. And I was good at it. It was a source of pride when people commented on how much I could hold. Most importantly, it was reliable. Alcohol worked every time. It could plug the hole that had somehow, somewhere been torn into my soul and keep the good feelings from seeping out.

But, like a trusted lover who had found another, alcohol began to turn on me. It took a long time before I noticed it and even longer to admit it was true. Over the years, it slowly took more alcohol to close that hole. The odds that I would be intoxicated before reaching euphoria had steadily increased, and by December 1965, it was a toss-up as to which would come first. This night, a remnant of the euphoria had been captured when I took the first drink shortly after work. The laughter and din of the bar crowd, the camaraderie of coworkers, the wisecracks and light sarcasm, all buoyed by alcohol made Mitch's the place where I wanted to be. I felt connected, alive. But, as the bar room emptied, the fantasies of fellowship, romance, and business success evaporated. A quiet emptiness stole in, and the good feelings gave way. Still, I didn't want to go home but with only a quarter in my pocket to get me on the bus, that one more drink I craved was out of the question.

Yet, this night, when stepping out of Mitch's door, I turned to the right, not wanting to face reality quite yet or feel the nascent guilt grow into despair on the bus ride home. I didn't want to think about my responsibilities to Marilyn, my young wife, and my three little children, or fend off from conscious thought the real reason why I wasn't home with them. I didn't want to think about the money problems and the latest of many futile household budgets, written in the ink of denial with their dollar-a-day allocation for alcohol, only to be abandoned before the week was out. I didn't want to think about the sleep I needed in order to get out of bed in the morning to start another day. This day wasn't yet complete to my satisfaction. In a hundred feet or so, I took another right and headed up 4th Street. For just a little while, home would have to wait. I'd catch the next bus. I couldn't face Marilyn feeling this downcast. If she saw this, she would ask what was wrong. Deep down I knew the answer but had lost hope of ever doing anything about it. Instead, I needed to get myself together and enter the apartment as if everything was not just fine, but great. And, most importantly, elude questions about why I was doing what I was doing.

The late-December cold can be bitter in St. Paul. With the temperature in the teens and wind swirling a light snow up and off the sidewalk, that night felt especially harsh. Yet, the weather didn't have my attention much at that moment. I was calling up an old defense mechanism as I walked. Whenever my conscience fought with the driving urge to repeat the experience of an alcohol high, I could let my mind go blank without making a conscious decision to drink. A sort of psychic numbness would set in. The freezing cold helped get me there faster that night. Hatless, I huddled as far under my collar as possible, not really knowing my destination. The fact is, I didn't need to know. When drifting like this, I always ended up where I had to be, in a place where I might get some small fragment of that feeling I desperately needed to make me whole. Slowly the urge would grow to a point where all defenses fell before it. I couldn't deny that I wanted to re-create that alcohol euphoria once more that night, if just for a moment.

My conscience, destined to crumble, didn't go down easily. Fighting one last losing battle, it told me that with the twenty-five cents in my pocket, I could still turn the next corner and three blocks away, hop on a bus and go home. The addiction told me to find a dive. I had long figured out how to get the most alcohol out of my money when I was nearly broke. In those days, skid row bars sold twelve-ounce bottles of beer for twenty-five cents, tap beer in eight-ounce glasses cost fifteen cents, and six-ounce glasses cost a dime. Any combination of tap beer meant more for the money.

Fourth Street was lined with office buildings, retail stores, the St. Paul Public Library, and a warehouse. Most prominently, there was the old St. Paul Auditorium where a few years earlier, under bright lights and amidst roars of a full house, my alma mater, Johnson High, won the state boys high school hockey championship, making our whole side of town proud. This night everything was dark, and a vicarious enjoyment of a decade-old feat of others was the best I could do to offset the despair. Years later the scene flashed back when first hearing the great Chris Smither tune, "Desolation Row." I was the only one out there. About to make another right at Exchange Street and head for the bus, I caught a glimmer of light in the middle of the next block. A tinge of excitement rose from my gut to my chest. There it was again — just the anticipation felt good.

On a site close to where the Xcel Energy Center now stands, I recognized the building and perked up as I approached it. It had once been a mortuary, then a music school where I had taken lessons as a child. The last I knew it had housed a bar and restaurant. Trudging inside craving one last taste, surprise and disappointment waited. There was no bar, no booths, and no tables, just a big, bare brightly lit room with rows of chairs and skinny black frames on the walls enclosing inane quotations. At the far end, a middle-aged man was cleaning out a coffee urn. We were the only ones there.

"What's this?" I asked.

He looked up and said, "We just had an Al-Anon meeting."

"What's that?"

He told me it was a meeting for the wives and loved ones of

alcoholics. By then he had had a chance to eye me up, and as he drew closer, he picked up on the smell of alcohol I had carried from Mitch's.

"Are *you* an alcoholic?" he asked. The question surprised me.

"What? I don't think so. I don't know ..."

"Here, take this with you. It will tell you whether or not you are an alcoholic."

It was the Johns Hopkins questionnaire. Today, it is still a good alcoholism screening tool. I stuffed it in my vest pocket and left, dismissing the encounter.

My dive, King's Bar, was a few blocks away on St. Peter Street. The only guy in there wearing a tie and three-piece suit, I spent my last twenty-five cents and walked the five miles home. When I got there, it was nearly 2 a.m., and the effects of the drinking were beginning to wear off. Marilyn never wanted the sun to set on her anger, so once again she had waited up for me, relieved that I was not hurt or lying somewhere frozen to death. Moments like that might have brought out anger and frustration in many wives. Marilyn was always compassionate. But her face and voice couldn't hide the concern and hurt. I had done it again.

Having a good story to tell when getting home late was part of my routine. Those "meetings" after work at Mitch's included officers of the company where I worked. Knowing them would help my career. I would recount the advice, the rumors, the gossip, some true, some embellished, some completely fabricated. She'd warm up the dinner, and we'd eat late after putting the kids to bed. We had three at that time. Tom was three, Linda was two, and Carmen, one. Twins — Caroline and Kelda — were to come three years later. But this night, the kids had long been put to bed and the dinner in the refrigerator.

While much of what I told Marilyn on these occasions stretched the truth, one connection I had made really was helping me. His name was Harry, and he was the corporate secretary and chief legal counsel of the company. I had been hired into a newly created position of assistant government contracts administrator. While he wasn't my boss, he still became my chief mentor. But, this night, Harry hadn't been at Mitch's. In fact, no one knew where he was. He had been gone from work for nearly two months, and Marilyn knew it. So what would I tell her? Why was I out, drinking, until the bars closed? Who discusses business that late? Who was I with?

Scrambling, I decided a little misdirection might resolve my dilemma. I would show her the Johns Hopkins questionnaire. Several months earlier, she had read an article on alcoholism and A.A. in the *Parade* magazine section of the Sunday *St. Paul Pioneer Press*. Until then, I had worked hard to convince Marilyn that her concern about my drinking was unfounded. It was the result of a difference in our upbringing, a conflict in cultures, particularly our religious backgrounds. She had been raised Baptist and I was a Catholic. Although she had converted to Catholicism, I pressed the case that she still suffered a hangover of sorts from her years in a religion that prohibited drinking. Basically, I didn't have a problem. Her frame of reference was out of whack. Ironically, at our wedding, the only person who had gotten drunk was my childhood buddy Phil, who was also Baptist. I had a solid explanation for that. I went so far as to suggest that Phil probably would not have gotten plastered if he had only had a little more practice drinking earlier in life. The article in *Parade*, however, blew the lid off that and all the other self-serving rationalizations and hypotheses. The tall tales were beginning to be exposed for what they were. Her concern that my drinking was a problem was being confirmed as she sorted things out. She suggested that I attend an A.A. meeting. My response was that I could handle alcohol, but if it ever did become a problem, I most certainly would do something about it.

One of the saddest and most devastating developments in a relationship with an alcoholic is the inability of the afflicted to resist putting the problem onto their partners. Marilyn loved and respected me in the beginning. She believed I was an honest person. Moreover, she had her own insecurities, which I played on without realizing it. So at first, she took me seriously when I concocted stories about the problem being her perception and background. To prove she wasn't shackled to her past, she cut me a lot of slack, only to see me stretch each new boundary further. It is little wonder that by the time a person who has lived under such conditions finally gets to Al-Anon, they are usually confused, often resentful, and sometimes bitter. Their love, no matter how deep, how fervent, how persevering, had been no match for their partner's addiction. That so many can rebuild their lives and find the "new happiness and new serenity" promised by the program makes Al-Anon as great a miracle as A.A. For the most part, those showing up at Al-Anon gave their best only to find betrayal at the end of the line. Many came from homes fraught with addiction, so the boundaries of appropriate behavior were indelibly obscured. Over time they may develop their own set of rationalizations, compromise their own principles, and even use the deep flaws of their alcoholic partner to excuse their own shortcomings. With some, the pain and frustration boil over into angry outbursts. Others just suffer in silence, either quietly seething or going emotionally numb from the pain. But all have one thing in common: They may not take the course in alcoholic pathology for credit, but they certainly are a classmate trapped in a schoolroom with the walls closing in and a padlock on the door.

This night I took out the Johns Hopkins pamphlet, and we sat in the middle of the living room floor and went through the questions. Answering "yes" to only seven of the twenty, I thought I was home free. Less than half seemed pretty good. Then Marilyn pointed to the legend at the bottom of the page. In short, it said, one "yes" and you may have a problem; two and you probably have a problem; three and you definitely have a drinking problem.

I was shocked. "Hell!" I scoffed. "No one could pass this test."

From one viewpoint, that was true. No one *I* drank with could have gotten through with fewer than three "yes" responses. But this wasn't Marilyn and her Baptist orientation saying I had a problem. It wasn't some writer at *Parade* "on a crusade," probably a closet Baptist himself, I had told myself. It was Johns Hopkins University, the founding institution of modern American medicine. How could I argue with that?

At that moment, it became clear what had to be done. The challenge was to go back over the questionnaire and figure out a way to reduce the seven to two so I could at least argue the point. As I write this, it occurs to me that more than fifty-four years have passed since that moment, and I still haven't been able to shrink those seven endorsements down to two. In fact, when I took that screen again after having secured the clarity of six weeks of sobriety, I answered thirteen of them "yes"!

I hadn't gotten what I so desperately yearned for that night. Instead, it turned out to be the start of what I gravely needed: an authentic life.

## HARRY

New Year's Eve fell on Friday that year. Marilyn and I went out with my best friend at work, Dick. His date was my boss's secretary, Diane. We spent the evening ringing in the New Year at a Prescott, Wisconsin, supper club, eating, drinking, and dancing to the music of a good little band and a great female singer who belted out a medley of rock-and-roll hits of the day. Marilyn was radiant; we were all joyful. But what impressed me most about that night is that I drank more than two fifths of wine by myself and barely felt it. From an alcoholic's perspective, it was a near-perfect New Year's Eve.

The following Monday when I got to work, Diane had some great news. Harry was back. Not only was he my mentor, but he was also my most reliable drinking buddy and one of a number of high-level problem drinkers at work who I pointed to in order to rationalize my own consumption. Years later, as the two of us reminisced about the hours we spent at Mitch's, we reflected on the delusional thinking that so characterizes alcoholism. Many nights we were the last of the work gang to leave. We would walk out together and go our separate ways; I would turn left, and he would go right. Often, I thought it was a shame that Harry, with all his ability and power, was undermining his reputation and effectiveness with his drinking. For his part, he saw me as an "up and comer" whose potential was starting to erode because of drinking. We each wondered why the other didn't try to drink less. We each saw the progression of a problem in the other. We were each blind to it in ourselves.

A guy named Duke was my boss, a thirty-five-year company veteran. He was a smart, kind, patient man. In bearing and manner, Duke was the antithesis of Harry. His office was on the thirteenth floor, and Diane and I had our desks just outside his door. He reported directly to the CEO. Harry's palatial office was on the floor below in the executive suite with the CEO and the other top brass. The law library, with the many volumes of Armed Services Procurement Regulations (ASPR) occupying most of one shelf, was on the outer wall of Harry's office. He introduced me to it.

For months, I spent most of my lunch hours there, reading from the ASPR in full view of the top execs who passed by on their way to and from lunch. Harry and his staff were always available to help interpret the law for me. What in the beginning seemed like a drab, unexciting job came alive as I studied and discussed the law governing my work. In time, I became the "go to" guy, outside of the legal department, on federal procurement law. Our company was the largest supplier of electric storage batteries to the federal government, contracting with all branches of the military. We manufactured everything from small communication cells no larger than a flashlight battery all the way to massive submarine batteries housed in large on-board battery rooms. Only Duke and one other person were higher than me in our department, and they were both in their sixties. I was in my mid-twenties with a powerful mentor, a supportive boss, and access to the CEO. The future was bright.

I hadn't been down to the law library for a while. It felt like I didn't belong at that table if Harry wasn't around. But now he was back. I went to his office, but he wasn't there. The number-two lawyer in the department was sitting behind Harry's desk.

"Where's Harry?" I asked his secretary. "I heard he was back."

"Oh, he's up on thirteen."

*On thirteen? That's my floor. What's he doing up there*, I wondered. I returned to my desk and didn't seek him out until the next day.

The first time I ever saw Harry, it was my first week on the job. He was leaving the office of a vice president on our floor. I was at my desk preparing a proposal when an explosion of laughter and conversation erupted. Harry's high-pitched voice carried across the floor, and his affect seemed "put on," as my mother would say. There was something a bit off about him, not only the way he broke the quiet but his appearance. All the executives and mid-level managers were well-dressed and neatly groomed. Not Harry. His suit needed pressing, it looked like he hadn't shaved that morning, and his shoes were scuffed and worn. He had the start of a beer belly that was beginning to overhang his belt. He looked ten years older than he was. Worse, he was attracting negative attention and obviously enjoyed it. A woman sitting at a desk outside the VP's door was pretty loud herself. She had a smoker's voice and a Kentucky accent. She and Harry were enjoying an inside joke. Her name was Shirley, and I was to learn that she was one of the most effective secretaries in the place.

"Who is that?" I asked Diane. She told me his name and added: "He doesn't look it but he's very important around here."

Later, Duke introduced us, and Harry invited me to have a drink at Mitch's with him and a gang from the office. I wasn't all that sure about him, but the invitation felt good. That night, I joined him, Shirley, a guy named Ed, and half a dozen others. Duke wasn't there. It turned out that he wasn't part of the gang. I called Marilyn to let her know I would be late for dinner and who I was with. She sounded impressed. As the evening wore on, I called her a second time and told her to eat without me and put the kids to bed. Mitch's was quieting down, and four of us were the only ones from our company still there. Then Ed left. When it began to feel like three was a crowd, I finally got up to go. Harry and Shirley stayed and seemed to be getting comfortable with each other. I got home around 8:30, eager to describe the evening to Marilyn. I was excited and imagined that she was too.

I was being exposed to information few outside the executive suite knew about. A few weeks later when Duke took some vacation time, I had direct contact with the CEO. Harry and Shirley schooled me on how to interact with him. The experience made me feel like I could belong, a feeling I had rarely felt in my life.

Now, three and a half years later and after hundreds of nights drinking with Harry, enhancing my career but undermining my marriage and my life, I found my way to his new office, a cracker box of a space stuck in a far corner away from the power center of the company.

"Harry, where in the hell have you been?"

I had privately asked myself that question many times in the past, but this was the first time I asked him directly.

Harry had a history of truancies. During my time there, he had gone missing at least twice a year for two, three, sometimes five days. But he always came back ready to roll. There were also times he showed up with a black eye or scratches and bruises on his face. It turned out that he and Shirley had spent many nights together after stopping at Mitch's. Well-proportioned at about five feet eleven and 170 pounds, Shirley was a piece of work, to say the least. Mitch called her "Shirl the Girl." She was smart, seductive, had a wicked sense of humor, knew what everyone was doing at the office, and could drink most guys under the table. More than anything, she was tough as nails.

Harry had a way of irritating people when he drank. Loud and sarcastic, he often put Mitch in a bind. He and Shirley brought a lot of business into the bar, and many were heavy drinkers. Shirley would corral a few secretaries, and that attracted the guys. Most of them had one or two drinks and headed out, but others drank through the grocery money and some through the car payment, keeping Mitch's cash register ringing well past the dinner hour. On the negative side, a few customers were driven away. Harry's mouth was his biggest weapon, an asset in the courtroom and a big liability in the bar room. One night he pissed off one of Mitch's patrons, and it looked like it would come to blows. As the anger escalated, Shirley slipped out of our booth and walked over to a nervous-looking guy sitting at the bar who was trying to ignore the fracas. She rubbed up against his arm and sweet-talked him a little.

"I need to borrow this, honey, okay?"

She emptied the beer from his bottle, topping off the glass sitting in front of him as well as the glasses of a couple of other patrons sitting at the bar.

"Don't worry, good-lookin', I'll buy you another one."

Then, with her hand wrapped around the neck of the empty, she walked over to Mr. Pissed. He was standing now, making threats and increasing the volume. I was pretty sure he was screwing up his courage to launch an attack on Harry. Shirley began the encounter with a few quiet profanities. He said something back to her, and she whacked him full force on the side of the head with the beer bottle. He staggered back and slid halfway to the floor, bracing against another patron to avoid going down.

"F___ with my friends and you f___ with me, ___hole."

That ended it. Mitch told the guy to leave. Holding his head, he stumbled out the door. I never saw him again. A couple of other customers left behind him, including the one whose beer bottle Shirley had borrowed. Smiling, "Shirl the Girl" returned to our booth, and in her Southern drawl, asked,

"Now, where were we?"

The secret source of Harry's bruises slid in alongside him, fully self-satisfied.

This Tuesday morning was different from all the other times Harry had returned to work. First, he hadn't been in Mitch's the night before. He was noticeably slimmer and better groomed than I had ever seen him. His eyes were clear; his voice was low. There were no signs of Shirley's mayhem on his face. Except for the office, he looked like a successful, thirty-eight-year-old executive instead of a disheveled downward-bound failure in his fifties. That was just the surface. When he answered my question, it was a clue to just how much different this occasion really was.

"Well, Jim, I have finally figured out what my problem is. I am a recovering alcoholic."

Suddenly it all became clear. Yet, it didn't seem like news. In the back of my mind, I knew from the beginning that Harry had a problem of some kind. I just couldn't understand why he didn't do something about it. The fact is he was powerless. Beyond that, he wasn't compelled to do anything, either in his personal life or on the job. As his friends pulled away, he had the gang at Mitch's. His wife's unhappiness and threats of divorce were no problem with Shirley on the side. On the job, he had a staff who covered for him and superiors who looked the other way. Like many high-powered executive alcoholics, he was so talented that transgressions which would get most employees fired were tolerated.

Years working in the EAP field revealed a typical course for top executives whose alcoholism hadn't been apparent until they reached the peak of their careers. Almost from the beginning, they were unusually bright and competent. Equally important, they had powerful mentors. Because alcoholism is nearly always characterized by its most blatant, late-stage symptoms, and in the workplace by serious job performance problems, these best and brightest can go for years before their performance becomes an issue, especially in large companies. Their mentors have a stake in the denial process, as well, which is usually enacted through a cover-up process that not only affects the alcoholics but those around them. As these stars rise in the corporation, they are being pulled up by their mentors while pushing their mentors up the ladder ahead of them. So it had been with Harry.

At that time, alcoholic jokes and comic routines abounded, but no one used the term "alcoholic" in polite conversation to describe a specific person known to the parties. And certainly, no one referred to *themselves* as an alcoholic. The skid row stereotype was prevalent even though both the World Health Organization and the American Medical Association had declared alcoholism an illness a decade earlier. But here was Harry, saying he was a "recovering" alcoholic. Not an alcoholic or a cured alcoholic or a recovered alcoholic, but a recover*ing* alcoholic. The adjective impressed me almost as much as the noun. Like most of us, except for the adjective, Harry would never have been able to use the noun to describe himself.

He went on to explain that he had gone through a three-week program at Hazelden followed by an extended stay at a place called "The Old Lodge." This was late in 1965. A few years later, experience with relapse rates and their patterns prompted Hazelden to lengthen their primary residential program to an open-ended approach averaging twenty-seven days for men and thirty-eight days for women. Those who weren't ready to navigate the waters of real life after primary care could spend weeks or months in The Old Lodge, which was much lower intensity, both in care and cost.

Harry said he hadn't had a drink since October 24. Two and a half months.

*My God,* I thought. *That's amazing!*

We touched on the disease concept and discussed his absences from work and his future. During many of those disappearances, he had been in the psych ward at St. Mary's Hospital in Minneapolis, drying out and getting expert psychiatric opinions ranging from manic depression to borderline schizophrenia. The drinking was but a symptom of a deeper-lying problem, they told him. But the Librium, Valium, and God-only-knows-what-else were no match for the primary affliction that was eating his life away. St. Mary's had no answer for people like Harry, until a few years later when Dr. George Mann, with consultation from Vern Johnson, started its alcoholism treatment program based on the Hazelden model.

Our company didn't have any answers in dealing with Harry, either. However, this time it had finally reached its limit. The CEO told Harry he could use the office on thirteen to find another job. His pay would be continued, but not indefinitely. They wanted him out, but they would give him some time. After hearing all this, I made a decision;

the motivation for which is still in question.

For years, Harry and I had played verbal one-upmanship at Mitch's. We talked about Kant and Descartes, Goldwater, Kennedy and Johnson, Arnie and Jack, Unitas and Tarkenton, Mantle and Killebrew, and scores of other topics. Each of us tried to out-do the other, or so it seemed. In retrospect, maybe it was just me trying to keep even with Harry. In truth, no one I knew had ever bested him.

Then, there were the stakes Marilyn and others had driven into my psyche, plus the vague, gnawing feeling that my life was getting away from me. In Harry's absence, I had been drinking alone. The false quilt covering my reality, stitched together by the lies I had been telling myself and Marilyn, was unraveling. Drinking wasn't a mere side feature of Harry's mentoring. Mitch's wasn't just an incidental meeting place made necessary because I could always find him there and discuss people and issues we couldn't talk about in the office. My drinking had been inappropriate for a long time, and one incident that I never shared with Harry or Marilyn would have set off alarm bells with anyone who was even vaguely familiar with alcoholism. A few years earlier, coming back from a trip to Washington, DC, I was denied boarding on a United Airlines flight because I was sick — sick from drinking. The agent was kind and allowed me to lie down in the boarding area until the nausea passed. Then she booked me on a Northwest flight home.

But now, I was drinking alone, just as I had in my late teens and early twenties, which was shrugged off as a "phase" most young guys pass through. Drinking alone, just as I had done while on break from college even though I knew I would need the money later when I was back at school. In those moments I opted for that magic feeling here and now. Alone, as when I trudged up 4th street a few nights before in the freezing cold. Years later, when I first heard the Willie Nelson classic about the loneliness of cowboys, I thought of how well one line described the life of alcoholics — how they never quite find themselves or catch up to their dreams. That was me. And for all his power and position, it had been Harry too.

Sitting across the small pedestrian desk from him in a spare, bare-walled office with a single-line telephone, I still do not know if I was just playing my trump card in a competition to tell a better story, or if the weight of my alcoholism pressed the truth out of me. The words just came out. I disclosed how I had wandered into an Al-Anon meeting thinking it was a bar. I told him about the Johns Hopkins question-naire. Whatever my motive, that small bit of honesty was to change my life but not without one last argument. No conversation with Harry was worth having without some kind of debate. I wasn't going to just roll over. He started things off.

"Well Jim, how about going to a meeting with me and finding out if you have a drinking problem."

"What kind of meeting?"

I knew full well what kind of meeting, but I needed to buy time to organize my rebuttal.

"An A.A. meeting. There's a good one this Thursday night."

"A.A.?"

"Yeah."

"But wouldn't that mean I'd have to stop drinking?"

"We keep it simple. We do it one day at a time. We just don't take that first drink."

They don't take that first drink! Shit — how can anyone get drunk *that* way, I wondered.

"And," he added, "it works."

"Well, Harry, I can see that. If *you* are sober, well … But there's a problem doing this right now. We gave Duke a fifth of Jim Beam for

Christmas, and just today he said Marilyn and I would have to come over and help him and his wife drink it."

"Oh, I don't think you need to worry about Duke. He's an understanding guy."

"Wait a minute! No one is going to talk to Duke!"

"Of course, no one will talk to Duke. But believe me, Jim, he won't miss *your* help drinking *his* whiskey."

"All right, Harry, but there's another thing. Just last week I learned there is a good chance I'll be offered a job in Washington to eventually take over Bill's spot when he retires. Now, if I quit drinking here and then get transferred to Washington, where they probably don't even have A.A. or, if they do, it probably isn't as good as it is here, and then I start drinking again, I could end up in worse shape than if I never stopped drinking to begin with! Maybe I would *never* be able to quit again!"

He just bellowed that old Harry laugh, no less annoying sober at work than half in the tank at Mitch's.

"Well, how about this?" he asked. "Come to a meeting, and if you find that what they are talking about doesn't apply to you, fine. You can go and drink some more."

*Go to an A.A. meeting and still have the option of drinking some more?* I had no rejoinder.

I went back to my desk and called Marilyn.

"Don't plan anything for Thursday night, honey. I am going to an A.A. meeting with Harry."

Going to an A.A. meeting with Harry?! For starters, Marilyn had long given up planning anything two days in advance that required my presence. Moreover, she was wary. Fresh out of affection for Harry, drunk or sober, she questioned his value to my career and our lives. One night months earlier when Harry, Shirley, and I came into our small apartment around 1:30 a.m., drunk and loud, arousing Marilyn and waking the babies, the last of the bloom came off the rose. She didn't see three professionals with important corporate responsibilities who needed to meet after work so they could refine their business acumen. We were just three drunks. Pure and simple.

An A.A. meeting with Harry? Was this the ultimate excuse for getting out of the house to drink?

## STEP TWELVE

A.A.'s 12th Step embodies the organizing principle for nearly everything in human experience. Much of the good that occurs in the world depends on it.

> *"Having had a spiritual awakening as the result of these steps, we carried this message to alcoholics and practiced these principles in all our affairs." (Alcoholics Anonymous, p. 60.)*[1]

During my lifetime, we learned to split the atom and splice the gene. Although we've been doing this for decades and have gone beyond those huge milestones to quarks and neutrinos, it is still astonishing. So are the iPhones that have more computing power than the old mainframes once housed on entire floors in large buildings, as they helped put humans on the moon. Or arthroscopic, robotically guided heart bypass surgery with the surgeon seated in a booth several feet away from the patient; not to mention artificial intelligence, online shopping with drone delivery, or self-driving vehicles. Whether it was these recent manifestations of human genius or those that came earlier — Edison's incandescent lightbulb, Dante's Divine Comedy, Tchaikovsky's Fifth Symphony, Henry Ford's Model T, E. L. Masqueray's magnificent Cathedral of St. Paul, or Marjorie Merriweather Post's brilliant formation of General Foods, which changed the way the world ate — the essence of Step 12 was at work.

The inventor, the scientist, the poet, the composer, the industrialist, the architect—all first had a spiritual awakening, a vision of what might be. But it didn't come out of thin air. Natural talent was important, to be sure, but it wasn't the entire story. The awakening came as the result of what they had struggled to learn from those who had gone before, ascending step by step in understanding, birthing the discipline and creativity those steps spawned in developing the God-given genius of their imaginations, and optimizing the resources at hand. Then, they carried the message of their vision — their awakening — to others and continued to practice the principles to refine their creations and move on to new ones.

The awakening, clear and unblemished, is spiritual. The practice, fraught with error and repetition, is human. The message is both.

The life of recovery with which I have been blessed did not start with *my* 1st Step, but with *Harry's* 12th. Having had a spiritual awakening as the result of A.A.'s twelve steps, he was carrying the message, both in his office and when he knocked on our apartment door the evening of January 6, 1966. Less than three months sober, "The Promises" of the program had taken root in his recovery, and he intuitively knew how to handle a situation that would have otherwise baffled him. He knew what to say to me without a script. But for the power of his spiritual awakening and what it enabled him to see in me, both as I was and as I could be, I could never have connected with any message he tried to convey about my drinking. Given our history, it just would have been more balderdash, like our arguments about sports and politics while getting drunk at Mitch's.

I had one last drink at 4:55 p.m. that Thursday after work. A vodka sour, and, of course, it was at Mitch's. I cashed a five-dollar check, walked out, turned to the left, got on the bus, and was home by 5:30 p.m. We ate dinner, I played with the kids, and we put them to bed.

Harry got there a little after eight o'clock. When he told Marilyn we would be back at around 10:30, she could only hope it was true. But, at long last, after the hundreds of phone calls from Mitch's that I would soon be on my way only to show up hours later, the countless daily vows in the morning with "see-you-for-supper" kisses, the Hail Mary's on the bus to work pleading for the strength to not get drunk that day, the endless plans and schemes to do better the next time, the fervent pledges to never do *that* again, finally, a promise was made that would not be broken.

## MERELY POWERLESS

The meeting was at the Uptown Club located at Cleveland and Grand Avenues in St. Paul. The place had once been a saloon. Today it's a restaurant and the Uptown Club has had a beautiful new home for several years in one of the old mansions on Summit Avenue. The weather that night was bad, and we walked in after the meeting was underway. Normally they would have gone back to Step 1 when a first-timer came in, but they had already gotten started on Step 4 — *the searching and fearless moral inventory.* Warren M. was leading the meeting. Unbelievable to me at the time, Warren had ten years of sobriety. While writing this, Warren died having enjoyed fifty-nine years of continuous sobriety without interruption.

We had missed the reading of the Preamble from *The Big Book* and the recitation of the steps. There were a dozen people sitting around the table, including three women. I still remember their names. Jan was about thirty-two, Arial was in her fifties, and Anita was in her seventies. There was Mark, and Dick, two Bills, and an elderly gentleman named Knight. A guy named Bob who owned a shoe repair shop was giving the lead. He spoke of how his inventory revealed the extent to which he lied, even when he didn't need to. Admitting he was a liar didn't come easy, but he did it, and it raised the curtain of denial that had shrouded the truth about the rest of his life. It resonated with me. So did all the other stories shared around the table. Finally, Warren asked if I wanted to say anything.

"I don't know if I am an alcoholic or not," I said, "but I thought I'd just come to check it out."

At the far end of the table, a guy named Bill B. replied,

"Don't worry about it, kid, we never saw anyone walk through that door who wasn't."

I believed him. I believed it all. Everything they said about what they had found in their 4th Step inventory resonated with me. No, I hadn't gone down the road as far as any of them had. The average age in the room had to be early fifties, and I was only twenty-seven. But I knew I was capable of all they had described; it was all waiting for me.

What I *had* done was more than enough: the neglect of my family, the infidelities, the cheating on expense reports. "Borrowing" ten dollars my son's godmother had given him for his first birthday and never paying it back. Working two jobs and still falling behind financially. The underlying guilt, shame, and self-loathing, and how it could all be wiped away for a little while with alcohol. And yes, as Bob had talked about, the many, many lies.

They also spoke of the promises they had broken, how they had hurt their families while never intending to, the dangerous situations they had gotten into, and the desperate worry they had caused to loved ones. We weren't on Step 1, but the tales told were all about powerlessness and unmanageability. They talked about the insidious progression of the illness and where they had been at age seventeen or twenty-seven or thirty-seven. How their "best friend," alcohol, had turned on them and how its manifestation in their behavior was a complete contradiction of their values. They told of how, over time, alcohol had been winning more and more battles whenever the choice was between meeting a responsibility or satisfying the urge to drink. Willpower didn't work. Then, somehow, like many small, watery deposits landlocked beneath the earth's surface which eventually seeped past the roots and weeds, through the muck and across the bedrock, they had each streamed into the great river of recovery to be carried forth to freedom. They had found A.A.

Through all of this, there was a powerful message of hope. I knew that I was just like the people in that room. It was clear where my life was heading if I didn't stop drinking. But, while they and I were profoundly alike, there was one huge difference. They were sober.

Woven into the stories of the wreckage of their lives, they laughed a lot, and it wasn't for show. They really were happy. Above all, they were grateful and expressed it. I wanted what they had, without having yet heard that phrase in *The Big Book*. There was no question that they were alcoholics, except they didn't have to drink, and they were building successful lives without it. I wanted to be like them.

Someone has said that union is the highest reach of the soul. I believe that. In everyday terms, we all need to be connected to something at a spiritual level. The question is, to what?

As far back as I could remember, my soul had been in a state of searching for union but rarely finding it. As an adopted only child, I had felt like an outsider most of my life. Margaret and Stanley were good parents, but it seemed as though we were from different planets. At some crucial level, we were a mystery to each other. We didn't connect, and we didn't understand each other. After I turned twenty-one, occasionally on a Saturday morning, I would drop in at Archie Schweitz's tavern on St. Paul's East Side to have a beer and a shot with my dad. It was the only time I had felt connected to him, and it took alcohol to do it. The rest of the time, we lived in separate worlds. The night I had wandered up 4th street, I was hopelessly in union with the disease of alcoholism.

But, that Thursday night at the Uptown Club, I knew I was where I belonged. These people, most of whom had never laid eyes on me until then, knew me in a way no one else did. My parents, my closest friends, even my wife didn't have their insight into me. They knew me better than I knew myself. This was the union I had long sought. I belonged. Walking into that meeting, I was hopeless, helpless, and powerless. Walking out, I was merely powerless.

We got back to the apartment at about 10:20 p.m. Harry remarked on the glow on Marilyn's face when we came through the door. She invited him to stay for a cup of coffee. He declined. He wanted to get up early to seek his new career.

As for me, I didn't need to go anywhere, or do anything else. I was home, starting a new life.

# HOLDING ON

No one knows how many first-timers in A.A. end up being one-timers, never to come back, but the number is great. And, notwithstanding Bill B.'s statement at my first meeting, non-alcoholics do occasionally wander into closed A.A. meetings. There are also short-timers who attend for a while and quit. Some stay sober for lengths of time that vary from a few hours to several years. Other alcoholics get sober without the benefit of treatment or A.A., and some experts think this number is significant. Back in the 1970s, alcoholism professionals believed that spontaneous remission rates were about 30 percent for those on treatment program waiting lists, and more recent studies[2] do not vary greatly from that estimate. I wasn't in any of these categories.

I no longer had any question in my mind that I was an alcoholic. At that first meeting, I found something I knew I needed, and I wasn't going to risk losing it. I believed the stories about old-timers with long-term sobriety who took that first drink and never made it back. Today, I advise my own sponsees not to take chances. I realize the choice is theirs. But I try to help them get to a point where whatever they decide is truly an informed choice.

So, who is eligible for A.A.? Tradition 3 defines it:

*The only requirement for A.A. membership is a desire to stop drinking. (Twelve Steps and Twelve Traditions, p. 139.)*[3]

There is no requirement that one be diagnosed as an alcoholic, either by themselves or someone else. Had it been a prerequisite, Harry might never have gotten me out of the house that Thursday evening many years ago. At the same time, A.A. wasn't established for the benefit of people who have no problem with drinking but are simply on a quest for self-improvement. Generally, people who desire to stop drinking do so. Those who cannot need more than their own personal resources.

Fundamentally, people have one of four relationships with alcohol and drugs. About one-third of the adult population does not drink or use illicit drugs at all. They are abstainers. Then there are social drinkers, people who drink responsibly, meaning that their drinking has no adverse effect on themselves or anyone else. They avoid getting intoxicated, often feeling uncomfortable when they get close to it. Like the abstainers, if social drinkers use medication at all, it is as prescribed, taking only the dosage recommended, for the time period specified, and for its specifically intended purpose. Roughly forty percent of the adult population falls into this category.

Neither social drinkers nor abstainers pose problems. The problems begin with the third group. Traditionally this group has been referred to as alcohol and drug "abusers." However, addiction scholars William White and others have launched a move calling on the profession to discard the term because it denotes willful mistreatment, connotes moral depravity, and evokes a response from therapists and lay-people alike which reliably produces an attitude of blame and punishment.[4] Rather than "abuse" or "abuser" we preferred the term "alcohol or drug problem use" or "alcohol or drug problem user." People in this group occasionally become intoxicated or drink inappropriately or at inappropriate times. Sometimes they drink too much and still operate a vehicle. They may occasionally use prescription drugs or over-the-counter medications in a manner other than as prescribed or for inappropriate purposes. Some use illicit drugs without becoming addicted, which by virtue of the illegality is a problem. But, *and this is key,* they haven't lost control. When they intend to have two drinks, they have only two, not three or four or eight. At any given time, about one adult in six, or 17 percent fall into this category. Some migrate between social drinking and problem drinking, but the problem drinking is usually for limited periods of time.

Finally, there is the relationship alcoholics and drug addicts have with mood-altering substances. Definitions of the disorder abound and may be complex or simple, depending on who proffers them. But over the years, after clearing away the confounding variables, the research[5] has been relatively consistent on this point. Starting with the work of Dan Cahalan, PhD, and Robin Room, MA, in 1972,[6] about 8 to 11 percent of the adult male population fall into this category, which computes to about 12 to 17 percent of those who drink.[7,8] Subsequent studies have shown that men have a higher rate than women. The common denominator, regardless of the circumstances and what they drink, how they drink, or what drugs they use, is that they are having trouble in their lives as a result of drinking and do not have command of their use. To a greater or lesser extent, they have lost control, and over time this becomes more apparent as the disease progresses.

Determining who is or isn't an alcoholic requires more than personal opinion. Many good screening tools are available by which to determine the need for a full evaluation or treatment. The CAGE, the TADD, and the US military's DD Form 2900 used in connection with the Post Deployment Health Re-Assessment program are all excellent screening tools. And, of course, there is my sentimental favorite, the Johns Hopkins questionnaire. No tool is 100 percent foolproof, but they do not need to be in order to be valid. Most have a false positive risk between 2 and 5 percent, and a false negative of about 10 percent. Alcoholics seeking to rationalize their way out of considering the need to quit will nearly always claim to be the exception to the rule and, as I did, try to dismiss the results. At the time I attended my first A.A. meeting, a good working definition of alcoholism was passed on to me, and I used it for years in my own recovery, as an A.A. sponsor, and as an EAP professional. Harry said it best:

*"If you're having trouble in any area of your life as a result of drinking and you continue to drink in spite of the harmful consequences, that's alcoholism."*

About nine times out of ten, people who meet this description are, in fact, alcoholics.

A key element in any definition of alcoholism is the loss of control. It may be as seemingly benign as the inability to take only one drink instead of two, or it may manifest itself in imminent life- threatening behavior. But, if a person repeatedly devises failed plans to control their drinking, or cannot predict what they will do once they take a drink, or breaks promises regarding their drinking, or lies about how much or whether they drink, or drinks more than they intended to, or has considered stopping drinking or cutting back but hasn't been able to, or has family or friends who have expressed concern about their drinking — they are probably in serious trouble. Any one of these symptoms points to a loss of control, and a professional evaluation can result in a confirmed diagnosis of alcoholism as often as nine times out of ten. The greater the number of these symptoms, the slimmer the chance that the person is not an alcoholic. And, if they are an alcoholic, they cannot safely use other drugs, including many prescribed by a physician. Conversely, neither can drug addicts safely drink. These and a host of other, non-substance addictions — food, gambling, sex — seem to run in bunches. Anyone afflicted with one addiction is far more vulnerable to developing another.

Although I was young when Harry took me to my first meeting and didn't fit the customary rehab patient profile with divorces, jail time, lost jobs, or homelessness, I would have been a good candidate for treatment had it been available. Not the contemporary managed-care pretense that has come to pass for treatment with its three to five days of initial authorization and then another two or three days if the case manager is generous. And not one-to-one counseling. I needed the core of what programs like Hazelden, Lutheran General Hospital, and The Caron Foundation (then Chit Chat Farms) provided and what Betty Ford, The Hanley Center, and The Retreat offered later. Had the essence of Hazelden's residential program been available on an outpatient basis, it would have been a near-perfect fit for me. But it is doubtful such a program would have helped Harry or most of the others we drank with, many of whom ultimately died from the disease. They needed the safety of a residential program without life's daily distractions and temptations, until they could acquire the tools to stop and stay stopped.

I was more sheltered than most alcoholics coming into the program at that time. We couldn't afford a car, so accessibility to bars and liquor stores was limited. Getting the urge to drink while on the bus ride home from work was a lot safer than if I had been driving a car where, in the flash of an eye, I could take a detour to one of the dozens of bars between work and home. Since Marilyn hardly ever drank, much less had a problem with it, I had no drinking partner in my family and therefore no trigger at home. Yet, in retrospect, a good primary outpatient program would have helped me to advance faster in my recovery. Regardless, I would not have been able to recover on my own.

## RECOVERY STARTS WITH "WE" NOT "ME"

Unfortunately, even in Minnesota, treatment options were limited at that time. There was Willmar State Hospital for the indigent, and I wasn't indigent. There was Pioneer House for Hennepin County street alcoholics, and I lived in Ramsey County. Then there was Hazelden but, as I have enjoyed saying, "It was too damned expensive: It cost $290 for three weeks!"

With so little treatment and formally structured "aftercare" still several years away, one might wonder how anyone got sober without perpetually bouncing in and out. The idea of ninety meetings in ninety days wasn't the staple it later became because there weren't enough meetings available. Then as now, many people did not make it the first time.

What saved the day at that time for many of us was "Black Belt" sponsorship. Virtually no newcomer left a meeting without exchanging phone numbers with several members. At the Uptown Group, at least two members followed up with phone calls and face-to-face contact during the following week. They didn't wait for the newcomer to call them. The only telephones in those days were landlines in homes, offices, and phone booths. There was no voicemail, call forwarding, or call waiting. Email, FAX, and cell phones were still decades away. Members talked with each other between and immediately before meetings. They reported on how the newcomer was doing, whether they would be attending the next meeting, and if not, why not. The focus was on what the newcomer needed in order to stay sober. Not in the way a typical psychologist or social worker might relate to a client in searching for underlying causes, but with a total focus on how to simply help newcomers to not take that first drink. One member would volunteer to take the lead role. The newcomer was his or her "pigeon." Most every newcomer had a "temporary sponsor" from the very beginning. If it seemed like a good fit, it evolved into a more permanent relationship. If, at any time during the early weeks, the fit seemed off, another member filled the role. As is true today, either party could cancel at any time.

Transportation to the first few meetings was almost automatically provided. It was an opportunity for the member to talk with the newcomer on the way to and from meetings, and to assure a safe route getting there and back home again without the temptation to stop off on the way. The sponsor's job, then as now, was to help the newcomer get through the twelve steps of the program. But it wasn't treated as a casual matter. The belief that if the person "really wants it, they'll get it," wasn't assumed nor used as a litmus test. The basic operating principle focused on powerlessness and how to deal with it. Then as now, early in recovery the new person's desire alone too closely resembled the many failed attempts to quit through "single-handed combat" referred to in the literature. The underlying concern, more than anything, was that this may be the alcoholic's only shot at sobriety.

Experience has taught me that when dealing with any temptation, if the choice is between desire and willpower, put your money on desire every time. Many newcomers were not considered strong enough to "really want it" without getting a few days or weeks of abstinence under their belts. This enabled them first to find that they would not die without a drink and then experience how much better life could be sober, even early on. Tradition 3 needed to be nurtured into operating mode. This was not left to chance or presumed to have occurred spontaneously before the person came through the doors of A.A. Sometimes it was present, of course, but many times it wasn't. Sorting out who had the desire and who didn't, or how strong or weak it was, simply was too hard to ascertain with any real certainty. For me, it still is. So, when a newcomer came to an A.A. meeting, it was assumed there was some level of desire, or they wouldn't be there. Nevertheless, no matter how impressive they sounded, it wasn't assumed that desire alone would be enough to get the newcomer to the next meeting, which could be as much as a week later.

Was this invasive? In some instances, perhaps. But newcomers could always say "no," and some did. Did it violate anyone's rights? No. In all likelihood, it helped struggling alcoholics avoid violating someone else's rights, such as abusing or neglecting family members, endangering pedestrians and drivers, shortchanging employers, or frustrating union reps. And the member who extended the hand of help benefited as much as the newcomer. The newcomers tried to hold onto what they found in their first few meetings, and the members held onto the newcomers. Sponsors didn't try to do all the work by themselves.

In the ensuing years, formal treatment has been a godsend for untold numbers of alcoholics and drug addicts. It helps people face their problems, gives them tools to cope, and gets them started in the right direction. Good treatment also identifies and addresses comorbid disorders — conditions in which two or more primary disorders interact and exacerbate each other. But it isn't the entire answer. Treatment takes place in a safe setting for a limited time. Recovery takes place in the real world for the balance of one's life.

The principles of sponsorship I learned so many years ago, thankfully, are largely practiced today. And they still work. So does the old

A.A. axiom, "Stick with the winners." Early on, Harry arranged for me to meet some winners, and their influence remains with me today.

## JOE, BILL, AND ANITA

The day after my first meeting, Harry and I had lunch and he introduced me to Joe. Joe was a top-notch personal injury attorney who eventually left the practice of law to teach transcendental meditation. It's a skill he still teaches and practices. Among others, he works directly with residents in recovery programs in Minnesota. The day we met, Joe had two and a half years of sobriety. Today, he's in his fifty-seventh year.

Joe shared three major messages during that lunch. First, he recalled how he had attended A.A. meetings for six months without opening his mouth. He went, he absorbed, he took what he needed to stay sober, and he left the rest. While sharing is essential, and some believe that even a newly recovering alcoholic *has* to share in order to get sober, this didn't apply to Joe. Second, at that time he questioned the idea of a hereafter and the conventional understanding of God. But he did admit he was powerless and that his life was unmanageable. So, where did the power to stay sober come from, if not from God? This accomplished courtroom orator, who could regale ordinary folks sitting in a jury box with logic and complex legal theory, didn't try to explain this apparent theological disconnect. It didn't bother him one bit. The founders must have had guys like Joe in mind when they said:

> *"First, Alcoholics Anonymous does not demand that you believe anything. All its twelve steps are but suggestions." (12 and 12, p. 26)*

Finally, Joe said he needed a different kind of A.A. meeting, one where people shared their feelings and didn't indulge in strident orthodoxy. He hated pontificating and long drunk-a-logs.

Serenity is essential to a happy recovery, and the ability to live with ambiguity and paradox plays a large role in acquiring it. So here was Joe, a highly rational and articulate man who had been mute in his first six months in A.A., now believing that openly discussing feelings in the "here and now" was crucial. To him, this was more genuine and more helpful than what he had been hearing. Without denying the importance of A.A.'s twelve steps, doctrinaire declarations, sermonettes, and obsequious endorsements of A.A. didn't impress him. They may have kept many alcoholics sober, but Joe wasn't among them. He wanted something else, something he felt was "real." He had searched for two years but couldn't find a meeting to his satisfaction. So he started his own.

Joe's new meeting met on Wednesday nights at the Unitarian Church on the corner of Holly and Grotto, right in the middle of St. Paul's Black ghetto. It was the first racially diverse meeting in town. Harry had commented that it would be good for me to see how the disease treats everyone the same, regardless of race. It was a discussion meeting, and one night the sharing evolved into the issue of sex and alcohol. A Black guy who introduced himself as Slim was talking about a woman, not his wife, whom he loved "being" with, but she was a drug addict. However, he thought he could navigate those waters. His buddy, Spike, who knew the woman, commented that Slim was probably a "goner" already if he thought he could resist having a little pot or a drink once he was under this particular lady's spell.

"She got moves just for *you*, man. Ain't no way you're gonna get outta that one alive."

The next week, the woman showed up at the meeting with Slim's wife! Somehow, after a few stops and starts, they all got sober, at least for a while.

The fact that the Unity group welcomed those who were addicted to drugs as well as alcohol was another distinctive feature of the meeting. Joe believed that anyone addicted to any substance, including alcohol, needed to abstain from all of them in order to recover. It was at that meeting that I first heard the term "chemically dependent person." In what proved to be a misinterpretation of Tradition 10, many A.A. meetings at that time considered drugs to be an *"outside, controversial issue,"* like politics and religion. A popular expression justifying the exclusion of drug-addicted people from A.A. meetings was:

*"If you can't smell 'em, you can't tell 'em."*

This interpretation failed to recognize a deadly reality. It wasn't uncommon for dually addicted people to celebrate A.A. dry dates while popping pills or smoking pot. Conversely, many drug addicts were convinced that it was okay to drink. The Unity meeting wasn't having any of that. Alcohol was considered to be a drug, and any drug was off limits. It followed the twelve steps of A.A., but with a focus on how the participants were feeling at that moment. The premise was that the feeling often preceded the thought that preceded the behavior that led to relapse. The Unity group was a mainstay for the first several years of my sobriety, although it never secured A.A.'s GSO acknowledgment as a legitimate A.A. meeting. We met anyway and followed the steps. It grew to several meetings, including two Al-Anon-type groups. As of this writing, it still meets every Wednesday night. It's still not listed in the local A.A. meeting directory.

A few years later, under the leadership of Leonard Boche and Governor Wendell Anderson, the state of Minnesota merged two state agencies — the Minnesota Commission on Alcohol Problems and the Drug Abuse Section of the State Planning Agency — into a single state authority called The Chemical Dependency Programs Division. The belief that if a person was addicted to one substance, they likely could not safely handle any mood-altering chemical became conventional wisdom, not only in Minnesota but throughout recovering communities and treatment centers across the country. I like to think that Joe's insight contributed significantly to the enlightened attitude that took hold on the issue of chemical dependency.

During the week following my first A.A. meeting, I attended the Wednesday night Unity Group and the Thursday night Uptown meeting. I liked them both. Already I was experiencing some benefits of recovery. I was thrilled to reach Tuesday before I spent the last of the five-dollar check I had cashed at Mitch's the previous Thursday after work when I had my last drink. I had gotten home on time every night for dinner.

Harry and I had lunch nearly every day, often with another alcoholic. One day, Joe introduced a guy named Bill from Hudson, Wisconsin, with more than twenty years of sobriety. He was intense, and it seemed that a lot of anger was always just beneath the surface. He was the opposite both of Joe, who was naturally mellow, and Harry, who had gained a large measure of serenity. Off-putting effect aside, Bill had years of experience dealing with demons that didn't automatically go away when he stopped drinking. His most enduring message was that after an alcoholic has been sober awhile, he or she may find problems with which A.A. is not capable of dealing. Many may dissolve, but some may persist or even get worse. If that occurred, Bill was convinced that we needed professional help. This was contrary to what many A.A. members believed at the time, which was understandable given the propensity of the medical profession to use addictive drugs to address a host of illnesses, including alcoholism.

While Joe and Harry had both been misdiagnosed as manic depressive (bipolar disorder) during their drinking days, Bill really was afflicted with that disease and probably more. Trying to control mood swings that he believed should have disappeared with sobriety, he struggled to figure out what he was doing wrong. Finally, after years of searching, he found a psychiatrist who understood alcoholism. The discovery of lithium was still in the future, so Bill underwent psychotherapy and electroconvulsive therapy. Neither did much to remediate the symptoms, but at least he knew that the problem did not lie in his attitude or how he worked the steps. Some twenty years later in an A.A. meeting in Palatine, Illinois, a young woman named Laura sitting next to me spoke of having two primary illnesses: alcoholism and bipolar disorder.

"So," she said, "when you suggest that I get off the pity pot and think positively, it doesn't work. When you suggest that I need to pray and meditate to get some serenity and come down from being hyper, that doesn't work either."

What worked for her was an insightful psychiatrist at the Lutheran General alcohol treatment program who had monitored her mood swings for several weeks so he would get the prescription for lithium just right and then managed the medication over time.

Unfortunately, most health care professionals, even today, do not have adequate training in addictions. Incredibly, a few still do not believe it is a legitimate disease. Then, as now, Laura's psychiatrist was a rare find. He did not make the kind of binary diagnosis that characterizes much of medical practice today, in which managed care forces primary care doctors into a practice pattern where they can only spend seven or eight minutes in front of a patient and try to narrow the 170 ICD-10 codes down to one or two by using branch logic. All too often, the branch they pursue does not include mental or substance-use disorders. So, these afflictions go undiagnosed and untreated even though they are present at least 40 percent of the time.

Laura's psychiatrist understood comorbidity, the condition where two or more medical or mental disorders exist simultaneously, each exacerbating the other. Current research[9] indicates that at least 30 percent of alcoholics have a comorbid mental health issue, usually an affective or anxiety disorder, in addition to various physical disorders as the addiction progresses. For poly-drug addicts, the comorbidity rate with a mental disorder is even higher. Years of experience in the EAP field has shown me that neither disorder in a comorbid condition is likely to yield to treatment without treating the other, as well.

Bill's psychiatrist made the effort to learn, but medical science hadn't yet provided him with the tools. Although he wasn't drinking, Bill was not really capable of developing the kind of connections with people that can make recovery enjoyable. When he shared his experience, strength, and hope, he often sounded like an angry drill sergeant, ready to knock your block off. Looking back, I realize that his recovery was quite heroic. It was based almost entirely on not taking that first drink and the intellectual satisfaction produced by that singular achievement. Sadly, when it came to just plain feeling good, it wasn't there for him. He was abstinent and had worked the steps, but without the emotional rewards that usually come with it. Yet, his wisdom was most valuable. In seeking psychiatric help and sharing it, he opened my mind to the benefits of therapy and the fact that I might need more than A.A. as time passed. Years later at the urging of a friend, I finally took Bill's advice and sought professional help. After a number of false starts, it made a huge difference in my life.

Anita was a mainstay at the Uptown meeting. She was almost as different from Bill as one person can be from another. A tall, elegant elderly woman of means, she was well-educated, articulate, very kind, and never raised her voice. At the time, she was seventy-two years old. When she shared, people paid attention. Not only was she always on target, but we knew that if someone with her gifts — spiritual, material, intellectual, and physical — could become an alcoholic, anyone could. Indeed, alcoholism was an equal opportunity disease. At the Uptown meeting, the essence of the life-destroying experiences Anita shared was practically the same as that disclosed in the stories of the poor African American drug addicts at the Unity group.

Anita was one of the oldest members of A.A. in St. Paul at that time, and I was one of the youngest. She took to me, seeing the promise of a full life of sobriety she hadn't had the opportunity to enjoy herself. One day, I commented that with a normal life expectancy, I would need to stay sober forty-five to fifty years! The meetings and the literature emphasize that resentment is a killer for alcoholics, and it is true. I've seen it. But it is often preceded by an unhealthy dose of self-pity. Anita picked up on that in my comment and offered this perspective:

"Darling, we can always think of why staying sober is hard. And we can always see ourselves as unique. I could say, 'My goodness, I've been drinking for fifty years, why quit now?' If I dwell on that, I'll be drunk in two weeks. On the other hand, you could say, 'Gee, fifty years is a long, long time to stay sober,' and you can be drunk in two weeks, too. We do this one day at a time."

The message was clear: Be grateful for what you have today. The past and future are out of our hands.

Anita's point proved crucial to my recovery. Everyone has tough luck and bad times during their lives. But, as someone has said, "10 percent of life is what happens to you; 90 percent is how you respond to it."

Self-pity can destroy our lives no matter what our lot. How I thought and what I thought would dictate how I would live and the kind of life I would have. I was an alcoholic, and I had no choice about that. But I did have a choice of either being a practicing or a recovering alcoholic. Further, even if I chose to be a recovering alcoholic, I still could be miserable. It was up to me. Anita gave me my first copy of the little black book, "24 Hours a Day." In the first few passages in January, it talks about alcoholism as a "soul sickness." I certainly understood what that meant.

Little did I realize how important those early lessons would be. From Joe, I learned that orthodoxy is but a guide and has limitations. Just because a newcomer is quiet doesn't mean the message isn't getting through. Just because someone questions the idea of a hereafter or the prevailing definition of God doesn't mean they cannot achieve a spiritual life and sobriety. And just because they may not sound logical doesn't mean they are in error. From Bill, I learned that it is a mistake to disregard the wisdom of people who have a disagreeable manner, and we shortchange ourselves if we do not look for the meaning intended when someone's words are inadequate. Moreover, there will certainly be moments, perhaps even long periods of time, when in spite of our best efforts, we still do not feel happy. We need to utilize all the available resources, which often means we need more than A.A. From Anita, I learned that anyone could become an alcoholic, regardless of privilege or stage of life, and whether one stops drinking early in life or later. This moment, right here and right now, is the only one we can control. There is no room for self-pity in a happy life.

A.A. is not Psychology 101, and recovering alcoholics are not therapists trained in transference, counter-transference, or how to empathically engage others. While some have such skills either naturally or through training, most do not. But, if we are sober, we all have something of value to share. Early on, with less than three months' sobriety himself, Harry helped me to understand that. So did Joe, Bill, and Anita. They planted seeds, producing fruit that has sustained me throughout my life. Each in their own way was a pioneer who neither abandoned the orthodoxy of the day nor allowed it to retard their recovery and their ability to share their true experience, strength, and hope with others. Each had a profound effect on my recovery.

## THE HOLE

It seems there had always been a hole in my soul, and it was there long before my drinking became a problem. The joy of life would penetrate to a place inside me, but then somehow it would leak back out through that hole, leaving an empty feeling and a pervasive longing to be someone other than who I was and yearning to be somewhere other than where I was. Years later, listening to Randy Newman sing "Guilty," the lyrics remind me still of those feelings and what I tried to do about them.

The song depicts a man who is drunk again and in deep despair. He knows he should not stop by his sweetheart's place, but he finds himself in trouble and has nowhere else to go. The final verse sums up the self-loathing and the belief that he needs alcohol or cocaine in order to make-believe he is someone other than who he is.

Even in early childhood, at age three or four, I had a feeling of being out of place. Early on, a recurrent experience was telling.

The Randolph-Hazel Park streetcar line ran a couple of hundred feet from our house. Late at night two blocks away, I listened as one of those old rattle-traps rumbled down the tracks, gaining speed as it crossed our street down the block to make it up a long grade, steel wheels screeching against the tracks that gently curved leftward halfway up the hill. At the top, it would pause before passing over a single-lane trestle that traversed the Chicago Northwestern railroad tracks.

There was a bright red window pane high in the rear end of the car and, as it reached the opposite end of the trestle and headed down the other side of the slope, I watched from my upstairs bedroom window a thousand feet away as that light slowly disappeared into the night. The experience could have been a metaphor for my life twenty years later as a practicing alcoholic. First the anticipation of the approaching streetcar, then the noise and excitement building as it sped up the hill, slowing to a crawl as it crossed the trestle. Then, the melancholy as that red light slowly faded out of sight. Sad as those moments always ended up being, I couldn't help looking out my window when I heard a streetcar coming, my heart leaping as it clanged into view. And, as the excitement ebbed, I couldn't turn away. I had to watch that red light disappear into the night, wishing I could go with it.

My daughter Kelly once summed up recovery by saying it mended that hole in our souls, the steps being stitches that closed it so the good stuff would not seep out. The meetings, the readings, the people like Joe, Bill, Anita, and of course, Harry, helped me to suture that wound, close the hole, and fill the emptiness. After that first A.A. meeting and nearly every meeting since, instead of a melancholy aftermath, I have experienced satisfaction without the fear of a letdown. I didn't need to be someone else, going somewhere else. Being who I was and where I was, life could be good after all.

## "WHY" VERSUS "HOW"

Early on, I learned that A.A. wasn't going to focus much on why we became alcoholics but rather on how we would stay sober. Harry and Joe, trained attorneys who always focused on the "why" question to establish motive in litigating cases, Bill and his insightful psychiatrist who would have rejoiced to find the "why" of his difficulties, and Anita, along with the others at the Uptown and Unity groups, not only accepted that we did not know "why" but that it probably would not have helped much if we had. This flies in the face of the way we usually approach problem-solving.

Name a problem and we usually try to find the cause and then work toward a solution. Answering the "why" question is at the heart of the process whether it is fixing a leaking pipe or triggering exploration that leads to stunning discoveries. And it is not confined to the past. Self-parking cars with driverless vehicles on the near horizon, and online shopping with drone-delivery to our doorsteps, were beyond our wildest imagination when I began writing this reflection. Today they are but a few of the breathtaking scientific achievements on a never-ending list. Virtually every area of our lives has seen the benefits of answering the "why" question. That is, until we get to the question of what causes alcoholism and many mental illnesses.

For years, I imagined a hypothetical, primitive matrix to try to at least frame the "why" issue of alcoholism. On one axis were three clusters of causative factors: Genetic, Environmental, and Psychological. On the other axis were two categories: Predisposing and Precipitating factors. The hypothesis was that if a person had enough painful or addiction-inducing experiences in a majority of these six areas, they were likely to become addicted. It seemed to fit one of my daughters who became chemically dependent around the age of twelve.

To begin with, she was the daughter of an alcoholic, and research[10] indicated that for children of alcoholics, the incidence of the disease was several times greater than for children who did not have an alcoholic parent. In terms of environment, many of the neighborhood kids her age not only drank to intoxication but smoked pot regularly. And, psychologically, she experienced a number of extremely painful episodes that particular summer. Her closest girlfriend moved away. A pet met a violent death. Far worse, a boy on whom she had a crush returned home to Vietnam to be with his father and died shortly there-after in a terrible accident. Finally, a picture she had of him was lost when her wallet was stolen at a roller rink. All things considered, had my daughter been able to escape the ravages of alcoholism, it would have been a miracle.

I gradually saw that the cells in my hypothetical matrix did not bear equal weight as potential contributing causes of addiction. The predis-posing physical cell, or genetic predisposition, appeared to be far and away the most significant. That seemed to be true in my own case, and research pointed in that direction with the children of alcoholics being as much as four times as likely to become alcoholic as other children. But, even at that, a host of other factors are often present and can vary in importance depending on the individual.

Today, I am not so sure that genetic predisposition, while still extremely important, is such an overwhelmingly dominant factor. A year working with the Department of Defense to launch the Post Deployment Health Re-Assessment program for returning combat veterans exposed me to the realities of trauma in a way I hadn't previ-ously understood. The very high comorbid relationship between Post Traumatic Stress Disorder (PTSD) and Alcohol Abuse/Alcoholism which emerged in our data indicated that environmental factors may be more important than I had previously thought. Medical surveillance of returning OIF Service Members showed that the greater the number of fire fights they had experienced, the higher the number of PTSD endorsements they reported on the DD Form 2900. the greater the number of PTSD endorsements, the higher the rate of alcohol problem endorsements. A single event, such as seeing a buddy blown up before one's eyes, often resulted in deep, long-last-ing trauma. Moreover, the military has combined its work on PTSD with its efforts to address Traumatic Brain Injury (TBI). While the two conditions may exist discretely in some instances, they are often closely linked. Indeed, the physical and psychological spheres never have been polar opposites, although they have traditionally been treated as if they were. Unfortunately, the various segments of health care are often provided in discrete silos rather than in an integrated, holistic system. We reimburse for procedures in units instead of outcomes, and those yielding the greatest revenue to providers tend to be used more frequently.

Shifting from the combat theater in Iraq to the emotional war zones children face at home living with an alcoholic parent, the genetic predisposition and a traumatic environment can work in tandem to laden a child with a host of mental and substance use disorders. Studies[11] show that the earlier in life a person starts drinking, the greater the chance they will become dependent on alcohol. Kids with an alcoholic parent are more likely to commence drinking at an early age. And, when the mother is an alcoholic, the child may be headed toward the disease while still in the womb. When I first started my recovery journey, the old-timers in A.A. believed that alcohol has a different effect on the brain of an alcoholic than it has on non-alcoholics. Current studies show that alcohol itself changes the brain, especially in children, and the more and earlier it is consumed, the greater the change. This suggests that early-onset drinking can cause alcoholism without predisposing conditions. It also suggests that there doesn't need to be abusive, violent, or even neglectful behavior on the part of an alcoholic parent for the children to be adversely affected. In some cases, either a genetic predisposition or early-onset drinking may be all that it takes. At age sixty-eight, upon discovering who my natural father was, I was not surprised to read in his obituary that he had been an active member of A.A. during the last eighteen years of his life. Moreover, my adopted parents, neither of whom were alcoholics, gave me small amounts of alcohol starting at age five.

During the past twenty-five years, more research has been conducted to shed light on this issue than ever before. Much has been funded by the National Institute on Alcohol Abuse and Alcoholism (NIAAA). The wonder of electronic brain imaging used in the work of Carlton Erickson, PhD, and Daniel Amen, PhD, opened eyes throughout the recovering community and in the addiction treatment profession. Some forms of mental illness — especially mood disorders — affect the same area of the brain as alcohol. The internet, with its remarkable search engines, makes the latest findings available to nearly anyone. But knowing what causes alcoholism and knowing what to do about it once it has taken hold are two very different issues.

Essentially, recovery from alcoholism continues to be a quest to answer the "how" question: Given the fact that I am an alcoholic, how do I stay sober? How can I be free of the bondage of self and this disease? How do I live a life that can be productive? How can I become happy? Pursuing the "how," I have been fortunate to be able to experience the riches of recovery. At the same time, the "why" question has loomed in the back of my mind all through the years. Why did I become afflicted with this disease? Could it have been prevented? More importantly, could anything have prevented it in my children?

I approached the issue with caution. Early in my recovery, I saw the effort to pursue an answer to the "why" as fraught with potential danger that could threaten my sobriety. I feared that the "why?" could slip into "why me?" and the "why me?" could become "poor me!" From my first days of recovery, I held tightly to Anita's message about the danger of self-pity. Yet, the "why" is a vexing question. Many years later, the last words spoken to me by an acquaintance who was a bank president before he died from alcoholism were, "I just have to figure this out. If only I could figure this out." He wanted to find the cause, eradicate it, and drink some more.

Without dismissing the importance of the "why" question, it seemed to have little practical use to me in getting on the road to recovery. I even conjured up an analogy which has been one of my favorite ways to avoid getting into the "why" of my own alcoholism. It goes like this:

"I'm heading down the interstate when I feel something wrong in the steering. I pull over and get out to find that a tire is flat, punctured by a roofing nail. Now it may be interesting to learn that the nail started out as a lump of iron ore on the Messabi Iron Range in Northern Minnesota and that the iron ore was hauled by rail car to the Duluth seaport from where it was shipped by freighter to Pittsburg, hauled into a steel mill, processed through a blast furnace, refined into high-grade steel, and ultimately punched out as a nail, which, along with millions of other nails, found its way onto the shelves of local hardware stores where a guy in my area purchased a pound of them, put the bag in the bed of his pickup truck, went out onto the interstate, hit a rough spot in the road causing one of those nails to bounce out onto the highway, where I drove over it and got a flat. Interesting information, but it does absolutely nothing to fix the tire and get me back on the road."

However, caution is urged here. This perspective is not suggested as a prescription for all recovering alcoholics and addicts. The matter is really quite personal. Others may take strength early in their recovery in knowing that science demonstrates this terrible disease was not self-inflicted, that they are not to blame. At this point, having had such a good life sober for such a long time, I no longer fear that exploring the "why" question will lead me to drink — that I will slip into the fallacy that once I understand the "why" of my disease, I'll have the insight and self-knowledge necessary to avoid the problem and therefore will have no need for ongoing support, such as A.A. And I am especially fascinated by the work on brain chemistry and the effects of early childhood trauma, especially sexual abuse.

But, for many years, I simply refused to take any chances. I knew how my brain worked, and how my thinking had gotten me into trouble. It is alcohol*ism*, after all. The term has been criticized in some professional circles because an … *ism* is a belief system. As such, some consider it to be antithetical to the disease concept, even unprofessional. Indeed, the Diagnostic Statistical Manual of Mental Disorders (DSM) does not use the term alcoholism. For years, it referred to "alcohol dependence" and most recently as a "substance use disorder." However, most recovering alcoholics I have known are fully aware that as it manifested itself in their lives, as they lived with it and struggled with it, whether on the road to perdition or the path to recovery, alcoholism is *both* a disease and a belief system — a false belief system — and the two are inextricably interwoven with an array of variables, with dependence and loss of control at its essence.

I am not ashamed of the fear that kept me from pursuing the "why" question for so many years. I respect it. I am grateful for it. It kept me out of a lot of trouble, not just with this issue but with many others that could have jeopardized my sobriety. At the same time, I am also grateful that today I can drill more deeply into the "why" of alcoholism and not only gain greater understanding of the disease, but of myself. I just had to put "first things first" as it applied to me. And, as it applied to me may not be the same for others. Moreover, what helps us to get sober in the beginning may not be sufficient to help us stay sober and enjoy the fullness of recovery. Years later, a deeper understanding of what Step 5 actually means caused me to rethink the value of addressing the "why" issue.

# RECOVERING IMPERFECTLY

I was raised Catholic and was practicing my religion at the time I attended my first A.A. meeting. Later, I was away from the church for over forty years before reconciling, but during that time, I still prayed continually. Harry was an atheist before A.A. and an agnostic afterward. But he worked the steps of A.A., and he, too, prayed because whether or not there was a God, he believed he couldn't stay sober by himself and said so many times. Harry believed that following directions and learning from those who had gone before were important. Joe was somewhere between the two of us. We were all liberal politically. Ideologically, life was comfortable with them in the early years of my recovery. Then a major change occurred in my life. I moved from St. Paul to the Chicago area, and I got a second sponsor.

## TOM D-1

Tom was a conservative Republican, a top executive in a major company, and gay. Politically we were polar opposites. Both of us were also headstrong, and occasionally we had heated arguments for which we were later compelled to make amends. It was a mystery to him how I could be an advocate of basic business principles such as free enterprise and the profit motive and still be an ardent Democrat. And I couldn't imagine any gay person supporting the Republican Party. Politically we had both made the mistake of falling in love with our own rectitude.

How could two people so different from each other unite to stay sober? It was because all the political and philosophical beliefs we held so dearly were not nearly as powerful or as critical in our lives as our desire to put to rest the false belief system that had once nearly brought us to destruction. It was the false belief system, among other considerations, that led the founders of A.A. to exclaim that alcoholism was ...

*"... cunning, baffling, and powerful." (AA, pp. 58–59)*

In order to successfully overcome that false belief system and recover from alcoholism, Tom and I needed to share our experience, strength, and hope. That meant putting our political differences aside. To do that, we surrendered to a new set of beliefs as expressed in A.A.'s steps and traditions. We needed them both — the steps *and* the traditions — because as a dear friend from Chicago, Mike C., once remarked:

*"The steps keep us from committing suicide, and the traditions keep us from committing homicide."*

Speaking only for myself, A.A. and the recovery it offers is not about winning arguments, but about solving problems. It is not primarily about the "why" but the "how." It is not about assessing blame, but about taking responsibility. It is not about making excuses, but about meeting obligations. It is not about winning a battle, but about surrender. And it is not about exercising willpower, but about nurturing the desire. Success is not measured by the volume of what we acquire, even years of sobriety, but by the quality of what we freely give others.

This doesn't mean that we can just sit back and not exert what is often an effort beyond what we once thought was possible. We do not abandon the strength of our convictions or dismiss the "why" question as irrelevant. We do not deny the effects of abusive authority figures in our lives or underestimate genetics and trauma. Nor do we ignore the committed, persistent personal effort needed just to get through some days.

But we do need to be grounded in a spirit of humility, forgiveness, hard work, gratitude, respect, and love. Some of my biggest failings over the years occurred when I forgot this, even though I hadn't taken that "first drink." Experience has clearly shown that trying to do it alone, I can easily forget. That's why I still attend meetings after fifty-four years. I do not need so much to be told, as to be reminded.

## THE YEARS SINCE

Again, my dear friend Mike remarked:

*"These 12 step programs don't solve all our problems.
But, they do help us to stop doing the things that make
us feel so terrible about ourselves."*

Over the years, countless experiences have transpired ranging from pure elation to emotional devastation. Two long-term, productive marriages. The births of my five wonderful children and the gain of three delightful step-daughters, fifteen grandchildren, and five great-grandchildren; being reunited with both sides of my birth family at ages fifty-eight and seventy-seven; the fruits of an unexpected college education from St. John's with a strong sense of social responsibility instilled with love and patience by the Benedictines; a marvelous career with lots of recognition; friends who go back to high school days; addicted people transformed before my eyes from "pitiful and incomprehensible demoralization" to a life of sobriety and integrity emanating from an ever-growing spiritual awakening. And a second chance at marriage with Janis, an unbelievable, courageous, marvelous woman. Indeed, there have been many wondrous experiences.

There has also been pain: The addictions and other challenges faced by several of my children, accompanied by the abject fear I carried for years of being jarred awake in the night by the worst of all phone calls telling me one of them was gone; a difficult, painful divorce from Marilyn after nearly twenty-one years of a marriage that had overcome a number of big challenges; the loss of three big jobs; other addictions that were equally cunning, baffling, and powerful; PTSD; acute financial problems; the suicide of my first A.A. sponsee; the passing of parents and several dear friends, especially the loss of Harry after a long bout with Alzheimer's. In between there were political victories and defeats, both of which I frequently took too personally.

There were times of family joy I could never have dreamed possible, and there were times of unimaginable pain; periods when I attended very few A.A. meetings, never having benefited from those spiritually dry times, to making them an integral part of my life; falling away from my religion for decades and slowly staggering back to it. I have yet to figure out whether it was me, running just slowly enough so I didn't get out of God's sight, or if He always moved just fast enough to keep me in view. Given my history, the odds strongly favor that it was He more than me who kept that gap from growing until it finally closed.

Through it all, my Higher Power, the program, and the steps were there for the taking, along with the love of my wife, and my family and friends both in and out of the program. The closer I held onto them — God, the steps, and the people — the better my life was. Their lessons have been too numerous to recount, many forgotten for the moment. But as always, they will come back to me when I need them most. Out of all of it, here is what comes to mind in thinking about how the miracle of recovery has unfolded in my life.

# STEP ZERO:
# TRADITION THREE

For many people, sobriety starts with Step 1. Its importance is emphasized in the A.A. literature and most contemporary treatment programs. The *Twelve Steps and Twelve Traditions* says it is the only step that must be worked perfectly. I do not argue with it. That's not how it happened in my case.

I was fourteen years sober and sitting in a meeting in San Francisco when it dawned on me that the first step reads, "We admitted we were powerless over alcohol, that our lives had *become* unmanageable." It didn't say "our lives had *been* unmanageable." This wasn't the only time I had made such a mistake. Over the years, I have been surprised and even amazed at how I could misinterpret or misread the wording in a step. Was it a subconscious denial of its true meaning? An attempt to not face the lesson it had for me because I cherished more the defects to which it pointed? Had I lost my edge by not consistently and continuously taking the steps and slipping from regular attendance at meetings into an irregular pattern of participation? Had I insidiously migrated from rigorous honesty in thought to a sloppy, lazy notion of what the step said? Or was it just further evidence that the journey on recovery road is truly one of progress and not perfection? Whatever it was, I pondered the discovery in that meeting and tried to examine how I could have erred so dramatically after being in the program so long.

Implied in that mistake, of course, was that once sober, I could manage my own life. While I would never have consciously admitted to that belief, one's attitude and actions are always a better gauge of what they truly believe than their words. Moreover, after I had gained a few years of sobriety, I hadn't persisted in studying the literature as diligently as I had either in the first several months of my recovery or later in life. And I wasn't attending many meetings. The truth is, I was imperceptibly backsliding, a fraction of an inch here, maybe a little more there.

At that point in life, I was approaching the apex of my career. I had come a long way since my first job out of college. The rewards were great. I had speaking engagements all over the country and abroad. I authored what was then the seminal book in my field and received a steady stream of invitations to provide consultation to companies, unions, and professional groups. There was a national award from my field's professional association and a special citation and financial reward from the CEO of my company. To my knowledge, I enjoyed the highest salary of any of my peers. At last, there was something I could do as well sober as I once was able to drink. It all served to convince me that I could *really* manage. It was heady stuff and satisfied a need that long preceded the onset of my addiction. That old nemesis — the hole in my soul — was back. Years later when a friend in the program, also named Tom D., suggested that an alcoholic is an egomaniac with an inferiority complex, I understood completely. Humility certainly wasn't my strong suit.

Powerlessness over alcohol was apparent from my first A.A. meeting. But acceptance of the need to relinquish the notion that I could somehow manage my own life was slow in coming. Deep down I clung to the belief that not only could I manage me, but virtually anyone or anything else, too, especially my family. Looking back, it is apparent that if one believes they can manage their lives, they will have trouble truly believing they are powerless. But at the time, I was blinded by ego and fear. Ego, which said I was responsible for my success and therefore I wasn't the failure I had so long believed myself to be. And fear, that I didn't deserve the success I enjoyed and could lose it all unless I defended and controlled it. It had to be *managed*. By *me*. Or it wouldn't turn out the way I wanted it to.

Yet, it wasn't just Step 1 that got short shrift. Just as alcoholism is progressive, so is recovery. We are talking recovery here, not just abstinence. Moreover, while recovery is spiritual, so is the disease. If there is a serious compromise with the first step, the synergies of recovery can end up reversing themselves, affecting both the practice and the efficacy of the rest of the steps. If one's grasp on the admission of powerlessness loosens, or the belief wanes that their life is unmanageable, what is the need for a greater restorative power as suggested in Step 2? Going to Step 3, if they manage everything themselves, it is antithetical to turn their will, much less their lives, over to God, regardless of what their understanding of God may be. And, taking a 4th Step moral inventory? What's the point, unless it would be to discover glitches that interfere with one's efforts at self-management? Many times a drunken relapse is the result of this type of thinking. But not always.

In my case, I earnestly went through the first five steps during the first six months of sobriety, although my Step 3 effort was weak. In Step 5, I shared with Father Raymond Slattery at St. Luke's Church in St. Paul (since renamed St. Thomas Moore) the findings of my 4th

Step inventory. This is not really what Step 5 suggests, but it was how I learned to do it at the time. Imperfect as my taking of the steps was to that point, it was still effective. Things were working. In a one-week period during May of 1966, Marilyn and I bought a car, our first home, and I got a new job. I drove twenty miles from the suburb where we lived into St. Paul to attend meetings, but not nearly as often as I had during my first months in the program, and I wasn't seeing Harry several times a week as I had up to that time. Marilyn and I were getting deeply involved in the community, and life was filling up. I was incredibly happy, and she was too. Then, I slowly went on a vacation of sorts from the program. I did not work Steps 6 and 7 until years later, although I gave them lip service. The first time through, I made a mental Step 8 list of persons I had harmed, but in the process confused it with Step 9, which is where we actually make amends. With Harry's help, I did make a few amends, but then largely glossed over Steps 10 and 11 and instead engaged in activity which I thought was working Step 12 — I was trying to recruit practicing alcoholics to the program. I also got involved in local politics, and in the next few years was elected to public office, re-elected, and elected chair of my political party. I believed a political future lay ahead and fervently wanted it. The adrenalin rush was as good as drinking. Meanwhile, work, family, and the program were all slowly being compromised.

I have learned over the years that practicing the entire twelve-step program of A.A. results in a life in balance anchored by serenity and acceptance. In addition, for me, practicing my religion in the early years reinforced this state of being, and today it has become co-equal to the steps in fulfilling the "promises" on page 83 of *The Big Book — Alcoholics Anonymous*. However, the forty-year absence from religious practice left a void and undermined the serenity essential to a truly fulfilling recovery.

But the question remains: How could anyone stay sober without having worked the first step continuously and "perfectly"? In my case, Tradition Three saved the day. Or as I like to call it, Step Zero.

*"The only requirement for A.A. membership is a desire to stop drinking." (12 and 12, p. 139)*

Early in my recovery, A.A. taught me that willpower alone did not work with alcoholism. My own experience was evidence enough. In the years since, as other addictions emerged in my life and in the lives of those around me, this principle proved true time and again. *Desire*, on the other hand, was a different matter. Whenever there was a choice between willpower and desire, I won every time I bet on desire. Whenever I put my chips on willpower, I usually lost. Desire and willpower usually complement each other, but not when it comes to dealing with addiction. For me, willpower only works when it follows desire.

Long before my first A.A. meeting, I had wanted to quit drinking but did not believe I could. Then, I saw that it had been possible for the people around the table at that first meeting, and the desire to not drink came alive in me. By the end of the first week, between the meetings with Harry, getting home for dinner on time every night, and money in my pocket from the check I had cashed days earlier, the faith mushroomed that I could not only stop, but stay stopped. The desire quickly grew into a powerful lifesaving force. It reached the point where I would rather have died than drink. To me it did not matter what I might have to give up — career, family, or my life — I would not take that first drink. I believed then and now that if I drank, I could end up losing it all anyway. Every morning for years, I looked in the mirror and prayed, "Lord, help me. I am an alcoholic. I won't drink today." That morning ritual eventually passed, but I still say it instantly whenever the slightest trace of a craving occurs. Today the desire to not take that first drink is as strong as it was in the beginning, and it has never waned along the way. But I stay on top of any urge with this declaration and surrender for help.

As will be apparent in the remainder of this story, I have worked each of the steps imperfectly. But, to quote Deepak Chopra, "*Intention organizes everything.*" Even more importantly, when it comes to addiction, desire alone fuels intention and puts it in motion. Without desire, whatever our intentions, however grand or noble, they are unlikely to be realized.

My first suggestion to newcomers is to fervently pray for the desire. If they are non-believers, I express respect, both for them and their belief system, but urge them to "make believe" there is some kind of power that will grant their wish, and to pray anyway. They can sort out their theology later. They first need to get some sobriety under their belts.

Harry would have approved, God love him.

## THE TWELVE AND TWELVE

Harry gave me two books during the first week of my sobriety: *The Big Book — Alcoholics Anonymous* and the *Twelve Steps and Twelve Traditions*. Both have been indispensable, but I have gravitated more toward the *12 and 12* over the years. At my A.A. meeting, someone will often comment how, after having read a chapter numerous times over several years, they still heard something new. That's been my experience too. Each paragraph is packed with meaning, and it is timeless. But, regardless of the times, in our society being a "winner" is essential to having self-respect. In contrast to that cultural norm, consider this question and the response to it:

"Who cares to admit complete defeat? Practically no one."

So begins the *Twelve Steps and Twelve Traditions* (p. 21), commencing a narrative on the steps of recovery that is unmatched, in my opinion. Oh, there are dozens of changes I would make to this book if God would only appoint me Editor in Chief of the Universe. I'd update it using contemporary language, with current metaphors and analogies. And some comments would be thrown out completely, clichés such as "Separating the men from the boys" and "Pure as the driven snow."

Good Lord, who uses those clichés today? Aren't they borderline sexist and racist? For those reasons, I do not use them in conversation and avoid them in conscious thought. Moreover, when was the last time anyone under the age of eighty has used the term "John Barleycorn" to describe whiskey? Or who would suggest in print that someone who has trouble breaking a dependency on parents needs to "grow up" and should "wake up to the fact." Or referring to someone who refuses to believe in God as "savage." Some of this stuff is just plain un-cool.

So how does a weather-beaten old liberal like me reconcile this? Simply put, I don't. The early A.A. members, nearly all men, were not "touchy-feely" types. Nor is there evidence that they were concerned about getting in touch with any softer, feminine inner self. They would likely have been aghast at the notion that they even had one. Politically correct in today's terms, they certainly were not, and neither was hardly anyone else at that time. However, the legacy of love, commitment, and acceptance they cultivated in the 1930s is present today in the meetings I attend: meetings in which the number of women is often equal to the men, and attendance by minorities is roughly representative of the community. More important, the principles of recovery they espoused have held up for these past eighty-five years. Dated words and expressions are common in most texts written decades ago. Both *The Big Book* and the *12 and 12* have been considered historical texts, and therefore the decision has been made to leave them unchanged. Nevertheless, would a good edit of the *12 and 12* be appropriate? As someone who would tweak the Lord's Prayer, I believe so. But that's beside the point. I ask myself: Is it a few phrases with archaic wording that are essential or the principles being advanced?

In my experience, those who get on the road to recovery the fastest and stay there generally do not get hung up critiquing the details of A.A. literature. It can feed a latent resentment about even needing to read the material, much less stopping drinking or drug use. We try to look for how each comment, thought, and principle applies to us and then follow the credo of virtually every successful person in any endeavor:

"We take what we need and leave the rest."

So, would I change anything in the basic literature if I were asked? Yes. But no one has asked me to, and I am no longer bothered by it.

# STEP ONE

S o, what about this notion of admitting complete defeat? There is little to nit-pick here. The basic fact is that when dealing with nearly any chronic personal problem, at some level, we win by losing. And to win when dealing with alcoholism or any other addiction, we start with the very core of the problem:

> *"We admitted we were powerless over alcohol, that our lives had become unmanageable." (AA, p. 59)*

This is where it all begins. But, like those of us in recovery, the steps, too, evolved. When Bill Wilson first drafted them, borrowing from the Oxford group, there were only six. Some of the final twelve were not even included. Others were considered too difficult to swallow all at once and were divided in two. But not Step 1. From the beginning "One" stood virtually on its own; however, not in its current form. An early draft read:

> *"We admitted we were licked, that we were powerless over alcohol."*

Apparently, the issue of unmanageability which took so long for me to comprehend did not occur spontaneously to Bill Wilson, either. But Bill knew it was a "we" program, and he sought the advice and counsel of the early fellowship members both in New York and Akron. They pointed out the need to include unmanageability right from the beginning.

In large measure, recovery from addiction requires us to do what comes *unnaturally*. Decades later, one of the world's most practiced curmudgeons, a loveable old guy named Bill B. at the Mustard Seed in Chicago, would say:

> *"We come into A.A. and this is where we tell*
> *the truth about ourselves."*

The truth starts with acknowledging our powerlessness and unmanageability, however haltingly. Of the thousands of people who have attended meetings where I was present over the years, none declared:

> "I woke up one morning and my life was absolutely wonderful.
> My spouse was happy, my job was great, my kids were doing
> well, I had plenty of money, and I was in total control of it all.
> So I said to myself, 'I think I'll go to an A.A. meeting today.'"

On the contrary, *The Big Book* sums it up best when describing where many of us were in our lives when we came into the program:

> *"All of us felt at times that we were regaining control [of*
> *our drinking]. But such intervals — usually brief — were*
> *inevitably followed by still less control, which led to pitiful and*
> *incomprehensible demoralization." (AA, p. 30)*

When finally getting into A.A., some of us still had a lot going for us: jobs, families, friends, even money in the bank. We hadn't lost everything. But, at some level, practically all of us either knew or strongly suspected that "we were licked." We just didn't know what to do about it. Something was wrong, and we couldn't fix it. Moreover, many of us did not want to do anything that might prove that our spouses, parents, friends, or others had been right all along, that we had a problem, and drinking was at its core. Some of us thought if we worked at it hard enough, or thought about it deeply enough, we could solve the riddle. Ultimately, we had to conclude that we had no choice but to stop drinking. While our own enlightened self-interest had to tell us this, the epiphany usually occurred after those around us has planted seeds and driven stakes.

Usually we had to hear the concern about what we were doing to ourselves and our families numerous times. For that reason, it is important for the friends and loved ones of alcoholics to set aside their fears and express their concern directly to the person whose drinking is getting out of hand. *But,* and this is huge, without expecting immediate results. When an alcoholic does respond positively, it is likely that several others had already expressed concern, often more than once. Even then, for some of us it took a month or more in treatment. Sometimes it took a calamity. At times, just getting fed up with ourselves was the key. Or it may have taken a growing sense of desperation accompanied by an awareness that we were in a trap from which we would never escape without help. Sometimes the call for help was made, not by us, but by a friend on our behalf. Rarely did any of us heed the first warning.

## "WE," AGAIN

It's no accident that the first word in the first step is "We." "I" didn't work. It was only when I admitted my powerlessness and unmanageability with others, and together *we* admitted this hopelessness to others and they admitted it to us, that together we were able to make progress. So, it is natural for me that memories of other alcoholics I have known and loved come to mind when I ponder Step 1. What they did to get sober and how they did it have been as important to me as my own efforts. I could not have enjoyed the recovery I have had if they had not walked the journey — some ahead of me, some with me, and some following. But all in their own way have been present in my struggle and essential to my recovery.

## MARQUIZ

The phone rang late one morning, and it was Wes. Wes owned a beauty salon on North Broadway in Chicago a couple of blocks from where we lived. Black women were ninety-five percent of his clientele. Of the remaining 5 percent, about 4.9 were Black men.

Shortly after moving into the neighborhood and while walking past his shop from the garage where I parked my car, I realized I needed a haircut. Not knowing where any traditional men's barber shops were in the area, I walked into Wes's place. He was doing a weave for a pretty, young lady and barely glanced at me while doing a subtle double take.

"How you doing, sir. Can I help you?"

"Fine, thanks. Do you do conventional hair?"

"Sure do. But that's okay — we can do yours, too!"

Three female customers, Wes, and a second younger Black male hairdresser all laughed. I did, too, and sat down and waited my turn. It was to be the first of many hours I would spend in Wes's shop, bantering, arguing, discussing everything from race, religion, and politics, to music, cars, and sports. Some of the liveliest and most enjoyable times for Wes were my arguments with a guy named Johnny, an upper-middle manager in a large bank. Johnny was Black, had worked hard his whole life, had a highly accomplished wife and two great teenage sons. He also hated public welfare, taxes, and government in general. Johnny was a Republican. Liberal white old me defended welfare and the role of government. Bemused at the irony, none of the spectators openly took sides. How could they? We created a dilemma whenever we held forth. I was defending a system many had counted on, but Johnny was a "Brother." Occasionally, I got my hair cut. The young guy working the second chair was Marquiz.

Marquiz was born in Michigan and raised by his grandmother. At age four, he was raiding mailboxes on his block for cough syrup samples and their alcohol content. He started drinking and drugging in elementary school. In his mid-teens, he became a father, having hooked up with a woman in her early twenties. By age twenty-three, he was the father of two and hustling any way he could to support them and their mothers. By the time I got to know him, he had become a gifted hairdresser and had built up a nice clientele.

I've never kept my recovery from addiction secret. Early on, I told Harry and everyone close to me to break my anonymity any time they thought it could help someone. So, in time, Wes and most everyone at his shop knew I was in recovery. On more than one occasion, he had shared his concern about Marquiz's drinking and drug use but wanted to wait with any kind of intervention. He had talked to Marquiz about it because it was beginning to affect his reliability, either showing up late or not at all, with Wes trying to work Marquiz's missed appointments into an already busy schedule.

Finally he saw an opening and called me. Marquiz was in trouble.

"Hey, Jim, Wes here. Can you come down to the shop? Marquiz is ready to hear what you have to say."

"About what?"

"About that situation we talked about — you know. He needs help."

I hung up the phone and walked over to Wes's. Too often, a serious event is needed to give those around the addicted person enough confidence to take action, hoping that it may be enough to convince the addict to accept help. Everyone is usually in denial about the many less-spectacular but equally diagnostic incidents that precede such an event. Sometimes the reality can no longer be denied, and the addict seeks help in anticipation to avoid being compelled by someone else to do something about their problem. They short-circuit a friend, relative, employer, or judge from forcing the issue. Sometimes, the "right" time doesn't come before the alcoholic dies, kills someone else, or ends up in jail, leaving a hurricane of personal and social damage in their wake. Marquiz, whose only support system was the shop and his career, was in a precarious situation. He made good money but was always broke. No car, no home or apartment, living with a series of women, and just marginally getting by.

Marquiz was short and Black. He liked big women, and color didn't matter. Towering over him, Sharon with brown hair and fair skin filled the bill just fine. She was independent, strong-willed, worked a regular job, and had a nice apartment. Marquiz was bright and sweet, a charmer, and she was attracted to his good side. But that wasn't always what she got.

Putting it mildly, Sharon and Marquiz had a tumultuous relationship. He had been drinking all through the night before Wes called me. They got into a fight, and she threw him out, as she had many times before. Only this time she wanted him to stay out. The next morning before leaving for work, she admonished her son to call the police if Marquiz showed up at the apartment. Later in the morning, he went back to get his belongings, and the boy did as he was told.

Police hate domestic calls, especially where alcohol or drugs are involved, which is most of the time. They never know what they are walking into. This wasn't the first time they had intervened in one of

Marquiz and Sharon's fights, and they were likely tired of it. When they arrived, Marquiz was gone, but they tracked him down less than a block away at a 7-Eleven store across the street from Wes's. Using anatomical phrases that had no medical significance, they threw him on the floor face down, one cop mounting him and holding a service revolver to his head while the other put the cuffs on.

When I arrived at Wes's, I had to walk around a police cruiser parked kittywampus on the sidewalk in front of the shop. The cops had gone there first before catching up to Marquiz across the street. I went into the shop and asked about the cruiser. Wes pointed to the back seat. There was Marquiz, roughed-up and shoeless. Wes bailed him out a day later, got him some shoes, and arranged the intervention. It was easy. Marquiz was ready. The problem was he needed the safe environment of some type of residential treatment, and none was available. Because he worked, he wasn't eligible for publicly funded treatment. And like many alcoholics, especially minorities, he had no personal resources to pay for private treatment, no insurance coverage, no family with the means to help. So, we had to come up with a plan.

Marquiz agreed to go to a 10:30 a.m. meeting with me every day. I would pick him up, go to the meeting, and then take him to Wes's immediately afterward, usually before noon. Since they both worked late — typically until around 9:00 p.m. — Wes would drive him every night to a 10:00 p.m. meeting. When the meeting was over, Marquiz would get a ride home from another A.A. member, usually after coffee, and turn-in around midnight. Then we repeated the process the following day. The men and women at my first meeting at the old Uptown Group would have nodded their approval.

An old friend of Marquiz's from cosmetology school also contributed to his recovery. Marquiz had no place to stay, so Shanice put him up in a little back room at her apartment. She had family in recovery and was familiar with the challenges. She and Marquiz talked into the wee hours most nights about many things, including the disease and staying away from the people, places, and things that could pull him back into it. She put him up for free for several months until he got on his feet. Her role was crucial. She provided a safe pad. However, "safe," like many other terms, is relative when applied to addicts.

Shanice's apartment was in a Chicago housing project. Each morning when I pulled up in front in my new Q45, the crack dealers and hookers were out there sizing things up, including me. At first, they thought I was a "trick," then a pimp, and finally Marquiz's dealer. Marquiz walked right past them and got into the car, and we drove off. Every night, he walked past them again, back into Shanice's apartment. Indeed, "Intention organizes everything." For alcoholics and addicts, substitute desire for intention, and the picture is the same. Both Marquiz and I had been praying that he would have the desire.

As sometimes happens, the most obvious threats do not turn out to be the biggest ones. After seven days, Marquiz had a slip, and it didn't occur anywhere near Shanice's place. One of his customers had been getting her hair done for free, sort of. They had a drill. She would strut through the shop door, a fancy handbag slung over her shoulder. When she sat in Marquiz's chair, she draped the bag over the back where he could filch drugs stashed in there for him, and he would do her hair for free. In his newfound sobriety, he hadn't prepared for this. He automatically followed the old routine and relapsed. Fortunately, he told me about it right away.

So, we amended our plan. The next time she came by, he told her the "do" really was free this time. She was to keep her bag on her lap under the apron. He didn't want any payment for his work that day. Next time, she had to pay him in cash. Eventually, she found a new hairdresser.

We worked the plan for more than a year. Marquiz found other meetings too. He became actively involved in the program, first setting up and cleaning up at meetings, then occasionally giving the lead. Eventually, he sponsored others with whom he had once drank and used. He steered clear of the sweet honeys who sauntered into the shop one hip at a time, adorned with drugs and the special moves with his name on them. Somewhere, Spike from the old Unity group was smiling. Marquiz had hit bottom — the turning point — and was heading in a new direction.

Marquiz was high on a list of people I wanted to spend time with whenever I visited Chicago. Over the years he had become like a younger brother to me. The last time was 2016. We had lunch at a north-side restaurant. He was enjoying twenty-four years continuously sober and clean, and a life he could not have imagined that day he wound up in the back seat of the police cruiser.

The following summer I was going to Chicago again and tried to call him. There was no answer, so I went to Facebook. There he was — his name followed by RIP. It was then that I learned that he had been murdered a few weeks earlier. Walking to his car late one evening on what was considered a relatively safe street, a car pulled up and the driver got out and buried a shell in Marquiz's chest. An hour later, he was gone.

*"Oh, God! Oh, God! Oh, dear God!"*

Some pain is too hard to talk about — or write about. Too hard.

## HITTING BOTTOM

When I came into the program, broken families, lost jobs, barroom brawls, jail terms, panhandling, even riding the rails were badges of honor in some quarters of the Fellowship. The misery was often embellished by great storytellers who mixed humor with the pathos.

For entertainment value, some rivaled Dean Martin and Foster Brooks, who in the '50s and '60s perfected TV comedy routines premised on the notion that drunkenness was hilarious.

Somewhere along the way between the time *The Big Book* went to press and 1966, the phrase "hitting bottom" took on a meaning that became part of the problem in recognizing the presence of alcoholism instead of a tool by which the afflicted and affected could be spurred to action. Then as now, the more sensational the descriptions are of "bottom" — replete with the kind of graphic drunk-a-logs that drove Joe to form the Unity group in St. Paul so many ago — the more they can be used to rationalize that a person who has quietly crossed the line from social drinking into alcoholism really doesn't have a problem with drinking and that their use of drugs is purely recreational. The reality is that most of us do not fit the old stereotypes.

Early in my sobriety, some A.A. "old-timers" did not ask if young newcomers like me were married, but if we were "still" married. They didn't ask if we had ever been in jail, but "which jails." Some bragged that they had spilled more than we ever drank. Carrying it to extremes with *The Big Book's* reference to "real alcoholics," one suburban Minneapolis group in obvious violation of A.A.'s third tradition even disallowed membership to anyone who did not fit the very-late-stage alcoholic stereotype. When I objected, it was explained that if they were the only group in the area, they would not insist on such a criterion. But since there were other groups, they only wanted "real" alcoholics. Many of the early treatment programs also subscribed to such late-stage symptomology. Breaking down the denial was easier with those who had roared through multiple marriages, jobs, and courtrooms. Beyond that, there was a fear that someone would be "accused" of being an alcoholic when they really weren't. Fortunately, over time, the signs and symptoms were modified to reflect the disease in its earlier stages. But many still suffer far too long after the indications of a problem are present.

Whether then or now, the single most crucial element in defining an alcoholic's bottom is that it is a turning point. It can come anytime in the progression of the disease. Moreover, the most important element in defining the disease itself is loss of control. By defining the disease in terms of severe dysfunction and personal loss, a wealthy, high-functioning alcoholic could progress for many years before evidencing the customary late-stage symptoms. By then, it could be too late.

A bottom can occur by reaching a level of defeat in any of life's crucial areas: physical, emotional, social, financial, or vocational. But the one that counted most to me was "the bottom of the mind." When I acknowledged that something was wrong and I couldn't fix it, and that I had to stop drinking but couldn't, I had hit my bottom. And, although I was comparatively young, my bottom wasn't all that high. I was keeping up a good appearance but struggling on nearly all fronts.

## JULIE

The *12 and 12* talks about the necessity of raising the bottom and sparing alcoholics the last ten or fifteen years of hell the early members had experienced. Nevertheless, even today in some circles, "hitting bottom" is characterized by an array of spectacular late-stage symptoms which may have made it easier to convince some that they need help and may reduce the chances of a false positive diagnosis by professionals. But, it certainly does no favors to alcoholics in general, their families, employers, or the communities in which they live. And it isn't a necessary prerequisite for many who have gotten on the road to recovery earlier rather than later. A good example is Julie.

A newly minted therapist who was starting an EAP career, Julie was pretty, smart, had a sparkling personality and a good sense of humor.

She was a conscientious mother and responsible in virtually all areas of her life. I never saw her drink to excess. One day she commented on how she always had to have two drinks, even when she really wanted to have only one. At the time, her father was approaching the late stages of alcoholism; the signs had become apparent to nearly everyone close to him. With genetic predisposition being such a large factor, the warning lights flashed with her disclosure.

Julie decided to take the "acid test," two drinks a day for ten days. No more, no less. To a social drinker, this is a piece of cake. But to an alcoholic, even one in the earlier stages, it is difficult. Some will redefine what a drink is. Instead of a twelve-ounce bottle of beer, a six-ounce glass of wine, or a one-and-a-half-ounce shot of whiskey, there is a "misunderstanding" in which the volume nearly always increases. Others do not consume the two drinks required each day, but will abstain for a few days and then, adding up the number of drinks they missed, drink up the cumulative quota in one sitting. Others try to "white-knuckle" it, sticking to the two-drink regimen but becoming irritable, resentful, anxious, or depressed in the process. Invariably, the test period is followed by excessive drinking.

After the acid test, Julie decided to attend A.A., just to see if what they had to say applied to her. Not being able to have one drink and stop was evidence of a loss of control. It didn't matter that she could stop after two. She wanted to stop after the first one, and she couldn't do it. Given the progressive nature of the illness, we were concerned that sooner or later she would not have been able to stop at two and then three. When I ran into her a few years ago, she was enjoying long-term sobriety, a fine career, and a good life.

Was she a "real" alcoholic but just a long way from the old stereo-typical image of one? Or was she a problem drinker, or maybe an occasional alcohol abuser? The overarching question I had to ask myself was: *Does it really matter?* She was concerned about her drinking at the time, and in the years since she has had a good life and successful career without alcohol, labels notwithstanding.

## BOB AND DICK

Not everyone was so lucky. Bob was a big, handsome, articulate guy with an engineering degree. He held an important management position at a Fortune 25 industrial company. He had a lovely wife, two kids, and a nice home in an upper-middle-class neighborhood in Minneapolis. By any standard, he was a success, but as a minority in 1966, his achievements were all the more remarkable. I was in my first year of sobriety and volunteering with a community action group established to increase opportunities for minorities. Bob's wife also volunteered there, and the program director referred her to me.

I became involved with the organization, believing that no matter what opportunities were afforded minorities, the combination of racism and addiction could be an insurmountable barrier. Like most generalizations, this one had its exceptions and, as I was to find out, Bob was one of them. He had managed to navigate the turbulent anti-Black tides of the time and succeed in spite of his alcoholism.

Bob's wife introduced us, and we attended an A.A. meeting at the Uptown Group. I couldn't have been more elated. Bob seemed to identify with what the group had to say, and his comments were near eloquent and on point. There was no hint of denial, no indication that he wanted anything other than to stay sober. He became my first sponsee. He read the literature, called regularly, and we attended more meetings. Then his phone calls gradually slacked off. After a while, he didn't return my calls. Finally, his wife told me he was drinking. We tried to arrange an intervention, but he didn't show. Within a year he was gone. He took his own life.

The wise program axioms, such as, "Carry the message not the person," and "You stayed sober so the sponsorship was a success" offered scant solace. I felt that I had failed. Harry's reasoning was that if I was powerless over my own alcoholism, certainly I was powerless over Bob's. But that was little comfort.

Before Bob's tragic end, I had acquired another sponsee. Dick was a young guy, maybe twenty-four years old, and referred to me by a mutual acquaintance at work. He didn't attend many meetings, rarely called to check in, and didn't read much of the literature. Still, he was staying sober. Then one day he called. It was a couple of days after the first anniversary of his sobriety. Dick had holed up the night before in a motel room with a bottle of Jim Beam and got wasted. His objective had been to prove he wasn't an alcoholic by staying sober a year. His drunken celebration only proved the opposite, as did his later difficulties with drinking.

So there I was. Two sponsees: one who committed suicide after looking and sounding so good, and the other who used a period of abstinence to prove he wasn't an alcoholic, only to spend years in denial in the face of mounting problems resulting from drinking. *Maybe I wasn't cut out to be a sponsor,* I thought. Fear and ego prevailed, and it would be several years before I would meet Marquiz and sponsor another alcoholic. In the process, I deprived myself of the many lessons sponsees always teach their sponsors. Even though I didn't drink, my spiritual growth was stunted, and my life became more difficult.

## THE DRILL

A number of beliefs and practices attend the first step. Starting with the desire to stop drinking, Harry told me that the key was to want sobriety more than that first drink. Marquiz taught me that if we are not planning to stay sober, we are likely planning, however unconsciously, to take that first drink. Julie demonstrated that you do not need to ruin your life before recovering. Joe, Bill, Anita, and scores of others demonstrated that staying sober often means doing what comes unnaturally.

Thousands of tips and ideas can help an alcoholic attain and keep sobriety, and no one does them all. But there is a general framework — a drill, if you will — from which the right practice and attitude can emerge to address the threat at hand. Given that we are all powerless over alcohol, and our lives had become unmanageable, how do any of us alcoholics attain and sustain sobriety? It helps to know what a majority of alcoholics do in A.A. to stay sober. Here are some personal observations.

- First, a majority of alcoholics who get sober and stay continuously sober in A.A. attend a lot of meetings, especially during the early months of recovery. Ninety meetings in ninety days will give nearly any alcoholic a good shot at sobriety.

- Second, a majority of alcoholics who get sober and stay sober in A.A. get a sponsor who has a sponsor who, in turn, has a sponsor, and all of them are working the program. This means they attend meetings, work the steps, and help others achieve sobriety. If the sponsor doesn't have time to talk or meet regularly, get a new one.

- Third, a majority read the literature and discuss it with their sponsors or other A.A. members.

- Fourth, virtually none play games with other mood-altering substances — sober requires total abstinence from all street drugs and any licit medication not prescribed for a specific medical issue and used in dosages and lengths of time that do not exceed the prescription.

- Finally, a majority work the steps as well as they can. In the beginning, it is usually best to work them in order, although some do not follow a strict sequential path. Later, specific steps can be worked to meet specific occasions.

## A DAILY REPRIEVE

*The Big Book* says we get a "daily reprieve contingent on the maintenance of our spiritual condition." This requires action, real work. On a personal level, it has translated into the following daily ritual that worked for me for many years, and I suggest it to my sponsees, as well.

1. **Upon awakening, start praying.** Do what Harry did: pray even if you do not believe in God. Just do it anyway. There will be plenty of time to sort out your theology after you have been sober a couple of years. Ask for a loving and forgiving heart and everything needed for that day to stay sober. Give thanks that you even have another day — given the paths so many of us follow, it could have been very much otherwise.

2. **Do some spiritual reading**. In the beginning, read at least a paragraph of A.A. literature, especially *the Big Book*, every day. It doesn't need to be read in its entirety all at once. Just read until you get to something that resonates, and then think about it, and let those thoughts go wherever they lead.

3. **Call your sponsor.** Discuss *any* difficulty you may be having, whether or not it seems to be related to alcoholism. Especially

discuss any urges to drink. If you cannot reach her or him, leave a message. Call again later and leave another message. If you leave three messages without getting a return call within twenty-four hours, it's time to have a talk with your sponsor to determine if the two of you are a good fit.

4. **Attend a meeting.** Any time you tell yourself you need to attend a meeting tomorrow, or later this week or next week, attend one today.

5. **Review the day**. At day's end, examine any difficulties you encountered: arguments, disagreements, distressful situations, getting hacked-off at other drivers. The main issue is to determine what your role was in it. Commit to discussing it with your sponsor. Equally important, review the good experiences and your role in them. Go to sleep with a prayer on your lips, giving thanks for another day without drinking.

In the face of additional addictions, in recent years, I have bolstered my prayer life to five times a day, and I usually make two calls a day just to check in. If my program contact isn't available, it doesn't matter — I leave a voice message.

Above all, gratitude is key. We can never be sufficiently grateful, and we need to express it to whatever Higher Power we have in our lives, as well as to our loved ones, sponsors, fellowship members, and anyone else who will listen.

Some final thoughts on Step 1. My second sponsor, Tom D., used to say:

*"In A.A. anything worth doing is worth doing imperfectly."*

I certainly do not do these things perfectly, and my sponsees don't either. We make the effort. If you cannot find a good A.A. meeting, go to a lousy one; if you can't find a good A.A. sponsor, find one who isn't all that good. If you can't work a step perfectly (and no one can), work it poorly. JUST DO IT. You always get another bite at the apple. In fact, repetition is essential to recovery, and we get better at it as we go. That includes the drill above.

## WRITING IT DOWN

We write out our moral inventory in Step 4 and we make a list of all persons we have harmed in Step 8. But we do not have to wait to start writing. It can be helpful to put pen to paper from the beginning, in Step 1. Along with the daily practice above, many of my sponsees wrote out their first step, taking a sheet of paper and dividing it into two columns. The first column listed the experiences that demonstrated evidence of powerlessness over alcohol and drugs; the second column enumerated acts evidencing the unmanageability. The specific instances of promises to cut back or stop drinking; to do better the next time in any number of areas; the missed opportunities and broken promises; the unreached goals; the wasted money; the anger that alienated others; the pain we never intended to inflict on others; the lies and betrayals. Breaking the list into five- or ten-year time frames can help us see the progression of the illness. Sometimes these overlap, but it doesn't matter. Such a list makes the words and deeds that brought us into the program more tangible and undeniable before our well-honed rationalization skills can minimize, marginalize, and ultimately remove them from our consciousness. Saving this list can prove valuable later on, as we will see.

## JOB ONE

There may be a million things or more an alcoholic can do to get sober and stay sober. Effort, however imperfect it may be, is rewarded. But, whatever the initial motivation for stopping, it must ultimately be done for the alcoholic him/herself, not for someone or something else. And, above all, job one is clear and simple from the first time we darken the doorway of A.A. until we die: don't take that first drink. We may be beset with numerous intractable problems involving spouses, parents, children, bosses, and authorities, and we may believe that "if only they understood," our lives would be better. But that's not how it works. Ron, a friend and longtime A.A. member, passes on what his sponsor told him in the early days of his recovery. His sponsor said:

> *"I really don't care what you say; I don't care what you think; and I certainly don't care what you feel. All I care about is what you do — don't take that first drink."*

Not only does this apply to newcomers and those returning from a relapse, but also to the person with fifty years of sobriety.

# STEP TWO

If I am really powerless over alcohol, and if my life is really unmanageable by me, then I am finished unless there is a power greater than myself to restore me to sanity. But this restoration doesn't happen overnight. So, the program gives us the second step:

*"We came to believe that a power greater than ourselves could restore us to sanity." (AA, p. 59)*

This step is not only essential to the recovery of the individual alcoholic but to the continued existence of the Fellowship itself. A.A. depends on its members to carry the message, but I cannot do that unless my thinking is sound. Sound thinking is the essence of sanity.

It took time for the message to get through to me. The first time I read Step 2, I was glad to see that the program acknowledged the existence of God, glossing over the fact that this step does not refer specifically to "God" but to a "power greater then ourselves." Many people new to A.A. come with an agnostic, atheistic, or even hostile view of God, and Step 2 allows a broader and more gradual approach to the issue. But I thought I had this part pretty well down pat. I had studied theology and automatically thought I understood what the founders were saying. I assumed it meant my version of God *would* help me, and I skimmed over the part about restoring me to sanity. I wasn't insane. That the step does not read that way, or necessarily convey that meaning, was to be revealed to me as time passed. But, in listening to what the older folks around the A.A. table were saying, I could understand why it might be a good thing to have such a step — for people like them, many of whom for decades had been ridden hard by the disease and put away wet. I was even grateful in a perverse way that I hadn't drunk as long as they had or I, too, might have gotten so "bad" as to be in need of the last four words of Step 2.

In sitting around the tables and listening, the curtain which hides the truth every alcoholic needs to acknowledge if they are to recover slowly opened ever wider, and I began to gain insight. Just as my awareness had expanded when I revisited the Johns Hopkins questionnaire a few weeks after coming into the program, I slowly began to recognize how profoundly those final words in Step 2 applied to me.

Drinking up my bus fare and walking home in the dead of winter; jaywalking while drunk, which stranded me for several seconds in the middle of a busy street while cars whizzed past a few inches behind and in front of me; meandering under the influence toward a flooding Mississippi River rising in the streets of lower-town St. Paul and needing to be ordered back and driven home by a police officer who knew me from Louie's store — were but a few of the irrational instances that slowly came back to me. Of all these recollections, one that convinced me I needed restoration to sanity was an event that had occurred a couple of years before my first A.A. meeting.

The process of looking for something that wasn't there often took me from bar to bar. One night after work, starting with three or four drinks at Mitch's and then wandering up to Wabasha Street a few blocks away, I was half-in-the-bag after a couple of more whiskey sours at a place called Alary's Club Bar. Alary's was a strip joint, and drinks were more expensive there. Concerned that I was running out of money, I left and headed north on Wabasha Street toward a dive where I figured I'd have "just one (or two) more" and go home. On the way, I noticed a building under construction a block to the right and, for some insane reason still unknown to me, decided to check it out. Somehow, I gained entrance and found my way to a set of stairs which went up to the third floor. From there, the means of ascent became less sophisticated, and I had to climb a series of wooden ladders until I could go no higher — either the fifth or sixth level. In the darkness, I could barely make out the steel rods and other building materials stacked on the concrete floor. I crept past them to the edge of what would eventually become a floor-to-ceiling window, but in which the glass had not yet been installed. As I looked out over the city, I thought to myself, *How existential!* A truly concrete human experience, devoid of any of the trappings of abstract philosophical or religious thought. The highlight of an evening that only a drunk could imagine had such meaning.

## RUTHIE

With his passion for civil rights, fondness for assertive women, and his silence at meetings for several months when he first attended A.A., Joe from the old Unity group in St. Paul would have loved Ruthie. She was a short, thick African American woman, a native of Chicago's West Side. The first time I heard her, she was giving a lead on Step 2 at the Mustard Seed. She referred to her new sponsees as her "babies." She didn't tolerate nonsense and wasn't much interested in hearing any original thinking on how to stay sober from newcomers who sought her sponsorship.

That night, in a raspy voice, she declared,

"I tell my babies unless you're asking how to work the steps, I don't wanna hear nuthin' from you for six months, cuz you ain't gonna be restored to sanity before then."

Ruthie knew all the street games and wasn't about to be hustled. She had a deep fundamentalist, religious-spiritual orientation and as much of her education came from those streets as from classrooms. Yet, when it came to the steps, she was just like Harry, my agnostic, highly educated lawyer sponsor. She didn't get cute with the steps or try to edit them to demonstrate some esoteric insight. She kept it simple. She wasn't into self-redemption and knew that none of the rest of us could save ourselves, either. Like Harry, she had become steeped in the need for the humility and faith that undergird Step 2.

Indeed, if the program stopped at Step 1, most of us would be out of luck. Powerless and unmanageable, our prospects were bleak, if not hopeless. As important as it is, an admission of powerlessness and unmanageability alone does not restore us, nor does it alone get us sober or keep us that way. Listening to the stories of others and observing the changes in them and ourselves enables us to come to believe in the restoration to sanity. We hear it, we see it, and we feel it. Finally, we believe it — not just for others but, most importantly, for ourselves.

But like all the twelve steps, 2 is an ongoing process, not a single event. If we do not continue to hear it, see it, and feel it, the belief can wane. One of the great promises of the program, that "we will intuitively know how to handle situations that used to baffle us," will be slow to materialize, if at all. Situations that trigger an urge to drink that is sometimes so strong that our whole being screams out, telling us that our attempts to abstain are hopeless and totally against nature, will make taking a drink seem natural instead of contrary to what we need to do in order to live. Without the restoration to sanity, at least to some degree, the intuitive forces that can guide us to the right path in such critical moments will not be there.

Another key Step 2 provides is the realization that since the inception of our addiction, a power greater than ourselves has been alive and active in our lives: alcohol and other drugs. The presence of such a greater power in our lives should not be a surprise if we were truly sane. It stands to reason that, in the face of that terrible destructive power that has undermined our happiness and threatened our lives, another force equally powerful will be necessary if we are to recover. Certainly, our personal effort will be essential, but by itself it will not be enough. It will take a restorative power greater than us to overcome the destructive power greater than us so we can live rather than die. So here we have it: two equally "greater powers," one destructive, the other restorative. Which way the scale will tip, which of the two will prevail, again will be determined by our desire — Step Zero. We get to cast the deciding vote.

## MURIEL

Hearing about a power greater than ourselves restoring us is one thing, but seeing it in action is another. Those of us who were raised with a religious belief had heard the clergy and other believers expound for years on the power of God and His saving grace. Yet, in our personal lives, the consequences of our addictions mounted despite our prayers, frequently even after having seen the same kind of devastation played out in the lives of a parent or others close to us. For many of us, the message was an abstraction, a hypothesis at best, maybe wishful thinking, or somehow discriminatory in ways that baffled us. Certainly, God wasn't biased, loving one person more than another, making one suffer while others flourished. Or was He? No, I told myself, God wouldn't do that; it must be something I am doing. I am just not trying hard enough, praying hard enough, do not want happiness enough, or not willing enough to "pay the price." Honorable as this self-effacement and introspection may have seemed, it was still part of the problem, because it was self-centered and presumed that I either had or should have had the power to solve my own problem. My addiction never got better; I just became more obsessed with how to do it right.

Before coming into A.A., I hadn't completely lost my faith in a restorative Higher Power, but was of the growing belief that I would probably have to wait until after I died to experience it. Then at my first meeting, I listened to people who had known my pain and dysfunction but did not sound or look like I felt. They were happy. I hadn't seen them when they had first showed up, so I had no basis for comparing where they were to where they had been. I hadn't experienced the contrast between their recovery and their active addiction. The change had already taken place by the time I first met them, so at that point, I hadn't witnessed the power of Step 2 in their lives. Then, a couple of weeks later, Muriel walked through the door at the Uptown Club, and in her transformation, I saw the light, and it permanently changed my understanding.

Muriel was in trouble. Although she was young and a woman, even the hardliners would have considered her to be a "real" alcoholic. Very quiet, mostly wary with a scared, faint smile, shabby clothes, bad complexion, and the only African American in the place, she was addicted to alcohol and Lord only knows what else. At her first meeting, she said very little, just that she had a small child and had to stop drinking but didn't know how. Jan took her under her wing.

She became a regular at Uptown, and in the weeks that followed, the changes in her appearance and participation were dramatic. It turned out that she was not only articulate but attractive. I commented on this to Harry. His response was typical and hit where needed most at the moment. I do not know if it was my tone or manner of expression, but Harry's first comment was that I needed to beware of being smitten. She wasn't there to get involved with a married man, and I wasn't there to jeopardize my sobriety by fantasizing about her. The group was very protective of newcomers, especially women for whom it was much more difficult to get help with addictions than it was for men. Once a woman finally gets to a meeting, the last thing she needs is inappropriate attention, especially with lame sexual overtones, from guys who are either new to the program or not working it seriously. And a recovering man does not need a woman with virtually no sobriety and a value system so weak that she would be attracted to him and his inappropriate overtures in the first place. Exceptions aside, even if one member has years of sobriety, and the other is in the first few years of recovery, the relationship can be fraught with risk.

To the main point, Harry said that he, too, had noticed the change in Muriel. But to him it wasn't as surprising as it was to me. He had had the benefit of primary residential treatment. In the weeks Harry had spent at Hazelden, he had seen many similar transformations among patients who, after being admitted in desperate need of detox and other medical care, had left a few weeks later looking and sounding like completely different persons. Years later while working there, I was to see scientific confirmation of these changes in the pre-post psychological tests administered to patients. But the biggest surprise in Harry's response was when he said he had seen the same transformation in me. It hadn't felt like there had been such remarkable progress in my life, but Harry enumerated the changes he saw, from work through my personal life including my marriage, and he was right. Not only did the changes need to be pointed out by another person, but I also needed the reminder of where I had been only a few weeks earlier in contrast with where I had come to be. It was vital in fostering my gratitude and increasing my awareness of both the hell of addiction and the beauty of recovery. As for Muriel, like many early on, she struggled. But after a false start or two, she went on to a better life, the essence of which was a solid recovery.

Writing out Step 1 by listing the examples of powerlessness and unmanageability can be a big help in gauging the extent to which Step 2 is working in our lives. Some of my sponsees who have done this rated the severity of each item on their Step 1 list, both at the time they came into the program and then later in their recovery when they were pondering what Step 2 meant in their lives. Many used a scale, with 5 being severe and 1 being mild. The contrast was often dramatic. Even after a short period of time, there were significant changes in some of the most vexing areas. This exercise can be a concrete reflection of the gains we are making and the areas in which progress is slowly unfolding. Awareness of this progress can be a great source of encouragement. In the day-to-day bustle of living, it's easy to lose sight of our how far we have come. Just as the progression of our addiction can be insidious, the progress we make in recovery may be largely silent and not immediately apparent to us.

Hope is an essential part of life in general and certainly in recovery. It was the principle gift I received from my first meeting and throughout these many years of sobriety, fraught as they have been with as many low points as high ones. At its essence is a vision, however bleary, that life can change for the better, and a situation largely unknown will end well. As time passes, and some of our hopes materialize, we begin to develop faith. A faith that works. And with this, we are ready to take the next step.

# STEP THREE

M any in the Fellowship have a step they find particularly difficult. For some, it is Step 4 or 5 or both. For others, 6 and 7 get
shorted. For still others, Step 9 seems insurmountable. And, for some
— especially those with an agnostic or atheistic resistance — any step
that mentions God is a problem. For me, the toughest one was Step 3:

> *"Made a decision to turn our will and our lives over to the care
> of God as <u>we understood Him</u>." (AA, p. 59)*

Starting my journey in A.A. with a meeting on Step 4 had a lot of
advantages, mainly because it enabled me to identify with the experiences shared by the people sitting around the table. Step 4 elicited a
level of detail about how the problem manifested itself in their daily
lives that was so palpable that I could not help but feel connected
to them. The big disadvantage was that it was almost four months
before we got around to Step 3 when I could gain the group's collective
wisdom on how they may have struggled with it. By that time, I was

feeling really good about the program, myself, and my new-found sobriety. And, I hadn't had to do anything so drastic as turning my life and my will over to God, or so I thought. But just the sloppy way that notion was constructed in my mind, and the way it misrepresents what the step actually says, was a crucial part of what would develop into a serious problem in taking Step 3. We'll examine that in a moment. But for now, let's look at one of the biggest hurdles nearly all alcoholics face: deep-seated, self-centered fear. And doubt.

Many who come into the program have had the sad experience of not having been taken care of by those to whom they were entrusted. Physically or sexually abused as children; neglected or abandoned by parents or guardians; betrayed by friends, lovers, or spouses; bullied and belittled by siblings or other kids; they learned to be wary, cynical, and fearful. When in persistent pain, it is difficult for any human being not to be preoccupied with themselves. Every morsel of strength in their being rallies to counteract the pain. Thinking of the best interest of others is not only difficult but may be out of the question. Self-centered fear can be the strongest defense mechanism one has.

This is not to ignore the fact that many people have had such unfortunate experiences and did not become alcoholics. Conversely, some who became addicted had experienced few, if any, of these adversities. But, increasingly, experts are learning what a major part trauma can play in the onset of addictions, mental illness, and social dysfunction. Many such victims came to believe that somehow, they were unworthy of the love and respect that seemed to adorn the people from happy, well-adjusted environments. This lent credence to the addict/ alcoholic "False Belief System" Patrick Carnes describes so well in his book *Out of the Shadows*. The fundamental premise is that "I am no damn good." Next, if anyone really knew me, they wouldn't like me. Therefore, I need to solve my own problems. The quickest solution is alcohol, drugs, inappropriate or compulsive sex, overeating, or other high-risk, self-defeating, self-destructive behaviors. Before addictive behavior became our problem, it had been *what we did about* our primary problem — a spiritual condition that was in tatters.

Many of us had prayed to no apparent avail. We prayed that we could be "good" so our abusers would relent. We prayed that our parents would stop fighting or stop drinking. We prayed that we ourselves would not get drunk. We prayed for the big break that would change things for us. Love, peace, money, happiness, success — we prayed for it all and not only for ourselves but for those we loved. It never seemed to materialize, at least not in the way we had hoped.

Some of us had doubts that God even existed. Others had dispensed of the doubt and simply concluded that there was no God. Yet, if we were powerless, then only a power greater than ourselves *could* restore us. What could we do? For me, after years of resistance, avoidance, and minimization, the only choice was Step 3. But it took heavy doses of failure, reflection, insight, and the recovery experience of others.

## VICTORIA

For many years, the Sunday morning meeting at the Mustard Seed in Chicago was my anchor. I loved that meeting. It was a step meeting, and regardless of the attendance, everyone got a chance to share. As a result, the comments were to the point, rambling soliloquys kept to a minimum. Victoria was a regular, an Irish South Chicago woman in her thirties. Like many in the program, the God of her childhood was a huge disappointment, a detached, judgmental, rigid, authoritarian figure who allowed injustice to abound in the world. I am not sure what happened in her life to cause her to view God in this way, but whatever it was, her perception was not uncommon. She knew she was powerless and that her only shot at a life with any meaning was if she could rely on a power greater than herself. But it wouldn't be the God she learned about while growing up. Struggling with the issue, her sponsor made a suggestion. Without arguing about the existence of God, her sponsor posited a hypothetical question:

> "Okay, let's assume you are right that there is no God. But, if there *was* one, what would he or she or it be like? Just consider this idea."

Victoria pondered the question. Later, she shared her thoughts about what God would be like, if there really was one — loving, fair, loyal, forgiving, comforting, protective, along with a host of other beautiful attributes. Her sponsor replied,

> *"That's it. That is God as you understand Him."*

God as *we* understand Him? How can that be? Wouldn't the one true God have but one description, one definition? Wouldn't this call for one belief system? A member at my current Sunday morning meeting, a guy named Jasper, had what was for me the key. He saw this part of the 3rd Step as a sign of true brilliance on the part of the founders:

> *"'God as <u>we understood Him</u>,' makes all of us right," he said.*

It doesn't invite arguments or hang-ups. It is profoundly respectful. On this critical matter, the foundation of Step 3, the step on which "the effectiveness of the whole A.A. program will rest" (*12 and 12*, p. 34), *all* of us are right.

Finally, the step does not say we turned our will and life over to God, but over to the *care* of God. *God cares.* For me. And for everyone else.

## FAITH AND DOUBT

One of the great actors of our times, and one of the great tragic figures attesting to the cunning, baffling, and powerful forces of addiction, was Philip Seymour Hoffman. In the movie *Doubt*, he gave a great speech in which he said part:

"Doubt can be as powerful and sustaining as certainty."

A daunting proposition. When doubt takes over, we can feel very lost. But then he added,

"When you are lost, you are not alone."

And that's both the paradox and the challenge: whatever our perceptions are of reality, however powerful the forces of doubt, no matter how lost we may feel, we are still not alone.

But frequently that message is anything but clear, even when we have some measure of faith. The *Twelve and Twelve* says,

*"We can have faith, yet keep God out of our lives."* (12 and 12, p. 34)

How can that be? Can one have faith and doubt simultaneously? Not if we are talking about a binary condition. However, there may be another way to look at the issue. Is doubt the opposite of faith, or is the opposite of faith "no faith"? Conversely, what is the opposite of doubt? Faith or "no doubt"? Moreover, is it possible to believe in the existence of God without believing He will be of any practical use to us? Personally, I cannot recall a time when I did not have faith that God existed, but often doubted he was really on my side. How could He be? Consider Him, and look at me. We do know that doubt, a potentially perilous human condition as old as Adam and Eve, had in fact long disfigured faith in many of us. Then, after years of self-doubt and knowing something was wrong with us that we couldn't fix, we find A.A. and finally come to a point where we have some modicum of freedom from the most severe effects of our addiction. Miraculously, we are sober. Yet, it isn't easy or natural to turn our will and our lives over to a God who, at some level, we had for so long believed had abandoned us or others we loved. The doubt can linger even after our lives begin to change, however dramatic and positive that change may be. Nevertheless, making that decision in Step 3 was absolutely crucial for me in order to experience the fullness of the miracle of sobriety, or anything even close to it. Again, for me at least, the *Twelve Steps and Twelve Traditions* says it best:

> "*The effectiveness of the whole A.A. program will depend upon how well and how earnestly we have tried to come to a decision to turn our will and our lives over to the care of God as we understood Him.*" (12 and 12, pp. 34–35)

A powerful and uncompromising statement, indeed, and one that did not sink in with me for decades.

## MARK

In early spring of 1966, I attended my first Step 3 meeting at the Uptown Club. A guy named Mark gave the lead. I was feeling wonderful. The change in seasons can be a challenge to many alcoholics, but for me this one was exhilarating. So was Mark's lead. The part that struck me was when he said that in his two-plus years in the program, he had observed that the people who were happiest in their sobriety had gotten a "good handle on the spiritual end of this program." We couldn't do it ourselves. He talked about the absolute need to surrender. At that time in my life, anything that affirmed God's existence was a comfort and a validation. Yet without realizing it, I had reservations. Not about His existence, but about what it would mean to let Him be in charge. Again, I did not contemplate what the step said nor comprehend its real meaning and applicability to me. It would be years before I realized and accepted the fact that surrender was the connective tissue running through recovery from beginning to end.

Mark also emphasized what A.A. taught in Step 3 — it was "God <u>as we understood Him</u>." This left room for interpretation. In my own case, I believed in the existence of God and if asked, would have said He was in my corner. This was what my head said. Yet, inexplicably, I was afraid that if left to his own devices, God would screw up something in my life. Either I would need to do something I didn't want to do, or I would need to refrain from doing something I wanted to do. I doubted things could get much better for me, especially in view of what my life had been before coming into the program. In a seven-day period during my fifth month of sobriety when we bought our first home, a car, and I got a new job making 30 percent more money, I felt like Jonathan Livingston Seagull. I was soaring. What I did not realize was that life could get pretty bad even without drinking if I did not "let go absolutely," as the Preamble in *The Big Book* says. It just took a while, and the slide was not only insidious, but camouflaged by apparent success.

Contrary to my interpretation, Step 3 does not say we turn our life and will over to God. It says we *"Made a decision"* to turn them over to "the *care* of God <u>as we understood Him</u>." And it has "will" preceding "life" in the order. The difference is no accident — it is more than semantics. Without turning my will over, it isn't possible to turn my life over. The literature stresses that willingness is the key. I had a tough time with that.

## A FAITH THAT WORKS VERSUS A DOUBT THAT CAN KILL

Buying our first home was a wonderful experience. Home ownership at that time was a rite of passage and much easier to do than it is today. I was twenty-eight years old, and Marilyn was twenty-five. One beautiful evening that first summer, I was out on our front lawn gazing at a sky full of stars with a heart full of gratitude. To have gone from a state of "pitiful and incomprehensible demoralization" in a life that was unmanageable to having a great new job, a car, and a home in such a short time was astonishing. Prior to A.A., dreams weren't coming true and hope was fading. Now, it had turned around. I recall thinking that evening that if our government could succeed in putting a person on the moon and I could get sober, anything was possible. Expecting the rate of change to continue and underestimating the down and gritty work involved in raising a large family, I prayed that God would tell me what I should do — give me a sign.

Shortly thereafter, we became involved in the community starting with church, civic affairs, and activities with the kids. But by far the biggest attraction was politics, especially for me. Many forces drove me. The social conscience formed at St. John's, with its emphasis on making a contribution, the inspiration of the Kennedy family, the civil rights movement, and the thrill of this great turn-around in my personal life all conjugated into a huge force seeking a purpose. That fall, I attended a meet-the-candidates meeting for the first time and made an immediate connection with the local political scene. I knew I would love the action. Marilyn got involved with the League of Women Voters, and together we were off and running.

We had moved into what had been an old and conservative farming community that was changing fast with hundreds of new middle-class affordable homes going up every year. By 1966, the demographics were flip-flopping, and it was becoming a young community with needs and a culture foreign to the old guard. Everything was in the formative stages. Sewers, curbing, sidewalks, and parks were needed. Comprehensive, professional planning, rezoning, infrastructure, charter revision, activities for kids, and equal opportunity legislation in housing and accommodations all had to be initiated. But the political power structure was still controlled by long-established landholders. We had only lived there a little over a year when I successfully ran for city council and was almost immediately seen as a leader in a fresh, new generation of local politicians.

It was heady stuff. Nothing feeds the ego more than winning an election for public office. Here I was, less than two years' sober with many of the deep-seated insecurities that characterize alcoholism yet to be exorcised, and the people elected me by a large margin even after I had disclosed that I was recovering.

I wasn't there to be a fixture — I wanted to get things done but was in the minority on the city council. Nevertheless, along with a small group of colleagues, we set out to make big changes across the board. However, I had doubts that any of it would happen without a strong, unrelenting effort from me personally. I didn't feel confident leaving any of it up to God. After all, wasn't I supposed to be an instrument in His hands? In truth, my trust in God was not strong enough to let go even moderately, much less absolutely. Public service can be incredibly hard work. But for me it went beyond that. In order to initiate change I believed things needed to be controlled. Therefore, while working a full-time job and trying to be a good husband and father of five, I attended 205 meetings in the first year, nearly all in the evening.

Aside from politics, the Jaycees gave us seed money for a not-for-profit Athletic Association to provide organized activities for kids. I was elected its first president. We got off to a great start, and it reinforced my political standing. Years later and long after our family had moved to Chicago, it continued to grow, becoming a major organization and culminating in a regional Olympic tryout site spearheaded by a friend, Gordon Voss, who had gotten elected to the state legislature. My work did not go unrecognized. Separately, a local newspaper awarded me "The Man of the Year," and the Jaycees did likewise. A large radio station gave me their "Good Neighbor" award. It was intoxicating. Like any addict, I wanted more. And I got it. We won a majority on the city council, and my colleagues elected me council president and eventually chair of our local political party. I played a significant role in helping a candidate for governor get the party nomination and ultimately elected. Various office holders and officials of both political parties consulted with me on a regular basis.

This scenario lasted nearly five years. During that period, I attended few AA meetings and largely neglected the family finances. From the outside it all looked great, but the reality was another story.

Marilyn may have summed it up best when she said:

> *"The trouble with being married to a politician is that*
> *everyone tells him how great he is, but when he comes*
> *home you [his wife] have to tell him the truth."*

At the same time, she had her own issues. She didn't think Al-Anon was her cup of tea and was resentful when they suggested she focus on her issues, not mine. She considered it unfair that with it being my problem, she should be required to do anything about herself. Moreover, caring for five children would have been a challenge for anyone, even with the reinforcement of a mutual help group and a husband who was home enough to be helpful.

One problem when an alcoholic is having such success, especially early in recovery, is that it can be difficult to separate what is healthy from what isn't. Was I a good, hard-working public servant or a control freak? Was it legitimate motivation or "self-will run riot"? Political astuteness or "instincts on rampage"? Was I a man of vision or "grandiose"? Was I a tenacious man of principle or stubbornly and narrow-mindedly hanging on? Finally, who was I really doing all this for — the betterment of the community or my own political self-aggrandizement? My political supporters might have said one thing while my adversaries took the opposite stance. Could either group, partisan as they were, be objective? Could both, in some ways, be right?

Perhaps the answer was in the fact that I was increasingly upset about one thing or another, with resentment and criticism of political adversaries fueling much of the hyper-activity. I was seldom satisfied, a self-promoter, and easily hurt. The Serenity Prayer was a source of mystery. I understood the parts about "the serenity to accept the things I cannot change" and "the courage to change the things I can," but the "wisdom to know the difference" baffled me. Who knows what can be changed unless there is a concerted effort to try? Really try! Also, I left off the last part: "Thy will not mine be done." Beneath it all, I had aspirations for higher office. I dreamed of becoming a United States senator, and I didn't want to leave that in God's hands. He might have other plans.

Looking back, two or three A.A. meetings a week and regular contact with my sponsor would have made a big difference, especially with an emphasis on humility and letting go. But I did not have time for that. The problem had become an intrinsic part of its own cause. An emerging conundrum took hold. Without trust that God's plan for me might be better than my own, I could not "Let go and let God." Therefore, I had to control all the more, which in turn depleted the time and energy for A.A. meetings and further reduced both the chance of letting God guide me and my own ability to follow the guidance that was apparent had I been open to it. Finally, I stopped going to church regularly.

Our finances, our marriage, the condition of our house, my job, my A.A. program, and my religious practice were all adversely affected. Increasingly, there were conflicts with almost everyone, even some of my supporters. But my ego was still being fed. How could anything that felt so good be bad?

## INTEGRITY

The words integrity and integration come from the same Latin root. If one's outside is not integrated with what is going on inside, there can be no integrity. Ignoring the downside, I believed what I was doing was admirable, and many others said so, as well. The contrast with what my life had been during my drinking days was beyond question. But again, something was wrong. I didn't like the person I was becoming. The Preamble to *The Big Book* says, "Half measures availed us *nothing.*" It does not say "Half measures availed us *half.*" I was shortchanging the most important parts of my life: family, faith, and recovery.

Thinking back, a great line from a G.K. Chesterton poem, "The World State," comes to mind:

> "This compromise has long been known, this scheme of partial pardons,
> In ethical societies and small suburban gardens,
> The villas and the chapels where I learned with little labor
> The way to love my fellow man and hate my next-door neighbor."

Ah yes. A scheme of partial pardons. And how I loved my fellow man while neglecting my family and fighting with those around me. And how the resentment was festering toward my political opponents and even some of my supporters.

Even though I had always prayed, it wasn't without qualification. Throughout this time and for several years thereafter, I started each morning in front of the bathroom mirror and, while shaving, saying to God: "I am an alcoholic, I won't drink today. Thy will not mine be done." Turning the drinking over to God was one thing. And, I would have said I was willing to turn my life over, as well. But my will? Well, that was another matter. As we will see later, a major problem was that Step 3 says we "made a decision" not that we actually carried it out to perfection. *The Big Book* asks, "Just what do we mean by this and just what do we do?" This is huge. The answer is that in order to turn our will over, we must take the remaining steps, especially 6 and 7.

As I encountered life's daily difficulties, many were the foxhole prayers like those I had said when drinking. They all pertained to God helping me with my *life*. After all, I knew what needed to be done; I had a plan, an agenda. And it was based on high moral principles, helping my community being foremost. It was just a matter of God helping me do it. When I was in trouble, I wanted to turn my life over, never realizing that as I lurched from one predicament to another, unless I first surrendered my *will*, my life would always find its way back into the quagmire, even when I seemed to be doing so many good and admirable deeds. These were prayers that mostly requested God's endorsement rather than guidance.

No one could go on like this indefinitely. After nearly five years of nonstop activity, I was getting burned out and feared that I would crash. On the city council with other liberal members, a strong core of volunteer constituents, and a great staff led by an excellent city manager, we did build the city's infrastructure, revise the charter, rezone a major portion of the town, attract a major regional shopping center, and witness significant population increase. On parks and playgrounds built by the city council, the Athletic Association provided activities to thousands of kids who fed three high schools that ultimately produced championship teams and some players who made it to the majors years later. Our town was becoming a political and economic force, a vibrant presence in the area. But increasingly, I began to question myself and where I thought I wanted to go. Technically, our family was bankrupt, and this secret weighed heavily on me. What if people could see the truth! The reality of my life did not match the appearance. Finally, little by little, I began to turn to the Power greater than myself.

## WHAT I DO VERSUS WHAT I AM

Again, the time between Christmas and New Year's Day proved pivotal. Only now it was 1971. My second city council term was coming to an end, and our team had lost the election six weeks earlier. Conservatives would rule again, led by a large landholder. What was worse, we had lost a human-rights referendum that I had personally spearheaded. Early in the term, I had decided not to run for reelection, hoping to move higher politically. But after these setbacks, more than anything, I needed to regroup.

I was no longer drowning in the sea of make-believe as when I was drinking, but I was still struggling to keep my nose above the water line. During my first term on the city council, I changed careers and started selling life and health insurance. The goal was to increase our income while providing more flexibility in my daily schedule to pursue politics. Three years later, it had become a grind, but it still looked like there could be a prosperous future now that I was taking a break from elective office. Again, appearances were one thing, but the reality was something else. Being the number-two producer in my agency and twenty-fifth in the company out of seven hundred agents satisfied the ego but not the pocketbook. Once more, my unwillingness to examine the contradiction fed the disease.

Feeling adrift and wanting to get away, late in December I decided to go up to St. John's for a few days and plan my sales activity for the upcoming year. The plan was to start with how much I needed to sell and the amount of premium it produced. Breaking it down to monthly, weekly, and daily activity, it would end with a specific number of telephone contacts and new appointments to be made each day.

The students were gone for Christmas break and I stayed in the monastery with the Benedictines. I spent most of the time walking the vast campus, praying, meditating, attending mass, and participating in community prayer with the monks. The beauty of the Gregorian chant and the holy silence of the monastery took me to a place I hadn't expected to be. I had difficulty getting to the task at hand, the purpose that took me there. It occurred to me that somewhere along the line, my view of myself had changed from that of a human being to a "human doing." I had come to totally define myself by *what I did* — my accomplishments — and had stopped reflecting on the bigger question of *what I was*. Politics and insurance were what I did, but what was I, really? In essence, I was an alcoholic and a man, a father, and a husband. And, although flawed, I awakened to the realization that I had value even if I never garnered another vote or sold another insurance policy. There had been grand sales plans in the past with wonderful goals but absent the necessary follow-through. I had gotten it backward: I loved the projected outcome but loathed the process required to get to it. Even the goals themselves tended to be superficial. My problem was earning enough money — commissions — not the face value of the policies or the premium generated, which was what our company emphasized.

I abandoned the grand plan in favor of a specific income goal for the following month. If I did not meet it, I would find another job, one that could provide for my family. If I met the goal in January, I would reset it for February and month to month thereafter based on our family's need. I made a decision that the first month I missed the goal, I would leave the business. That was the plan. It wasn't necessary to delve into the mechanics of how I would do it. In truth, I knew what needed to be done. I'd either do it or I wouldn't.

A burden had been lifted. Upon returning home four days later, I called my boss, told him my plan, and shared it with Marilyn. At the end of January, I came up about a hundred dollars short. Only one hundred dollars. I resisted the temptation to rationalize. Instead, I called a political friend whom I had met working on the governor's campaign eighteen months earlier. He suggested contacting a mutual acquaintance who was a close advisor to the governor. A month later, while still retaining my insurance business on a part-time basis, I began a new career with the State of Minnesota Commission on Alcohol Problems. A few months after that, I was asked to take a newly created position that would require me to travel the state. This provided a clear opportunity to establish political contacts that might enable a run for statewide office. Little did I know that it was to catapult me into a new field of human service that would ultimately establish innovative systems in thousands of employment settings around the world. Its purpose would be to help employed alcoholics and their family members get into treatment. In time, it became known as the Employee Assistance Program, a term I have been credited with coining. It would assist employed people and their families with a broad spectrum of personal problems, including alcoholism.

The new job did take me around the state and beyond. I became part of a national network of professionals trained by NIAAA, starting in Pinehurst, North Carolina, in the summer of 1972. For a while I still held hope of a political career. But surprisingly, that aspiration ever-so-slowly began to fade as I found the promise of this new career to be an almost-perfect fit for me. Elements from nearly all my previous professional experiences, my political career, and my recovery had a positive bearing on the work in the new position. Yet, the dream of serving in the US Senate still called out to me.

## WARREN

Really listening to the Power greater than me during those few days at St. John's paved the way to listen more to others. A year later, having made numerous contacts statewide that could be helpful politically, I met with various officeholders and party leaders to test the waters about seeking higher office. They were encouraging, but the one I respected most was cautious. The attorney general was widely admired. He had been the state party chair, had run for governor, and had seen many political aspirants succeed and fail. While my focus had been on my political future, he framed the issue in terms of the impact it could have on me personally. Could I win a statewide office, perhaps secretary of state, and use it as a launching pad to the US Senate? Possibly, he said. During these meetings, I did not want to explore anything negative or disclose any potential weaknesses I might have as a candidate, but he saw right through the pretense. He went straight to the financial risk and the fact that if I lost, I could be paying off huge debts for the next ten years or longer. While winning was possible, the party's nomination would first need to be secured, and that would require personal resources as well as contributions from supporters. And it would mean nonstop campaigning outside of work for more than a year.

He hadn't told me anything I didn't already know deep down. But facing him eye to eye made it impossible to avoid the issue or even skirt around the edges of it. Just as had been the experience when taking the 5th Step, another person now knew where I was and what I was up to, and that made all the difference. I finally admitted to myself how tired I had become of living in near poverty, the effect it had on our family, and the stress it created in our marriage. I liked having a consistent, adequate paycheck, the additional income from my part-time insurance sales, and the excitement of providing tangible help to alcoholics and others in distress. It was exciting to be in a fresh, new field that showed such great promise. I was to remain involved in politics and community affairs for the remainder of my life, but I never again sought elective office. I had changed course. Yet, "letting go and letting God" was still a challenge. While never seeking public office again, my fantasy never really died that someday I might hold office. Like all the steps, 3 is not an event but an ongoing endeavor both required by and reinforced by the steps yet to come.

## JOHN

Early in my Employee Assistance Program career, I made friends with a guy named John. I was thirty-four with about seven years of sobriety. John was in his sixties and had twenty years of sobriety, all in A.A. We were part of a federal effort to combat alcoholism in the workplace. Established by legislation shepherded by Senator Harold Hughes (D-IA), an icon in the recovery community, the National Institute on Alcohol Abuse and Alcoholism (NIAAA) had funded two Occupational Program Consultant (OPC) positions in each state to establish intervention programs in the workplace — one for public employers and one in the private sector. We became known as the "Thundering Hundred." John was the private sector OPC in Pennsylvania, and I held that position in Minnesota. The iron ore mines in Northern Minnesota were operated by the big steel companies headquartered in Pittsburg, so John and I were able to share two perspectives of our common professional interest: mine from the field and his from the corporate office. We also shared our challenges in recovery.

After getting to know me, he described my struggle with Step 3, saying:

"Jim, you are like the guy who has received an offer to enter into a cooperative venture that shows great promise. But you're gonna have to make some changes in the way you do business. So, you confer with your business buddies and do some research and then you write a letter agreeing to accept the offer. You put the letter in an envelope, seal it, put a stamp on it and walk down the street to the mail box. You open the lid to drop the letter in the box. You are holding the letter at the corner of the envelope between your thumb-nail and forefinger, but you just can't seem to let it go. You stand there, just barely holding onto the letter, but you do not 'let go absolutely.' The deal never gets done."

My watershed experience at St. John's notwithstanding, I was slipping back toward the "scheme of partial pardons." Going through the motions. Pretending. Giving it lip service.

Although the new career was a genuine success and I was in the middle of what was to become an international EAP movement, years passed before I finally found a way to "let go absolutely." Until then, I used a number of avoidance techniques to get around the level of surrender that was essential to taking this step. One of my favorites came right out of my drinking days. Just as I had so often allowed my psyche to go numb, like when I wandered up 4th Street that cold December night many years earlier so as not to face the fact that I was headed for another drink, I used this ploy as a way to not think about the fact that I was avoiding making the Step 3 decision. When it didn't work, I pretended. At A.A. meetings, I talked a good game — about how we didn't need to know what or who God was, only what He wasn't. He wasn't me: "God, The Great Not Me." How immensely knowable God was and so we couldn't really know Him/Her completely. Or how there was a difference between religiosity and spirituality. It was all true and sounded good but, given where I was spiritually, it was also a wonderful way to deflect attention from my own specific difficulty in taking this step, and shine the attention on the problems others were having with it. I was taking Step 3 vicariously at best, but mostly I just played around the edges.

Being able to turn a phrase or make a clever comment has always had a kind of seductive appeal in A.A. meetings. Joe at the old Unity meetings would never have stood still for this. He and the group would have cross-talked and made me focus on where I really was with the step "here and now." They all had a good sense of humor, but the primary purpose of meetings was to strengthen our sobriety, not to entertain or pontificate. I was stuck in a dogmatic slumber with clever lip service which would not allow me to "let go and let God." But why? The answer was fear and ego.

I was afraid I wouldn't get what I wanted. What did I want, besides a US Senate seat? A lot of things, but mostly I was in love with my own rectitude. Subconsciously I wanted the luxury of harboring resentments, initially toward political opponents. Later this morphed into anger toward civic and church leaders, child abusers, environmental polluters, the "super-rich," bought-off government officials and media outlets, and politically oriented newscasts that didn't share my viewpoint. You name it. Regardless of one's belief system, especially on social issues, resentment can be powerful fuel in driving personal ambition. It made me feel alive. However, I was loathe to admit that these were resentments. I told myself that I just had a refined social conscience. Beyond that, I wanted to shine, to be special. I wanted to display my unique analyses of what was wrong with the world and how it should be fixed. After all, I could see clearly now that I had been sober for a few years.

But gnawing away in the back of my mind was a troubling question that wouldn't go away: *What if God disagrees with you on this?* As if in a telephone conversation with my conscience, I responded by asking: How could He disagree? After all, I was right! *Okay, Jim, if you are "right," why are you so upset?* Because these other people won't listen! *Oh, really? How about the fact that you are not getting your way?* Click. Mysteriously, the imaginary call always got dropped at that point. Facing my fear was not easy. The biggest fear was, "If I let go, what will I have left?"

## TOM D–II

After years surrendering my will and taking it back, surrendering again and rushing to retrieve it, I had a wake-up call. I've already mentioned my first two A.A. sponsors, Harry and Tom D. Later, I had a third sponsor whose name was also Tom D. A big, handsome Irishman, he had been an excellent athlete, very intelligent, and an accomplished attorney. More important, he had a keen insight into the core of some of the more vexing problems alcoholics face, and he could articulate them in a direct, yet kind manner. Although he was less ideological and politically partisan than I was at that time, we shared many political views which left us far more in agreement than Tom D.-I and I had ever been. However, an occasional area of disagreement would surface. On one such occasion, we got into an argument with most of the heat and frustration coming from my end. Try as I might, I couldn't argue him into changing his position. Not getting my way, I did the next logical thing: I got pissed off. The following day, he sent me a note. He apologized for his part in the unpleasantness, which I thought was very nice of him and only appropriate. But before I could break into my happy dance, he spoiled the whole thing by suggesting that I look at *my* part. He said that there had been a number of occasions when the manner in which I expressed my views drifted from passion into "serious arrogance." With this note, Tom did two things that good sponsors do: First, he worked the program himself before assessing my part in the disagreement. Second, he didn't co-sign my behavior.

This most recent episode was only one instance. I didn't like hearing what Tom had to say, but it sunk in. This was my friend and sponsor, a person who truly wanted the best for me and had helped me on many occasions to consider alternative ways of looking at things. If he was put off by my attitude, maybe there was more to the problem than all "these other people" being obtuse and not listening.

Sometimes, a message like this comes through, sinks in, and calls to mind similar instances when other people tried to convey the same concern. Over the years, my wife, Janis, had commented that I did not want to listen to others once I made up my mind. I would over-talk and go on until others just fell silent, not wanting to argue their viewpoint when my mind was obviously closed. One of my favorite quotations from the late Senator Patrick Moynihan had been lost on me: "Everyone is entitled to their own opinion, but not their own facts." And this wasn't a new development. Years earlier at the old Unity Group, another guy named John told me, "Your pride is keeping you one inch tall."

I wish I could say that I had gone from point A to point Z on Step 3, that having logically seen it as a natural progression from Steps 1 and 2, I made the decision and then "just did it." But that wasn't the case. Even a long-practiced staple in my recovery did not work for me. I learned that when having trouble with a step, going back to the previous step and retaking it often helped, but not for me on 3. I was stuck. And many of the old shortcomings were emerging once again.

## THE "BONDAGE OF SELF" WAITS PATIENTLY ... BUT SO DOES GOD

Referring to prayer in Step 11 of the *12 and 12*, the author says,

*"... the great men and women of all religions have left us a wonderful supply." (12 and 12, p. 99)*

At this point one might ask where the Third Step Prayer was in my life all this time.

*"God, I offer myself to Thee — to build with me and do with me what Thou wilt. Relieve me of the bondage of self that I may better do Thy will. Take away my difficulties, that victory over them may bear witness to those I would help of Thy Power, Thy Love, and Thy Way of Life. May I do Your Will always." (AA, p. 63)*

It wasn't part of my daily life. Several years later it would become a staple in my prayer rhythm, but at that time, through all the battles when it could have helped me most, I rendered it missing in action. I had disguised my avoidance of the Third Step Prayer by claiming the virtue of integrity, no less. I told myself I didn't want to be a hypocrite by saying something or asking for something I could not be totally sincere about. In other words, I was just too honorable to say the Third Step Prayer! I could have used the admonition of Ron's sponsor. It wasn't what I said or felt or thought that mattered; it was what I *did* — or *did not* do. Once again, I needed to do what came *unnaturally*, but instead I chose to go with my own thinking — thinking which, uninspired by my Higher Power, would invariably lead me astray.

Our defects of character and indeed the addiction itself in its many alluring disguises will always call us back to the *"bondage of self"* — to the slavery of *"pitiful and incomprehensible demoralization"* — especially when we are most vulnerable. And we can be deluded into seeing only the narrow, immediate ray of pleasure which seems to fade to darkness so shortly after we give into the temptation. So, what was I going to do; where was I going to turn?

The words of a true heroine who knew the pains of slavery better than I could ever imagine, Harriet Tubman, come to mind as I recall my situation at that time.

"If you hear the dogs, keep going. If you see the torches, keep going. If there is shouting after you, keep going. Don't ever stop. If you want a taste of freedom, keep going."

With the mad dogs of addiction tracking me, I had a choice: I could either remain stuck in the quagmire of self-will and ambivalence to be eaten alive ever so slowly, or I could struggle forward as best I could.

It turned out that I had to go forward if for no other reason than to face how limited my efforts were in taking Steps 6 through 10 as a result of not having *"let go absolutely"* — of having turned my will and my life over and then taking it back, cherry-picking the issues I would turn over to God's care while hanging on to the rest.

Ultimately, I did both make the decision and actually turn my will and my life over to the care of God, but it took a long time. The seed had been planted years earlier when, as a result of working Step 11 poorly, I began to pray only for knowledge of God's will for me. In the years that passed, I went through the balance of the steps a number of times, with each pass taking me a little closer to the surrender Mark had talked about so many years earlier at the Uptown Group. I began to realize, and said it at meetings, that if God didn't want something for me, I'd be a fool to insist on having it. The key of willingness described in Step 3 of the *12 and 12* had been imbedded somewhere deep in the recesses of my psyche as a result of taking Step 11 imperfectly, and the door had been unlocked. Even though self-will had slammed it shut on many occasions, once unlocked, it could still be opened again and again.

A lot of "dis-ease" clung to the walls of my soul like barnacles on a ship's hull. Looking back, the pride, lust, anger, greed, gluttony, envy, and sloth were all present, and their corresponding virtues were in short supply. In addition, there was the self-pity, the abject fear, the despair, and the dishonesty.

## A LOVING AND FORGIVING HEART

Ultimately, I grew tired and disgusted having to admit to the same defects every time our Fitchburg Serenity Group came back around to Step 10. About that time, while saying the Lord's Prayer one day when out walking, the plea to "forgive us our trespasses as we forgive those who have trespassed against us" really sank in as never before. I began to pray in earnest for a loving and forgiving heart and with that, my life began to change. Almost immediately, the promise of *"a new freedom and a new happiness"* began to take hold, and I began to *"comprehend the word serenity"* and began *"to know peace."* (*AA,* pp. 83–84)

The first tangible evidence of it was patience with other people in general and, astonishingly, with other drivers. Inexplicably, I was no longer engaging in imaginary races with other cars and was backing off when they wanted to change lanes. Most surprisingly, when cut off, I didn't respond by flashing the international single-fingered salute. I went back to church, which is a story in itself, and I went to confession for the first time in years. I found myself continuously saying a prayer set I had abandoned decades earlier, finding that it was no longer monotonous but full of meaning and a wonderful inspiration for meditation. I was saying the rosary daily.

To sum up, for me the essence of the decision to turn my will and my life over to the care of God was to come to believe that letting God lead me through the remaining steps and through the remainder of my life would be better than obstinately trying to run my life my own way. At long last, I began to truly let go moment by moment, episode by episode and, contrary to what all those old fears told me, my life was better every time I did it. My fears really were little more than *"bogey-men"* as the *12 and 12* says, my pride a mortal enemy falsely disguised as a guide and friend. Rarely had my fear or my pride ever told me the whole truth, just enough to lure me into the wrong direction and, once I was on my way, abandon me.

# STEP FOUR

Holding forth at the 10:30 a.m. Saturday morning meeting at the Mustard Seed in Chicago, an old curmudgeon named Bill B. liked to say: "In A.A. we tell the truth about ourselves." For the most part, that's right. But in order to do it, we need to know what the truth is. And so we take Step 4:

> *"Made a searching and fearless moral inventory of ourselves."*
> *(12 and 12, p. 42)*

One of the beautiful experiences of fatherhood comes after your children are grown and you can learn from them. I am reminded of what my daughter Linda told her daughters when they were young and got caught engaging in some sort of unapproved activity. As they hemmed and hawed before answering a question about what they had been doing, she would tell them:

"If you aren't telling it all, you aren't telling the truth."

Knowing the truth about religion, or the truth about psychology, or even the truth about the twelve steps couldn't by itself get me where I needed to go. But when I learned the truth about myself and despaired, it was the beginning of a lasting recovery which all the other truths were able to support.

It was a bright, mid-summer day during my first year of sobriety. Our family was settled into our new home. The neighbors were young and friendly and had dozens of children the same ages as our kid. The new job was working out well. We were elated. The promises of the program were beginning to materialize.

## A CALL TO WORK

No longer working or living in St. Paul where Harry was based, I wasn't seeing him daily as I had during the first five months of my sobriety, so he reached out to me.

I was at work and the telephone on my desk rang. Harry was on the other end.

"Jim," he started out, "I have been thinking it's about time you did a 5th Step."

Taken aback, I responded:

"Step 5? Harry, I haven't done a 4th Step yet!"

"Well, I have been meaning to talk with you about that, too," he replied. Good old Harry.

Like the other steps of the program, I believe 4 is perfectly positioned. Taken later, our defects, unrecognized and unacknowledged, could undermine the chances that any initial joy we experienced from being sober could blossom into recovery. Taking it earlier, we would not have the benefits of Steps 1 through 3 that establish the foundation needed in order to do a thorough 4th Step.

We need the power implicit in the promise of *"the __care__ of God"* offered by taking Step 3. In order to get that power, we need to *"come to believe"* that the care and the love it implies really is available, and we get it when we take Step 2. But, in order for that belief to have any relevance for us, we need to face our condition and admit that we are personally *"powerless,"* and our lives are *"unmanageable"* in Step 1. In the process, our understanding evolves.

Getting to 4, I found that:

- Step 1 told me *what* I am

- Step 2 told me *what* I need

- Step 3 told me *who* I need and, finally

- Step 4 told me *who* I am

## THE TRUTH WILL SET US FREE

In Step 4, I learned the truth about myself in a way in which I would otherwise never have been able to. And the simple truth is best described in the *12 and 12*, referring specifically to the newcomer but applying to anyone in recovery, regardless of how long:

> *"that unless he [she] is now willing to work hard at the elimination of the worst of these defects, both sobriety and peace of mind will still elude him [her]; that all the faulty foundation of his [her] life will have to be torn out and built anew on bedrock."* *(12 and 12, p. 50)*

Many in A.A. have found Step 4 to be difficult. To begin with, we can't bob and weave around it; it can't be faked. Either we write it out and there it is on paper in black and white, or we don't. The written inventory, or absence of it, proves that we have either taken this step or not. Getting started is often the biggest challenge, and just having an idea of how to do so can be crucial. Perhaps that is why, in the years I have been in A.A., I do not know of anyone who was able to do Step 4 without help, usually from a sponsor or addiction professional. Somewhere there may be a recovering person who did it alone, but I haven't met them.

While I was surprised by Harry's call, I also was pleased that he thought I was ready to take 4, and I got started on it right away. A popular 4th Step tool, the Hazelden guide, hadn't yet been written, but *The Big Book*, the *12 and 12*, the meetings, and Harry's sponsorship gave me the guidance I needed. The all-consuming community involvement that characterized so much of my life in the early years of my recovery was yet to come, and I was still attending two A.A. meetings a week, driving the twenty miles from our home to St. Paul. Sharing with the groups that I was getting started on 4 helped reinforce my resolve to complete it.

Religion was important to me at the time, as I hadn't yet gone on my forty-year hiatus from it. Since childhood, I had gone to confession regularly after making an examination of conscience. It was cleansing and a source of new hope. But Step 4 was different. It wasn't about "sin" per se or seeking forgiveness in order to reach a level of spiritual acceptability that allowed me to receive God in the Eucharist at Sunday Mass. In other words, it didn't have the feeling of a transaction, which was how my religious practice had evolved as I labored under a code of moral theology expressed in a way that felt increasingly restrictive and judgmental. And it went much deeper than my typical examinations of conscience, which in time had become somewhat perfunctory. Years later when I came back to my religion, I used Steps 4 and 5 as models for how to truly examine my conscience and confess my sins. Instead of a series of periodic transactions when I was in some sort of spiritual trouble, both my A.A. program and my religion became a means of gradual transformation and a thorough moral inventory without fear as the basis of it.

Over the years, I have come to believe that the manner in which the 4th Step is taken should evolve as one gains years of sobriety. There are always exceptions, of course, but initially, Step 4 is more about identifying defects than assets, because it is the defects that will lead one back to drinking. Having borrowed the concept of an inventory from the Oxford Group, the founders knew from experience that:

*"no one can make much of his life until self-searching becomes a regular habit, until he is able to admit and accept what he finds, and until he patiently and persistently tries to correct what is wrong." (12 and 12, p. 88)*

While this quotation is from the narrative on Step 10, the life-long process of self-searching starts with Step 4. And, although every human being has personal assets, before the restoration to sanity in Step 2 begins to take hold, they may be hidden so far from consciousness that the newly recovering person has difficulty believing they even exist. But as time passes, it is just as important to identify the assets because they will form the bedrock on which a new life can be built. Moreover, to refuse to identify the assets may be little more than thinly disguised self-pity, a potentially deadly shortcoming.

Harry was concerned when he called that day, even though I wasn't displaying signs of a relapse or experiencing any prolonged cravings. In fact, I was relatively serene, enjoying an ongoing natural high. However, in the eight months or so he had been sober, Harry observed something that major treatment providers were to later acknowledge. In the *Twelve and Twelve*, Bill Wilson wrote about how our natural instincts often far exceed their proper functions. Instincts for sex, security, and society ...

> "so necessary for our existence ... [p]owerfully, blindly, many times subtly ... drive us, dominate us, and insist upon ruling our lives." (12 and 12, p. 42)

Again, sometimes a potential disaster can be camouflaged in apparent success. After the alcohol was out of my life, my sex drive did increase. Moreover, my desire for security, not only for myself but, more importantly, for my family, became much more finely tuned. I had developed a greater sense of responsibility. And companionship that no longer included drinking buddies but extended into the community was a welcomed new experience. Each of these was a good thing, and I enjoyed them. The problem is that each of them can also become an obsession in itself, replacing alcohol in order to get a high and create that exciting adrenaline rush. At the same time, as these new experiences were unfolding, an occasional sense of excitement still passed through me when involuntary images of the "good old days" crossed my mind. But I would say the mantra I used while shaving in the morning: "Dear God, I am an alcoholic, I won't drink today," and the image and craving would pass.

## DON'T DRINK OVER IT

This was one of the many times when Harry's sponsorship shone through brilliantly, based as it was on his spiritual awareness and intuitive knowledge of how to handle situations that were once baffling. While we had a lot in common, Harry and I did not entirely share the same moral code. His philosophy was that if you were going to steal from the company, cheat on your wife, or tell tall tales, it certainly

wasn't a good thing, but "do it sober ... don't drink over it." He emphasized the A.A. axiom that:

"There is nothing so bad that a drink won't make worse."

But he also realized that with my religious background, I might not
have the kind of tolerance for ambiguity he enjoyed. Equally important,
he did not try to persuade me to adopt his moral code. It has occurred
to me that an Irish Catholic without shame is likely to have an identity
crisis unless he can have a drink to mourn it. Harry knew that all the
people, places, and things accompanied by the self-defeating, self-destructive behavior that had characterized my drinking needed to be
identified early to prevent them from simply taking new forms. A
thorough house-cleaning starting with Step 4 was essential. This was
so important that Hazelden, one of the world's truly great centers for
the treatment of alcoholism and drug addiction, actually changed its
program in the early 1970s.

More than anyone, Dan Anderson, PhD, was responsible for
the development and widespread adoption of the multidisciplinary
approach to the treatment of addiction. This later became known as the
"Minnesota Model" and is used worldwide. As president of Hazelden at
that time, he and Sister Mary Leo Kammeier, the director of research,
conducted a modest study on relapse in the late 1960s. One of their
findings was that patients who had not completed a 4th Step after
discharge had much higher relapse rates than those who had. Dan
decided that every patient coming through Hazelden would do a 4th
and 5th Step before leaving treatment, and they added seven days to the
program to accommodate the process. Subsequently, they completed a
major study in 1972 which indicated that the overall relapse rates had
gone down significantly.

Important as it is to take the 4th Step, procrastination abounds
among recovering alcoholics. One of the big questions, and a frequent

stumbling block, is where to start. The answer is simple: start anywhere. Just get started: just start writing. Harry suggested starting with the worst thing I had ever done. I don't know if it really was the worst thing or not, but I started with something of which I was very ashamed. I had an aunt who was my son's godmother. On his first birthday, she started a savings account for him and gave me the passbook and a ten-dollar bill. The ten never got into the account. On one of the many occasions when I was short on drinking money, I "borrowed" it. I wrote this down first, and the rest of the inventory followed.

## ANYTHING WORTH DOING IS WORTH DOING POORLY

It would be nearly twenty years before I would meet Tom D. after moving to Chicago. But, of the supply of great little sayings he used when sponsoring me, one summed up the challenge for any alcoholic who finds difficulty taking any of A.A.'s twelve steps, especially Step 4:

*"In A.A. anything worth doing is worth doing poorly. If you cannot do a great 4th step, do a lousy one; if you cannot find a great sponsor, get a lousy one; if you cannot find a great A.A. meeting, attend a lousy one. It won't be the end of the world. You'll always get another chance as long as you keep moving forward and don't drink."*

Harry didn't give me a prescription for doing Step 4 but just referred me to the suggested format in *The Big Book* — if I wanted to do it that way. I looked it over and didn't feel quite right about the way it fit what I perceived to be my moral shortcomings. Without rejecting it altogether, I went in a modified direction.

At Louie's corner grocery where I worked part time, we sliced luncheon meat for customers and sold hamburger and hot dogs in bulk, wrapping them in thick butcher paper that came in rolls ten inches in diameter and two feet wide. I tore off a piece about eighteen inches long and folded and refolded it in half several times until I had a number of neat panels. I entitled the first panel "Stealing," entered the incident of the "borrowed" ten-spot and was on my way. From there, I wrote down everything I could think of, using the panels to demarcate the various categories of defects based roughly on the Seven Deadly Sins. I didn't worry about overlap. I wanted to be rid of anything that could take me back to drinking. If it was a threat to my sobriety, I didn't want it in my life. I took seriously the word *"searching."* To me it meant looking hard and long, not just taking a brief sidelong glance. To the best of my ability, I wanted my relationship with the truth to be an engagement leading to long-term marriage, not a brief flirtation.

I also needed to ponder the word *"fearless."* It didn't mean ferocious, screwing up my courage to a point that enabled me to grab a defect by the throat, choke the life out of it, throw it overboard, and be done with it forever. It simply meant "without fear." Though I hadn't truly surrendered once and for all in Step 3, I had still left the door of willingness open "ever so slightly" and had not yet slammed it shut. I was graced with enough trust to look at myself and my defects without fear when taking Step 4.

## THE ABBOT AND THE RECTOR

The word *"moral"* also caught my attention. First, the founders chose the word "moral" as opposed to ethical. The difference is significant. Both ethics and morals relate to right and wrong human conduct. But ethics is generally regarded as a series of rules provided by an external source such as a profession, religion, or other rule-making body. Morals refers to a set of principles regarding right and wrong that come largely out of a person's own conscience.

More than four decades later, a great theologian, a past Benedictine Abbot Primate, told me that there are two dimensions to morality: the law and the human conscience. It was his opinion that a clergyperson could not be a good pastor if they overemphasized doctrine while shortchanging the importance of the individual conscience. To paraphrase what he said:

> *"Knowing doctrine will get you 'As' in the seminary, but it will not assure that you will carry God's message, which is love."*

Of course, we need rules and guidelines, too. Without following strict accounting rules, we end up with an Enron scandal. Without following reasonable engineering maintenance and design rules, we have an I-35 bridge collapse or, worse, a space shuttle disaster triggered by something as seemingly small as an "O" ring — an "O" ring that failed and didn't need to. But, in the area of morals, things are not that clear-cut.

So, what is a moral inventory? For me it largely goes to my conscience, a conscience that has been formed in part by the example of others, plus an assortment of rules, regulations, laws, and theology, with all their nuances, ambiguities, and contradictions. But there is also something deeper, more personal, and more mystical. Some call it "natural law." Somewhere deep in my heart was the capacity to discern the moral quality of a concrete act. In deciding what was a moral transgression to be included in my 4th Step, Harry summed it up best for me, and I did not need to be an accomplished theologian or philosopher to understand it:

> "If it is troubling you, write it down."

He went on to say that I may not know exactly why it is troubling me. There may not be a clear-cut rule that has been violated or an easy explanation for including it. Scrupulosity may blur the picture. But it wasn't necessary at that precise moment to figure out why it was troubling me. If I knew why, fine, but if not, I could get to that later. If it persisted, professionals could help me sort it out. At that moment, he said, "Just write it down."

More important, "What if I leave something out — something that really is serious, but I do not see it as such?" Don't worry about it, Harry told me. As I grow in the program, or as the program grows in me, more will become clear and I'll catch it next time I do an inventory or later in Step 10. It is:

> *"progress, not perfection." (AA, p. 60)*

Some may think this borders on moral relativism where everyone decides for themselves what is right or wrong. I call it diversity of human understanding. The words of another respected theologian I have been privileged to know, my pastor at Cathedral Parish in Madison, are worth noting. In one of his Sunday homilies, he said:

> *"If 90 percent of the people followed their conscience 90 percent of the time, the world would be a much better place."*

Before there were any written rules or laws, there was the human conscience. But it isn't always right. It can be hardened or overly scrupulous. The question is: how can we engage it to honestly guide us? The answer is: we need help.

## ARE WE AS SICK AS OUR SECRETS?

Once we start writing these things down, we can no longer escape them or rationalize them away. We often hear the phrase, "We are as sick as our secrets." There is a lot of truth to it, but it is not an absolute. Some things we know about others should be held in confidence even if we were involved with them. Perhaps even some things we know about ourselves need not be recorded in our inventory if they would harm us. But these are extremely rare, and we still need to face them. At a minimum, whatever it is that we are debating putting into our 4th should be able to pass all of the following tests:

1.  First is the TV test: If you would have a problem should *60 Minutes* disclose the issue on their Sunday night show, it is a likely candidate for the inventory list.

2.  Next is the Mom test: Assuming that your mother understood the full dimension of what you did, if she would disapprove, write it down. Or looking at it another way, would you be comfortable if your own child did what you did? If not, write it down.

3.  Finally, the smell test: This largely involves what others might think, or what you would think about someone else doing it. You may not have a coherent reason, but it just doesn't seem right. If either they or you would not approve, or have questions about its morality, write it down.

It is a good rule of thumb to discuss any questions we have with our sponsor; otherwise, it is easy to either blow some things out of proportion or minimize them. When taking the 4th the first time, we usually haven't advanced far enough in our new recovery to decide, without guidance, the appropriate disposition of each and every issue. Even for those of us with long-term sobriety, our sponsors can help with these questions.

Above all, anything that might lead us back to drinking must be identified. Anything we are ashamed of or feel guilty about should go into our inventory. It is *our* inventory and *our* conscience. It will be *our* life going forward, either clean or continuing to be contaminated by guilt and shame.

## ORGANIZING THE INVENTORY

A few years later, I did a cursory version of Step 4 from memory, sitting across a desk from Harry in his office with no forewarning of what I was going to do. In fact, I hadn't planned on doing a 4th, it just happened.

When I was finished about fifteen minutes later, I said, "There, I just did a 4th or maybe it was a 5th."

It was never easy to startle Harry, but I think I succeeded this time. All he said was, "Really? Well, okay." This may have been what Tom D. had in mind years later when he said, "If you can't do a great 4th Step, do a lousy one." While I wouldn't say that this "inventory" was of no value, it certainly did not leave me with the sense of freedom I felt after taking any of my other 4th and 5th Steps, before or after. But it did provide a segue to discuss where I was spiritually and emotionally at that moment.

Preparation and organization can greatly enhance the impact of Step 4. It is doubtful that many people taking the 4th folded a piece of butcher paper into small panels to organize their inventory, but it showed a level of seriousness and commitment that paid dividends when I took the 5th and subsequent steps. Over the years, I have either taken or helped sponsees take the 4th employing a number of organiz-ing strategies. These are some of the most effective.

### The Narrative Story

After I had been sober about eight years, Hazelden hired me to head up a new Consultation Services Division. Even though I was not going to be part of the treatment team, they wanted me to be familiar with the program, and so I spent several days on one of the rehab units with the patients. During that time, I took another 4th. The head coun-selor on the unit told me to just start writing. This one was searching and thorough and done in a narrative story format that ended up being thirty-two pages long.

Our problem is much more complex than simply identifying one or a few major issues, isolating them, and then ultimately eradicating them in Step 7. In my own case, my shortcomings are so intimately interrelated that it has been nearly impossible to totally address only one without also working on the others. The advantage of the narrative approach was that it enabled me to more clearly see how one defect fed upon another and created a negative synergy that undermined my spirit and eroded my soul.

### List the people with whom you have had a conflict, and identify your part in it

During our drinking and using days, many of us found our lives fraught with conflict, nearly all of it involving other people. While not as frequent or severe, even after we are sober, our relationships are often less than ideal. One of my sponsors, Tom D.-I, suggested that I start a 4th by identifying anyone with whom I had had a conflict in the past six months. On second thought, he said, why not just list everyone with whom you have had contact in the past six months and eliminate those with whom you did not have a conflict. *What a "wise guy,"* I thought. But he was right. I had had some conflict, however innocuous it seemed at the time, with nearly everyone. Not working Step 3 thoroughly and truly letting go seems to have a way of haunting us in all our affairs going forward, particularly our interactions with others.

The key question to be answered was this: Did that person on my list feel better or worse after my interaction with them? Forget who may have been right or wrong. In any conflict, each party always thinks they are right. The reality is that whatever point we were trying to make, whatever our objective may have been, most people will forget what we have said, and many will forget what we have done. But no one will forget how we made them feel. That's the acid test.

This approach to organizing Step 4 usually proves to be good preparation for Steps 8, 9, and 10.

### The Seven Deadlies and Four Uglies

This is my favorite and, in addition to framing my 4th Step, I use it daily to practice Step 10. For me, at the head of this parade of shame and guilt was pride. Low self-esteem is a pretty natural consequence of the personal failure that attends active addiction. But working directly on low self-esteem as though it was an entity unrelated to my defects of character was like trying to fill a flat tire with air without repairing the leak. Fraught with self-doubt, I *had* to be right — all the time. My sponsor Tom D.-I summed up my all-to-frequent status when he said:

*"We are frequently wrong, but never in doubt."*

For many of us, lust can also be a source of guilt and can become a full-fledged addiction in its own right if not successfully addressed in the context of the A.A. program. Likewise, gluttony in its many forms is a major addictive disorder in our society, food being one of the most prevalent. In fact, as addictions, these are so widespread that twelve-step programs modeled after A.A. have long been established to help those so afflicted, going all the way back to Bill Wilson's friend and mentor Father Ed Dowling, SJ. He suggested applying the twelve steps to those with eating disorders, calling it OO (Obese Obvious). Because of moral and social stigma, like alcoholism and drug dependency, a great deal of shame and guilt attend these addictions.

However, if given exclusive attention without sufficient vigilance for other defects, these, too, can camouflage the remainder of the "Seven and Four." In my own case, many of them run together, each feeding several of the others. Anger, greed, envy, sloth, plus the "Four Uglies" of self-pity, fear, despair, and dishonesty.[12] Individually, each can be devastating to my spiritual condition, but when taken in any combination, they have a synergy which absolutely confirms the assertion that alcoholism is "cunning, baffling, and powerful." It is often deadly, as well.

### The Big Book

When all else fails, read the instruction manual and follow the directions — in this case, *The Big Book*. Personally, I have always liked specific formats using columns and cells. The outline on page 65 of *The Big Book* does this. It combines a list of people along with a specific shortcoming, as well as the cause and effect. Thoroughness is emphasized without ignoring the fact that some of the people with whom we had a conflict had their own problems. So, in addition to the mechanics of the inventory, one major feature it emphasized is the need to ask God to help us show others ...

> "*the same tolerance, pity and patience that we would cheerfully grant a sick friend.*" (AA, p. 67)

Since we ourselves have often been a few bricks short of a full load, it should be no surprise that many of the people we associated with had their own problems, some as vexing as ours. Well- adjusted people do not usually seek out alcoholics to be their buddies. Personally, it seems that compassion is the only response that will work if we want to enjoy the fullness of recovery from this disease. Otherwise the pain of resentment and self-righteousness will be an unrelenting burden, sapping our energy and blurring our vision of the reality of our own shortcomings. Left to itself, resentment is a killer, and self-pity is its equally lethal handmaiden. Prolonged doses of either can lead us to drink again. If not, as in my case, they just left me and the people around me feeling miserable. On the other hand, when I ask God repeatedly, sometimes like a mantra, to give both the other person and me everything we need, the burden is lifted and its power evaporates.

### The Twelve Steps and Twelve Traditions

The Oxford Group, an evangelical ministry from which A.A.'s twelve steps were derived, practiced a moral inventory based on a member's deviation from "Four Absolutes" — Humility, Purity, Unselfishness, and Love. In a similar fashion, the *12 and 12* organizes the inventory around some of our greatest blessings rather than our curses: our basic instincts for sex, security, and society. While we could not be complete human beings without them, when misdirected the instincts can far exceed their proper function, and ...

*"our great natural assets, the instincts, [turn] into physical and mental liabilities." (12 and 12, p. 42)*

The *12 and 12* probes these issues broadly with a number of pointed questions based on some of the most vexing problems alcoholics experience, both while drinking and after they have gotten onto the road to recovery. Within the context of probing these instincts, it covers the "Seven Deadly Sins." At the core of the discussion is a basic premise:

*"Every time a person imposes his instincts unreasonably upon others, unhappiness follows." (12 and 12, p. 44)*

It touches on our motives, the payoffs, the minimizations, and rationalizations we have frequently used to justify the misuse of our natural instincts. Thus, without offering a cut-and-dry prescription, the *12 and 12* asks us to evaluate those aspects of our behavior that most frequently plague alcoholics, both practicing and recovering.

### The Hazelden Guide

Given its history of having treated more than 100,000 alcoholics and addicts, and its willingness to do a self-assessment of its own operation, it isn't surprising that Hazelden would develop one of the most comprehensive guides to the 4th Step inventory. Using a four-column matrix, it asks us to identify people, places, and things like institutions, principles, or ideas which have either been the object of or a trigger for our defects. That's column 1. Column 2 asks us to identify and list the specific causes of the defect. Column 3, which is a matrix in its own right, identifies seven specific areas in one's life which are affected, and column 4 asks us to identify where we were to blame. The inventory is worked column by column, top to bottom. There is a separate worksheet for each of three major defects: resentment, fear, and sexual conduct. Moreover, this format could be used for each of the Seven Deadlies and Four Uglies, plus any others.

Again, alcoholics are often plagued by a false belief system leading them to act in self-defeating, self-destructive ways. In order to remove them in Step 7, they must first be identified. The *Hazelden Guide* is great preparation for the overall "housecleaning" to which we are invited by Steps 5 through 10.

### The Simple Two-Column List: Defects and Assets

A number of my sponsees have started the inventory by taking a piece of paper, diving it into two columns, listing the defects on the left-hand side and the assets on the right. Most of them have had far more trouble identifying assets than defects, especially early in their recovery. But, if they think deeply enough and with a sponsor's help, they can nearly always find something in themselves that they can feel good about. Many times, our assets are just the opposite of our defects. For example, while we may list resentments, we also can think of times when we were loving. Or while we may have been greedy, there are likely instances when we were generous. In order to qualify for entry on the list, it is important to write out two specific instances of a defect or an asset, including the people who were involved and the place or occasion when it occurred.

### The Ten Commandments

Some alcoholics use the Ten Commandments as the basis for doing a 4th Step inventory. While presuming a Christian religious orientation, some who would identify themselves as agnostics or even atheists have used them as a starting point. Harry was an example.

## FREEDOM FROM THE BONDAGE OF SELF

While taking a 4th Step inventory can be painful, it often proves to be an occasion of peace and freedom. Any of the approaches listed above, and others as well, can be effective. The best one is likely to be the one that most resonates with the individual. Any of them work as long as they help us to take the step, first searchingly and then without fear. Without grandiosity or melancholy, we simply try to tell the truth about ourselves as best we can. And, as the *12 and 12* points out, the truth means that our experiences are not written entirely in red ink.

My business experience helped shed light on how to approach Step 4, starting with my job at Louie's grocery store in my teens. Every year at tax time, we took a thorough inventory of the merchandise. While some stock was old, stale, or beginning to rot and had to be thrown out, the preponderance was good and could be sold to customers. Years later when involved in mergers and acquisitions, my company formed teams to conduct a thorough due diligence. Our objective was to get as accurate a picture of our would-be partner as possible. Certainly, we wanted to know about anything that could jeopardize our future success, but we also needed to carefully weigh the assets and determine how they would help us form a better enterprise, which was the primary purpose of the undertaking. Just as we would build the new venture on the assets, so do we alcoholics build our new lives on our virtues.

## DEFECTS OF CHARACTER AND CLINICAL DISORDERS

Not only do addictions run in bunches, but character defects also feed on each other. In my case, pride and anger are frequently entangled, as are lust and resentment, as well as sloth, despair, and fear. Self-pity and envy frequently trigger resentment, while greed, gluttony, and shame nearly always play on each other. So do non-addictive clinical disorders.

Comorbidity is rampant among addicts of all descriptions, and many of us suffer simultaneously from other mental disorders that can exacerbate our condition. Research[13] shows that depression and anxiety are at the top of the list. Like addiction, these can also be primary conditions, not just a symptom of a deeper-lying disorder. As such, they will not yield incidentally when we stop drinking. More importantly, they do not fall into the same category as willful inappropriate behavior. If someone is clinically depressed and cannot get out of bed, it doesn't mean they are lazy. If someone suffers from an anxiety disorder, the fear they experience doesn't necessarily mean they are lacking in faith. But, in the beginning of our journey, it may be difficult for either our sponsors or us to distinguish between a defect of character as described in the A.A. literature and a clinical disorder, since neither of us is a trained mental health professional. The key issue is to be patient, open, and non-judgmental.

Early in his career as a young psychologist, Dr. Dan Anderson recognized this and, in the late 1960s, included psychological testing of all patients upon admission to Hazelden. The Shipley-Hartford and Minnesota Multiphasic Personality Index (MMPI) were the instruments used at the time. A patient evidencing psychosis was transferred to a psychiatric hospital to stabilize them before being admitted for addiction treatment, so they could actively engage in the addiction treatment process. Anderson also administered these tests at the time of discharge and, interestingly, usually recorded a significant decrease in the frequency and severity of psychological symptoms. However, in some cases, there was little change, and the need for care specific to the disorder was arranged after discharge. Many of the better rehab programs follow this protocol today, and some offer comprehensive mental health care onsite. This component of care can be a concrete reflection of the gains we are making in our recovery, as well as the areas in which progress is coming slowly. Truth be known, each of our defects of character may be related in some way to a DSM disorder. If so, then the main question is the level of severity and whether or not professional help will be needed.

While many people come into A.A. after having completed formal treatment, most do not. For that reason, I will suggest that a sponsee get a psychological workup if self-defeating, self-destructive behavior persists over time, or if they disclose having had traumatic experiences. Fortunately, some therapists are experts in both addictions and other mental disorders and do not subscribe to the notion that by treating one, the others will automatically be remediated.

## THE CAPACITY TO BE HONEST

A.A.'s founders did not have the benefit of modern psychology. Nevertheless, they did recognize that some of us suffered from *"grave emotional and mental disorders"* (*AA*, p. 58). As *The Big Book* says, many of us do get well if we have the capacity to be honest, but that does not mean that all others struggling with reality are morally dishonest. In discussing Step 4, both *The Big Book* and the *12 and 12* emphasize thoroughness and honesty. But, in an absolute sense, who has this gift of honesty? Does a misperception of reality necessarily constitute dishonesty? And before recovery, when was the last time we were thorough in examining anything, given our preoccupation with the next drink or hit? Practically no one at the beginning of their journey toward sanity and sobriety is rigorously honest or thorough; neither are we totally devoid of these qualities. At some level, we know when something is not right. So, to reiterate what Harry said, if it is bothering us, we need to write it down.

Most importantly, we do not have to walk this road alone. Most of us can't, in reality. We all need help — from other alcoholics in and outside of meetings, from our sponsors, clergy, and therapists. Some of us are fortunate enough to have supportive spouses, children, friends, coworkers, and others with whom we regularly have contact. Janis, my wife, has been the most helpful person in my life, both when it comes to looking at myself and in countless other ways. Those who care about us neither want to see us suffer nor do they want to be left bewildered and hurt by our behavior, and that includes our employer. If there is an EAP at work, it can be a great source of support.

Tearing out the faulty foundation of my life and trying to build it anew on bedrock has been a lifelong project. It started in earnest with my first 4th Step inventory when the telephone rang that beautiful summer day in 1966, and Harry's friendly, high-pitched voice was on the other end. I didn't realize it at the time, but it was a call I would never have wanted to miss.

# STEP FIVE

Having written out the 4th Step, it was time to fulfill the ostensive purpose of Harry's phone call and take Step 5.

**"We admitted to God, to ourselves and to another human being the exact nature of our wrongs." (AA, p. 59)**

God, me, AND another person. The *12 and 12* concludes its narrative on Step 8 by stating that, for many in A.A., it was *"the beginning of the end of isolation from our fellows and from God."*

For me, that turning point started when I completed Step 5.

At that time in our area, clergy were as likely to hear 5th Steps as A.A. sponsors. Clergy had played an important role in A.A. almost from the beginning, when in the late evening on a cold November day in 1940, Father Ed Dowling, SJ, slowly climbed the stairs to the tiny apartment Bill and Lois Wilson rented above the A.A. club in New York City and began a lifelong friendship with Bill. Twenty-five years later, in the multidisciplinary approach to treatment that Dan Anderson installed at Hazelden, a clergy was part of the team and heard 5th Steps. Two of the early ones, Rev. Phil Hansen and Rev. Vern Johnson, went on to distinguish themselves in the addiction treatment field. For anyone thinking their defects are unique, Phil Hansen related an experience that stuck with me over the years. Of the thousands of 5th Steps he heard, he said that after the first half-dozen or so, he never heard anything new.

Although he was more familiar with my recovery and the contents of my 4th Step than anyone else, it never occurred to either Harry or me that he would hear my 5th. That role was to fall to a young priest at what was then St. Luke's Catholic Church on Summit Avenue in St. Paul. His name was Father Raymond Slattery, and he had developed a fine reputation in the A.A. community.

I set up an appointment with Father Slattery and a few days later was in his office with the folded piece of butcher paper that wrapped up all the wrongs I could think of in my 4th Step. Father started out by saying this wasn't confession, and it wasn't about sin. If I wanted absolution, he would accommodate me after we finished Step 5 and hear my confession. I went through each panel on the wrapping paper, drilling down as deeply as I could, trying not to leave anything out. It took about an hour and a half.

It's hard to estimate just how much energy — psychic, spiritual, and physical — is consumed by the defects of character we carry around with us. But I gained serious insight through an analogous experience forty-eight years later when recovering from heart bypass surgery. The burden of my heart disease had taken a toll that frequently left me short of breath and eventually with chest pain. Unaddressed, it would have killed me. After the surgery, as I lay in the intensive care unit too weak to walk, it occurred to me that my entire being was rallying in response to the huge medical insult my body had endured on the operating table. At the forty-eight-hour point, the nursing staff had me up and walking, just a little at first. In spite of the discomfort and the weakness, I could feel the tremendous difference the surgery had made. I was breathing easily and deeply.

It was then that I realized what the disease had been slowly doing to me. The contrast helped me realize how insidiously my functioning had declined. This awareness was similar to what I experienced spiritually after leaving Father Slattery's office so many years earlier. In 2014, the slowly increasing bondage of my clogged arteries had been relieved through modern robotically guided arthroscopic surgery. In 1966, the bondage of self had been lifted through a decades-old recovery step that simulated an act that had been a staple for centuries in the lives of men and women who wanted true freedom to be the best person they could be. The result of these two events in my life were very much the same. And so was the lead-up, fraught with denial, minimization, and avoidance of the facts regarding what was slowly becoming of me as my diseases progressed. The angiogram and stress test were the physical equivalent of my A.A. 4th Step. The surgery, during which the secrets of my heart disease were exposed to the cardiology interventionists, was the equivalent of Step 5. True recovery of each would require a lifetime of work beyond those events.

## EXACT NATURE VERSUS SPECIFIC EVENTS

There was more. My initial 5th Step and several that followed were largely an enumeration of wrongful acts I had committed and written down in a 4th Step inventory. I hadn't yet formed the notion that they were preventing me from being the best possible version of myself. The focus was largely on surface stuff, the behavioral episodes. But Step 5 itself says we admitted the "*exact nature of our wrongs*." In other words, what were the real issues, not just the manifestations. Maybe I am just a slow learner, but I was sober more than forty years before the stark difference between the two struck me while waiting my turn to share, thinking about what I would say about Step 5 in a FSC meeting. What *was* the exact nature of my wrongs as it pertained to the shortcomings disclosed in Step 4? I had to examine each of the Seven Deadlies and Four Uglies to begin to find out. I had to look deeply at the diseased attitudes and beliefs that were driving my life. This was when I began to gain a real appreciation for addressing the "why" of my behavior, a notion that I had largely discarded so long ago.

*The Big Book* says,

> *"We get a daily reprieve contingent on the maintenance of our spiritual condition." (AA, p. 85)*

What was my "spiritual condition" that determined whether or not I would enjoy the daily reprieve from my illness? It turned out that my shortcomings were inseparable from the exact nature of my wrongs, my spiritual condition, the immediate payoff, and what it ultimately did to me and others — the price. Speaking only for myself, in part, this is what I found.

| The Shortcoming | The Exact Nature | My Spiritual Condition | The Payoff | The Price |
|---|---|---|---|---|
| I *have* to be right. So I get into arguments with people, even about issues where I really have little knowledge. | Pride | Tom D. often said: "An alcoholic is an ego-maniac with an inferiority complex." I need always to be "right." Why? Is it because for so long, I believed I was wrong? My failings had destroyed my self-esteem; am I still ashamed and guilt-ridden? | For that brief moment I can paper-over my insecurities and delude myself into thinking that I am actually convincing someone that I am better than I really believe myself to be, that I know more than I know. And, of course, any validation can be exhilarating. | Others get turned-off and reject the arrogance that attends such a defect, often quietly. Ultimately, they do not want to be around me. Isolation follows and self-pity and resentment often tag along. |
| Sexually objectifying another person. Drinking-in images. Sexual and romantic fantasy. Infidelity. | Lust | Emptiness. "The hole in my Soul" that causes me to want to seek a connection to what is most powerfully and immediately gratifying. | Instantaneously feeling alive without making a true connection and just commitment to the person themselves. | A letdown from not having made a true connection. The guilt of breaking the faith and the shame of taking advantage of someone who is vulnerable. Self-loathing from having created a demand for behavior of others that is destructive to them. Abject fear of being found out or contracting an STD. Loss of trust of those who love me. The risk of developing a powerful sexual addiction. |

| The Shortcoming | The Exact Nature | My Spiritual Condition | The Payoff | The Price |
|---|---|---|---|---|
| A resentful, negative temperament with put-downs and angry outbursts. Rudeness, especially behind the wheel. | Anger | Unwillingness to accept reality in some form — something either did not go my way or is not likely to. | It makes me feel powerful, especially if others go silent or cower. It makes me feel superior by pointing out the faults of others. | Isolation from others and God. The "Hole in the Soul" grows. |
| Taking something to which I am not entitled, from a parking space to someone else's spouse. | Greed | Subscribing to the false belief that I either do not have or will not have enough of what I need and therefore compelled to get all I can while I can get it. | A rush of adrenaline similar to what I felt when anticipating a drink. A perverse feeling of satisfaction that I "put one over" on someone. | Fear I will be found out and wondering if others really know about it and are discussing it behind my back. Erosion of my ethics. Guilt. Shame. |
| Overindulging in anything I enjoy: food, sex, exercise, the internet, high-risk behavior. Seeking credit to which I am not entitled. | Gluttony | The false belief that there is "never enough." If I do not grab-off as much as I can, I won't get my share without honestly considering what my just share is. | Short-term pleasure from the taste and/or feeling. | Chronic dissatisfaction and always needing more. Risk of developing another addiction: eating, sex, gambling, the internet, etc. Loss of self-control. |
| Unreasonable longing for something or someone to which I am not entitled and feeling sad or angry about not having it. | Envy | Dissatisfied with the gifts I have received; feeling shortchanged or entitled to more. | I can rationalize any of my other defects, especially self-pity, because "I've been wronged, deprived, unlucky." | Never feeling blessed or fulfilled. Persistent dissatisfaction with my lot. Soul-sickness blocking out gratitude. |

| The Shortcoming | The Exact Nature | My Spiritual Condition | The Payoff | The Price |
|---|---|---|---|---|
| Not doing something I need to do or doing something I know is wrong. | Sloth | Locked-in resistance. | Just sitting, doing nothing at all, or doing something designed to help me avoid doing what I need to do. | The ongoing burden of guilt of not having met my responsibility. |
| Dwelling on my sorrows and misfortunes, real or imagined. Believing that I have suffered more than is reasonable or fair. | Self-pity | An ongoing state of dissatisfaction, devoid of gratitude, and therefore without peace or joy. Inability to empathize with those less fortunate than I. | The belief that I have something coming to me — the world owes me. Therefore I can rationalize behavior that illegitimately seeks pleasure or material goods to which I am not entitled. | Failure to recognize and be grateful for my many blessings. As a result, I am never truly happy. |
| Conjuring up future scenarios in which something terrible happens to me or where I do not get what I want. | Fear | Resistance in doing what I need to do or avoiding doing something that is healthy for me spiritually and losing trust in myself and God. | I can convince myself that meeting my responsibilities really will not make any difference. | I fall short of the mark due to my own inaction and forgo the pleasure of achievement and the confidence it provides. |
| Pessimism, negativity, critical of others. | Despair | Having failed to solve my own problems but pridefully refusing to call upon others to help, I lose hope. | Self-pity and denial that I was responsible. Self-justification. An excuse not to put forth an effort. | Despair is its own price: lost hope. |
| I embellish, exaggerate, rationalize, omit, or flat-out lie, often to make myself look good, or innocent, or intelligent, or important. | Dishonesty | Failure to perceive and accept the "upside" of reality. Fear that the truth will reflect badly on me, combined with the thrill of "getting by" with something. | Avoiding perceived conflict. Relief from the fear of what someone will think of me if I tell the truth. Believing I have convinced someone that something isn't really the way it is. | Carrying around the burden of worry that they will find out the truth anyway. |

As the *12 and 12* says, this emergence from isolation through the open and honest sharing of my terrible burden took me to a resting place where I could prepare myself for the following steps toward a full and meaningful recovery.

It may work differently for others, but for me, the shortcoming, the "exact nature," and my spiritual condition are at the essence of Step 5. Thoroughly examining the payoff and the price are the segue for Step 6.

The critical question is this: Is the payoff for any of these shortcomings worth the price I have to pay?

# STEP SIX

Sitting in an A.A. meeting in Chicago, waiting my turn to share, I was struck with the idea that the twelve steps of A.A. are like a family — a very large family. Like many families, the eldest and youngest members get a lot of attention, in this case, Steps 1 and 12. In between, some can be loud and a bit boisterous, demanding a lot of maintenance, like Steps 4 and 9, and indirectly, their closest siblings 5 and 8. Some seem to have an uncanny knack for provoking an argument, like 2 and 3. Then there are the quiet ones, like Step 6 and its close companion 7. Step 6, like the middle child in a large family, can almost go unnoticed.

> **"Were entirely ready to have God remove all these defects of character." (AA, p. 59)**

There it is, the middle child and shorter than most of the others, easy to overlook, especially after encountering the huge presence of 4 and 5.

What's more, it is easy to look beyond Step 6 to Step 7 and in the process, run them together. In fact, in some recovery literature and even at A.A. meetings, 6 is combined with 7. And, as was true for me, sometimes it just gets a passing glance as the alcoholic rushes past it on the way to Step 9. Yet, the words of Joe many years ago at the Unity meeting come back to me:

> *"These Steps — 6 and 7 — are the 'change' steps."*

If we do not change, the promises of the program will never materialize. In other words, these two steps are a BIG deal.

And they are as difficult as they are profound. It is possible that as much as any other step, the founders may have been referring to Step 6 when saying, "Many of us said, 'What an order. I can't go through with it.'"

Just look at the wording! *"entirely"* And *"all"?* That is awfully uncompromising language.

## EACH STEP STANDS ON ITS OWN, BUT ALL ARE INTERDEPENDENT

During my recovery, I have worked the steps individually but have also linked them around ideas or principles, and it seems that many others in the program do the same thing. Steps 1, 2, and 3 are the "getting started" steps; 4 and 5, the "inventory" steps; 6 and 7, the "cleaning house" steps; 8 and 9, the "getting right with others" steps; 10, 11, and 12, the "maintenance steps." Even some of the literature, especially pamphlets dealing with specific steps, often breaks up the middle six into three pairs, and that is mainly how I viewed them. But in recent years, a deeper look has changed my perception. Altogether, the steps are more of a gestalt to me than a series of silos only serially connected. While I found that many steps, if worked thoroughly, segue naturally into the one immediately following, at the same time, I have found that a later step can help me with an earlier one. For example, 10 and 12 motivated me to work 6. But, while 6 and 7 are usually coupled, I found an equally, if not stronger, relationship between 5 and 6. So, where does Step 5 end and 6 begin? I think it is in the process of examining the payoff and the price exacted by each of my shortcomings.

After taking Step 5 for the first time, I felt an incredible sense of accomplishment and freedom. Then I went on vacation. When I did take 6 and 7, the effort was miniscule in comparison to the work I had done on 4 and 5. That was a big mistake, but the fact is that few people I knew at that time were doing it much differently. Treatment programs did not go beyond Step 5, and virtually none of them had a formal aftercare effort, particularly one that was based on Steps 6 through 12. Very few did a professional assessment before discharge to identify issues that could jeopardize recovery, much less an accompanying plan of countermeasures. Ideally, follow-up to track progress against these measures — the remaining steps and the issues requiring professional help — should be integrated into an outcome evaluation system that gives a true picture of recovery rates and the issues attending relapse. It not only helps the individual addict to focus on issues most likely to trigger a relapse, but it also can improve overall outcomes for the treatment program. Wherever an outcome evaluation did exist, it usually did not specifically include Steps 6 through 12.

Throughout the 1970s in Minnesota, many new members were coming directly into A.A. from rehab programs that had taken them through Step 5. Some had sponsors, some didn't. But even if they did, chances were that the sponsor had not drilled down very deeply into Step 6. A nodding glance was often the most it got.

Beyond that, other factors reinforced the benign neglect of 6 and

7. I loved some defects and so I had glossed over them. A look at the payoff readily tells why. Others evolved into an addiction in their own right, lust being one of the most common. Still others had a utilitarian value, having once provided a defense for me when I was drinking that may well have saved me from harm. Since I hadn't looked at both the payoff *and* the price of my defects, I didn't feel compelled to change them much. Instead, I found new applications for some and simply continued the old modus-operandi with others. Overall, my life was so much better than it had been when I was drinking, so I drifted into a state of complacency. This seemed to be true of other recovering people around me, as well, as they drifted in and out of relationships and jobs. Finally, without having seriously turned my will and life over to the care of God in Step 3, it was difficult for me to become *entirely* ready to let go of *all* the defects — perhaps even impossible.

Not realizing it, critical questions had to be answered:

- Did I want a full and meaningful recovery, or did I want to just get by?

- Did I want to be the *best* version of myself, or was I satisfied to be just good enough?

- What kind of life did I want, really: one of aspiration or one of mere settling?

- And what *was* a full and meaningful recovery?

That a full and meaningful recovery is essentially the same as a full and meaningful life didn't occur to me until years later. So, how do we get it? I wasn't sure of that, either. But eventually, I came to understand as the restoration to sanity, promised in Step 2, kept slowly unfolding.

## FATHER ERIC

It was 2009 and I was in my 43$^{rd}$ year of recovery. There I was, surrounded by a throng of young people packed into the pews for evening Mass at St. Paul's Catholic Center on the University of Wisconsin campus the first Sunday of the school year. The joy and energy in the place were palpable. Over the years, I had stopped by church sporadically, usually at Christmas or Easter. But this was different. This time there was a level of intentionality that hadn't been present before. It had been a long road back, taking decades for me to get there.

I had been in therapy for a couple of years, had been attending A.A. meetings regularly for more than forty years, had a great wife who loved me deeply, had no money worries, and I was optimistic about a new real estate venture. All that notwithstanding, I was still caught in the throes of a low-grade depression and general feeling of dissatisfaction. Many mornings I awoke feeling so downcast that only repeatedly saying The Lord's Prayer as a mantra could lift me to the point of getting up. Life was bland and held little meaning. Various paid consulting projects and volunteer civic activity weren't helping much. Politically, the dream of a lifetime, less than a year after coming true, had found our first Black president facing a recalcitrant congress that was turning a great plan for health care reform into a patchwork of limited improvements written by the insurance industry and fraught with design and administrative challenges whose complexity was costly and often beyond understanding. More importantly, personal issues stemming from shortcomings I had battled most of my life continued to plague me. I was still struggling with Step 3, which limited the benefits to be realized in Steps 6 through 10. Every six weeks or so, when our FSC meeting came around to an inventory step, the same old stuff kept showing up in my share. Pep talks to myself aside, I felt pretty miserable overall and did not see things changing. Then, one of my heroes died. After nearly fifty years of public service, Senator Ted Kennedy was gone.

I read his autobiography, "True Compass," and was struck by the fact that with all his personal problems and the public humiliation that attended them, he never stopped practicing his religion. Along with many other high achievers with notable shortcomings, his plight had provided comfort to me over the years, reinforcing my rationalization that I could make valuable contributions to society even though I was deeply flawed. The truth is, I had pretty much conceded that my defects were here to stay, with little hope that they could ever be substantially mitigated, much less removed. I was resigned to living my life as best I could, doing as much as I could despite my flaws. Dark as that sounds, it was the beginning of acceptance of myself as I really was. But who was I, *really*? What did I really believe? What did I really need?

For some reason, a conversation I had had years earlier with Mike C. came back. He related how he had said to Cathy, his wife: "Wouldn't it be great if Jim came back to the church?" So, I opened the door of willingness just a crack, prayed just a little about it, and discussed it with my therapist and my sponsor, who by that time was Mac, a great guy and a great friend who now has more than sixty-four years of sobriety. Finally, I just said, "God, if you want me to go back to the Church, I will, but you're going to have to show me how." And I let it go at that.

At that point, one of AA's most important lessons emerged. Step 3 of the *Twelve and Twelve* stresses the critical importance of willingness.

*"Practicing Step 3 is like the opening of a door which to all appearances is still closed and locked. All we need is a key and the decision to swing the door open. There is only one key, and it is called willingness. … Once we have placed the key of willingness in the lock and have the door ever so slightly open, we find that we*

*can always open it some more. Though self-will may slam it shut*
*again, as it frequently does, it will always respond the moment*
*we pick up the key of willingness." (12 and 12, pp. 34–35)*

Not long after, placing the key of willingness in the lock brought me to St. Paul's, with its brutally modern architecture. The celebrant was Father Eric, the pastor. He gave a great homily based on his first humble days as a civil engineering student at the University of Wisconsin, showing up without a place to stay and only twenty dollars in his pocket. It hooked me just enough to get me to come back. A few weeks later, he gave a homily about a young student who asked him how he could be as good a Catholic and as successful a human being as was possible for him. Father Eric's response was, "First, you need to get the sin out."[14] Not to freak out those who prefer not to practice a religious faith, sin is used here in its classical, orthodox definition: It simply means "falling short of the mark." It doesn't mean brimstone and fire and eternal damnation loaded up with heavy doses of shame and guilt, although that's pretty much how it felt at the time, rational definitions notwithstanding.

Anyway, this was something I did *not* want to hear. "First, you need to get the sin out." I said to myself, *Who the hell does that!?* Having resigned myself to the idea that I might have value, while virtually laden with shortcomings that were not going away, I had finally found some modicum of comfort. Now this guy says I need to get rid of them! I wondered, *Had his training as a civil engineer overcome his under-*
*standing of life? Was he still in some bridge-designing mode? Getting all*
*the defects out of a physical structure that would bear millions of tons*
*of weight at high impact may be imperative to the long-term safety of*
*travelers and truckers, but who does this in their personal lives?*

Upon reflection, it became clear that that was *exactly* the point. In the course of everyday living, professionals of all descriptions do this. Physicists, architects, auto mechanics, and computer programmers all strive to this end. The cardiology interventionist who did my bypass surgery did it. One slip and I would have been a goner. Then it occurred to me that the best professionals I knew did not confine their desire to do their best only to their professional lives but carried it into their personal lives, as well. Or perhaps it was the other way around and had started with their personal lives first, and this formed the foundation for professional success. In thinking about Father Eric's words, it was clear that I had nowhere to go. I needed to get the sin — the defects of character, my shortcomings — out as best I could. It wasn't going to happen just by wishing them away. I needed to prepare, to become entirely ready. I needed Step 6 in its literal sense.

There may have been a time in life when I would have thought the payoff from my defects was worth the price. But having lived with some of them for more than fifty years, it had become clear what they had done to me and my capacity to have a positive impact on the world around me, not to mention peace and joy in my own life. Equally important was the issue of what my defects had done to others, especially those I loved most.

As my sponsor, Mac, had said, "I am not free from the consequences of my actions."

## THE CASCADING SYNERGY OF SIN

If addictions run in bunches, certainly my defects do as well. Just as the steps of recovery are interdependent with each reinforcing the others, so are my defects. Approaching them as independent entities to be eradicated one by one didn't get the job done. Nor did it work to see only one major defect as the culprit needing to be prosecuted and forever jailed. That only led to preoccupation with that one issue, which camouflaged all the others. One typical scenario that had recurred over the years started with pride.

Having been recognized for my professional expertise, I wanted the same deference in other matters. I *had* to be right, no matter what the subject or occasion. Naturally, this led to conflict with others who had trouble stomaching the thinly veiled arrogance. While some just turned away, not wanting to waste their breath, others stood their ground. Sometimes an argument followed, and I would get upset. But the other party wouldn't budge and might even call me out. Then my feelings would get hurt, self-pity would well up, followed by resentment toward the person, fear of how I looked to others not having won the argument, and despair from not getting my way — much of it based on an exaggerated sense about what I really knew about the issue at hand to begin with. Finally, when the dust settled, I would feel deep embarrassment at my behavior. Being an addict and feeling miserable, a quick fix that would accelerate my spiritual descent looked good and would call to me. In that one encounter, I had acted out seven of the eleven Deadlies and Uglies, each fueling the others, and I wound up needing to marshal all the strength I could to fight off the allure of active addictive behavior. All this because *I had to* be right and was so insecure that if others didn't acquiesce, I felt defeated.

Here is where Step 10 was crucial in helping me take the 6th. Until I began examining my conscience through a daily inventory based on the "Seven Deadlies and Four Uglies," I had no idea what a huge defect pride had been in my life, especially at home from little spats with Janis to big blow-outs. When I had begun to realize the price I had been paying and began to recognize how much my defects depended upon each other for their existence, I finally started to become *entirely ready* to have God remove *all* of them. But I wasn't there yet. There was the fear of becoming the "hole in the donut" as it says in the *12 and 12,* and this fear, at least partially, was based on reality.

True or not, I believed that the behavior that constituted many of my defects had helped me achieve goals and had gotten me through tough times in life. What would happen if they were suddenly taken away? Without pride, anger, and fear, would I have the fuel necessary to keep my engine going in the drive for success? Without lust and gluttony, how would I feel alive? Without envy, where would my inspiration come from? And in political matters, if I could no longer take the other side's inventory, exclaim "Ain't it awful?" and stoke resentment and fear in my colleagues and the general public, how could we ever defeat those on election day who had used these same tactics so effectively against our side?

Bottom line, if all my defects were removed, could I still get what I wanted? And what was it I really wanted? The truth is, what I *thought* I wanted and what I needed were not the same thing. And until the defects were removed, at least in part, I did not have a clear idea of what I really needed: namely, peace and joy. Call them whatever you want: defects, shortcomings, sins, maladjustments, it doesn't matter. They undermine my spirit and erode my soul. They largely destroy my peace and joy.

Without peace and joy, I could never be spiritually healthy, and I could never experience that "daily reprieve." Except for a few fleeting moments, I didn't even know what it was and certainly didn't realize that if I could attain it, very little would bother me. I didn't realize that the energy being squandered in a series of mini-conflicts and their aftermath could, instead, be used for positive ventures, large and small. Moreover, everyone around me would be affected for the better. Our behavior can either bring out the best in others or something far less. Everything counts. All of our actions have unintended consequences, for better or worse.

## PROGRESS

How to get ready? A great analogy from a meeting years earlier comes to mind:

"If an alcoholic isn't ready, you can shout the message at the top of your lungs three inches from his ear, and he won't hear it; when he is ready, you can whisper it the length of a football field, and he will take in every word."

Looking at the twelve steps, becoming ready in Step 6 is like a linchpin to the rest of the program. It completes and reinforces Steps 1 through 5 and without it, all the gifts provided by Steps 7 through 12 are either reduced or denied.

Again, I can only cite my own experience, which doesn't always come in big chucks but often in a series of events, mostly small ones punctuated by a big one here and there. The irritation of seeing the same old stuff every time we came to Step 10 in our FSC meeting; the realization that the spiritual state implicit in Step 12 was as much asleep as awakened in me; the fact that Ted Kennedy had something inside him I didn't seem to have, something that enabled him to carry on in spite of his shortcomings; all told me that the hole in my soul was still there and needed to be stitched up and filled. Something important was missing in my life. The question was, what? And how would I know it if it came to me? And how would it feel?

Then a different kind of feeling showed up, one that was both familiar and unwelcome: shortness of breath, even while at rest. I called my doctor and went in for a treadmill test, which showed that three minor blockages we had seen four years earlier had gotten worse. I would need bypass surgery. I also needed another stent, this one in the left anterior artery, balancing-off the one that had been inserted in the right coronary artery four years earlier.

The day before the bypass, I went to confession. One of the great things about the Catholic sacrament of reconciliation is the belief that God totally blots out the offense — it's as if it never existed. This belief did not originate with the Catholic church but was part of Jewish tradition centuries earlier, as seen in many of the Psalms, particularly the 51$^{st}$. A day later, I lay on the operating table immediately before the surgery, totally without fear, in a state that I could only call perfect peace.

Just as we do not recognize the insidious nature of our disease, sometimes we are not completely aware of our progress in recovery. It turned out that over time, at some deep level I hadn't been totally aware of, I had truly turned my will and my life over to the care of God as I understood Him. And, as I understood Him was beautiful beyond words. This doesn't mean that on each and every occurrence in my daily life I turned it all over, but at some profound level I trusted Him and knew that He cared for me beyond anything I could imagine. I had absolutely no fear of how the surgery would turn out or about where I would end up if it failed. Not that I was certain of seeing the face of God, but rather I took great comfort knowing that my God would treat me fairly, maybe even more than fairly because of His mercy. It was truly indescribable. There was no fear of pain or complications; no regret of things undone; no worry about my family; no despair about the world; no anger toward anyone; no lust, no cravings, no envy. As the anesthetic was about to be administered, I joked with the surgeons and nurses and thanked them for all they had sacrificed to attain the great skills they were bringing to me. I pictured Janis's gorgeous face and could hear the sound of her voice that I so loved, telling me she loved me. This was peace. This was it. This is what it felt like. This was what being without my defects of character could be. This is why Father Eric had said, "You need to get the sin out first." Then the anesthesia took hold, and I was out.

## "ENTIRELY READY" AND "ALL"

Becoming entirely ready started with an honest look at the payoff and the price of my defects, but it didn't end there. When I began to realize that the price — the overall pain — outweighed the payoff, a degree of willingness emerged. It moved me to a place where I was no longer willing to accept the pain as a given. But I still didn't know how I could manage without the payoff. Even with a leap of faith that I would be all right if I let go, it turned out that cleansing myself of my faults wasn't the end of the story. In fact, it wasn't even possible for *me* to do, but I tried.

Getting the defects out and keeping them out are not the same thing. With some, like lust and food, trying to rid myself of them meant short-term hope and elation, only to be followed by an uneasy yearning for something undefined, both the object and the attribution of which were at first unclear. Then would come a feeling of emptiness, followed by depression and finally the urge to again act out the defect to get a short-lived, exhilarating high in order to relieve the depression. With other shortcomings, such as anger or pride, the scenario was different. Certain conditions provoked an immediate knee-jerk response, welling up as if out of nowhere, leaving no time for resistance and against which I felt almost defenseless. With still others, such as envy or sloth, there was no big dramatic event. Instead, they sneaked up on me and quietly gnawed away at my spirit, and before I realized it, they were having their way with me.

I couldn't get them out. Trying to, even when it appeared that I was successful, only left a void that had to be filled, and they would come right back in again. The core problem was that I was jumping the gun. I was trying to do *God*'s work in Step 7 without doing *my* work in Step 6. I had to return to the words in the *12 and 12* cited earlier in Step 4 and rebuild the faulty foundation of my life. To take Step 6, I needed to turn to Step 11 and improve my conscious contact with God through prayer and meditation.

Whenever I wrestle with my problems, even when praying and asking God to remove them, I am largely living in the problem. Sometimes that is the most I can do, but it doesn't usually last long. In order to live in the solution, I found that I needed to take two deliberate steps — the act of surrender and the conscious practice of virtue.

1. **Surrender in the heat of the action.** Doing it in advance can set the stage, but if that's all I do, it doesn't work. At the moment I sense the allure, the payoff, of acting out a defect, I need to surrender it as quickly, deliberately, and completely as I can. Playing games with it by trying to control and enjoy it, especially through fantasy or euphoric recall, only leads to failure. Feeding the defect, however little, only makes it stronger. Moreover, fighting it doesn't work either because it fights back and is stronger than I am. The message in the *12 and 12* on page 22 regarding Step 1 applied to all my defects in getting ready:

   *"Few indeed were those who, so assailed, had ever won through in single-handed combat."*

   Keeping the act of surrender short and sweet so I can get my head going in the right direction works best for me. No pep talks, no arguing, no debate. If I get into a long prayer or dialogue, I can easily be distracted and slip back into the problem, even as I pray. Instead I simply say:

   "I am powerless, please help me, God."

or

"Please help me. Thy will not mine be done."

or

"Lord, please remove every single trace of this temptation — I surrender any satisfaction I might get from acting it out to You. Please take it."

Repeating any of these until the urge passes always works. So does talking to my Higher Power, telling Him what's troubling me and my hopes, and then imagining what He is saying back to me. This isn't easy but it works, and the peace that follows is worth the effort. It gets the defect out — temporarily.

2. **Practice the virtues.** It's easy to say we love someone or that we believe something, but the words are often meaningless. Backing up our beliefs by taking the actions of love is the only thing that counts. Returning to what Ron's sponsor told him:

"I really don't care what you say; I don't care what you think; and I certainly don't care what you feel. All I care about *is what you do* — don't take that first drink."

I had to practice the virtues, filling up my being with them as best I could, and not just in response to a craving or temptation. I needed to practice them when I was at peace, as well. As much as anything, I had to avoid getting into the quagmire, wrestling with my defects.

For me, practicing the virtues in order to become "entirely ready" meant practicing behavior that was the polar opposite of my defects. In other words, doing what came *un*naturally. I learned over time that my defects could not take root unless they were fed by the soil in which they were planted. Likewise, the virtues. I had to change the soil so the virtues could flourish. The soil needs to be nourished — it needs to be watered — and pure water cannot flow from a contaminated well. Watering the soil of my life with unclean water would sustain the quagmire, and nothing good could grow there. In order to decontaminate the soil, the water needed to be pure, and that meant the well had to be clean. The well was my mind, the water my thoughts and aspirations, the soil my behavior from which my life would be formed. The consequences of all this: the fruit.

So, let's look again at the "Seven and Four" and what cleaning the well, purifying the water, and enriching the soil consists of. Cleaning the well starts with working to rid my mind of the diseased attitudes, thoughts, and beliefs. That's where the battle has to start in order to get ready. The problem isn't with other people or circumstances that trigger me. It isn't the world we live in, whatever its problems. It isn't the alcohol, the drugs, the food, the women, the casinos, the advertisements, or any of that. It is me. The spiritual me — my mind. Again, let's start with pride.

For me, actively practicing humility has been the only effective substitute for pride. It started with two short statements: "I don't know" and "What do you think?" This sounds simple, but for me it was a big deal. I had always thought I had to know the answer to any question, and when I didn't, I would get frustrated. Sometimes I would start talking anyway, hoping to stumble across something that made sense. I was always more interested in letting people know what I thought than in finding out what they believed. But, inspired by the prayer of St.

Francis of Assisi, "Lord grant that I may seek rather … to understand than to be understood," this new approach bore fruit almost immediately. It turned out that people did think I was pretty bright, and when I said, "I don't know," they felt both a connection with me and better about the fact that they didn't know, either. When I asked them, "What do you think?" I not only learned from them, but it made them feel good that I would seek their opinion, that perhaps they had something to offer me. In that respect, they were just like me.

It didn't end there. I had to listen to their responses from beginning to end without interrupting to edit or interject personal pearls of wisdom. The acid test was whether or not I knew more at the end of the conversation than I did at the beginning. For most people, this is common sense, but for me, it was a revelation. It occurred to me that everything I had ever known came from someone who saw things differently than I did.

Above all, I was relieved of the bondage of self — my deep insecurities that led me to believe that I would not be acceptable unless I had all the answers. It turned out that the opposite was true.

These were small acts of kindness. They involved humility, patience, and respect and helped launch another virtue, one that was essential in dealing with an equally vexing shortcoming. The virtue was love in its highest human form — forgiveness — and the defect was anger. Love, in its most fundamental form was, perhaps, best described by Alex, a guy in my FSC meeting. On an operating level, he said love is simply this:

*"If I can help you I will, if I can hurt you I won't."*

Anger, along with fear, had long been the chief ingredients in the fuel that propelled my drive toward success. One of the big problems with anger is that it demands that I take someone else's inventory when things do not go my way. Also, it helps to justify the depths of my love for my own rectitude. I especially thrived on looking down on people who looked down on people, particularly those who tended toward any form of racism, however slight or unintended. Then there were those, too, who were cruel or selfish, and the list went on. I self-righteously detested the self-righteous, even though I had many times read the passage from Step 10 in the *12 and 12* that says:

> *"For us of A.A., these are dangerous exceptions. We have found that unjustified anger ought to be left to those better qualified to handle it."* *(12 and 12, p. 90)*

My anger could not be contained only to the self-righteous or others whom I thought deserved it. At some level, however seemingly insignificant, it permeated my relationships with nearly everyone. Building on the experience with saying the Lord's Prayer, more continued to be revealed.

For most of my life, I said common prayers, like the Lord's Prayer, pretty much by rote without thinking about what the words meant. But the part about "forgive us our trespasses as we forgive those who trespass against us" struck a chord permanently. Continuing to pray that God would give me a loving and forgiving heart produced almost immediate results nearly every time. My relations with everyone, whether I knew them or not, became more relaxed and pleasant. I was able to see more clearly that many of the annoying things people did were things I myself had done. I sensed that people were attracted to me in an easier manner than before.

Having said all of this, I do not need to become a Pollyanna, excusing or ignoring the harsh realities of the world around me and the people who, left to their own devices, would make it worse. Without an unsparing view of poverty, war, racism, sexism, homophobia, economic injustice, hunger, global warming, and the many other problems, we have no chance of improving our existence. We must speak out. But how we do this is critical. The Prophet Ezekiel urged, "Speak out to dissuade." To *dissuade*, he said. Anyone can just speak out and, as Paul the Apostle said, be little more than a resounding gong or clanging cymbal. But if we are to be effective and either dissuade or persuade others, we need to figure out *how* to speak out. For me, this was tough. Years ago, my son, Tom, said to me:

> *"Dad, we will always listen to what you say even*
> *if it doesn't seem like we are. But, when you*
> *tell us something, do it with love."*

The truth is that most people will not remember what I have done, and few will remember what I said. But virtually no one will forget how I made them feel.

While everyone has their own path to recovery, for anyone wondering where to start when getting "entirely ready," kindness, compassion, forgiveness, indeed love, is a safe bet while surrendering the anger, resentment, and self-pity.

Then there is fear. Self-centered fear is one of the killer defects cited in the *12 and 12*. It can be both a driving force and a crippling malady. For me, it is just a different side of the same coin as anger. While anger is being upset because something didn't go my way, fear is being upset because I do not believe something will go my way. One looks to a past which cannot be changed and the other to a future which is not here yet. When I finally looked back on my life and realized that the vast majority of my fears were never realized and that I lived through those that were, trust began to grow. My sponsor, Tom D.-I, once helped me at a time of great worry.

First, he told me to just take care of today, and God would take care of my future. Second, he suggested that I imagine everything I feared would come true — that I would lose everything I had. Then he told me to, just for the moment, believe that I would survive and visualize how I would get through it, thinking back to the crises I had already survived throughout my life and with far fewer resources.

At this point, we could go into detail with each of the remaining "Seven Deadlies and Four Uglies," but it would risk being too prescriptive. Everyone needs to work through these issues with their own sponsors and support system. But naming and nurturing the virtues opposite the "Seven and Four" have been essential to the serenity — indeed the joy and peace — I am enjoying.

## BUT WAIT! THERE'S MORE!

It has happened too many times to count. Just when I think I have something neatly buttoned down, especially a belief, another notion comes along that changes it. In this case it changed the "Seven and Four."

### The 5th Ugly: Self-centeredness

A few years ago, I made a new friend through my involvement in politics. He was a great policy expert and political organizer, and it turned out he was also in "the program." During a discussion of the steps, I mentioned the "Seven Deadlies and Four Uglies." He liked the addition of the Four Uglies and asked about them from time to time. A year or so later, he said, "There's one you missed – another "Ugly." He also pointed out that adding it would give me a total of twelve.

Ah, the magic number: twelve! My first thought was, *C'mon! Why does everything have to add up to twelve? We already have the 12 tribes of Israel, the 12 apostles, the 12 Steps, the 12 Traditions, the 12 Promises. We don't need another 12 of anything spiritual.*

Then I asked what he had in mind. "Ego," he replied. I quibbled about the word and we alighted on "self-centeredness." But isn't self-centeredness a part of each of the "Seven and Four"? And isn't it reinforced by each of them, as well? Good questions, perhaps, but they didn't convey my real concerns. I had ulterior motives. By the time I gave it serious consideration, I was coming down the homestretch in getting this book published, and I didn't relish the work of making a major change in it. Moreover, it was a bit embarrassing; it reminded me of that night many years ago in San Francisco when I became aware of how I was misinterpreting Step 1 after fourteen years of sobriety. How could I not have thought of this — self-centeredness — especially given my background? Finally, and what bothered me the most, was that in my recovery I hadn't consciously addressed the issue, per se, and I didn't feel I could write about it as part of my own experience, strength, and hope the way I had done with the "Seven and Four."

As it says in the *12 and 12* (page 49), these fears were little more than bogeymen. To the first concern, I had already written more than eighty-eight thousand words; a few more weren't that big a deal. Second, and most importantly, no one has a complete handle on anything when it comes to recovery. All of us are continually learning. Perpetually, we know only a little. More will be revealed, unless we let pride take over. Finally, I turned to my wife and asked where she would rate me on a scale of 1 to 10 when it came to being self-centered, and she said, "You are at the low end; you are always concerned about others." This surprised me.

So just what is self-centeredness? It's probably best described as a persistent personal state and attitude in which an individual sees everything and everyone through the lens of their own self-interest. It is an intense focus on one's own needs, feelings, and aspirations, and a lack of consideration for other people. The self-centered person has little interest in people, ideas, or activities which cannot be enlisted for their personal satisfaction or gain. They are often self-referential in their thoughts, words, and behavior.

When I thought of where I was in the early days of recovery, when I so wanted to become a US Senator, when I expended so much of my energy and activity with that end in the back of my mind and compared it to what my life and outlook had become, I was awakened to the change that had occurred. The promise of Step 2 was being realized. Sometimes we do not work the program — the program works us. There's also what I see when I look around.

The world stage is splattered with the debris of human brokenness left in the wake of widespread self-centeredness. Consider any major problem facing us: the environment, poverty, racism, hunger, homelessness, social-economic and judicial injustice, threats to democracy, and, of course, he worst pandemic the world has faced in modern times, COVID-19. We have the knowledge and technology to solve every single one of these problems if we were each willing to think in terms of the common good. But, when self-centered fear, frequently abetted by pride or greed, drives our decisions, problems that are solvable can become intractable. The price we pay individually and as a society for self-centeredness is enormous.

On balance, by nature the human species is remarkably cooperative. But many factors can lead to self-centeredness. Fear, insecurity, loneliness, anxiety, depression, grief, and a host of other issues can cause a person to turn in on themselves. Any of the "Seven Deadlies and Four Uglies" can cause us to think about our own problems and ourselves before all else. A particularly powerful cause of self-centeredness is addiction, with its unpredictability and the obsessive-compulsive behavior that often attends it. The preoccupation with where one will get the next fix — be it alcohol, another substance, or the relentless craving of addictions to food, sex, or spending — can block out any awareness we may naturally have for the needs of others. The hole in the soul needs to be filled somehow. But that void is spiritual in nature. Nothing material — money, possessions, substances — can fill it nor can any of the other addiction-driven substitutes. At their core, all of them are based on fantasy, and after getting the quick fix, we often feel let down. Before long, we find ourselves right back where we were, wanting more.

But whether addicted or not, whether we suffer from other mental or physical disorders or not, whatever our social-economic plight may be, we all need real connections with other people and their needs, not the self-serving misconnections of fickle substitutes for reality that we use to try to mend the hole.

Down through the ages, religious leaders have warned against self-centeredness, including Buddhists, Muslims, Jews, and Christians. Most recently, Pope Francis addressed the issue directly in major messages this year. In "Urbi et Orbi," he calls on us to "banish self-centeredness" in the face of COVID-19. Earlier in his Easter message, he said, "We need solidarity, not indifference, self-centeredness, or division" in addressing the plight of refugees.

In raising this issue with my friend Tom D.-II, he referred me to pages 60 through 63 of *The Big Book*:

> *"Selfishness-self-centeredness. That, we think is the root of our troubles. Driven by a hundred forms of fear, self-delusion, self-seeking and self-pity, we step on the toes of our fellows and they retaliate."*

It goes on to say:

*"Above everything, we alcoholics must be rid of this selfishness.
We must or it kills us! God makes that possible." We could not
"reduce our self-centeredness much by wishing or trying on our
own power. We had to have God's help." (AA, p. 62)*

A therapist could conclude that my personal background includes
a lot that could lead to self-centeredness. Indeed, it is still ever present, Janis's generous comment aside. Most of my thoughts and ideas
— even my prayers — are about me, at least in part. Ever noisy, my
head is often in a place remote from the reality of the moment. In an
A.A. meeting or even during the most important part of the Mass, my
mind wanders, and I can find myself in an imaginary argument about
something with someone a million miles away from what is happening
around the tables or on the altar.

As with each of the "Seven and Four," there is both a payoff and a
price. The payoff is the rush of self-indulgence and feelings of clever-
ness — winning every phantom argument, imparting knowledge to an
imaginary world. The price is in depriving myself of what the sacraments
of the Mass and the experience, strength, and hope of other alcoholics
could give me. Once aware of the problem and its effect, the question
was what to do to ameliorate it, and I didn't have the foggiest notion.

Except for my belief in a loving God and the hope forged from progress
I have made, however slow, there could have been food here for despair.
But again, my Higher Power — the God of my understanding — provided
everything I needed. As usual, I had it even before I knew I needed it.

Several months earlier, I had sent a copy of my daily prayer regimen
to a friend, Jayne. She is an active member of my parish and fellow A.A.
member. She read it and sent back the Litany of Humility in return.

The Litany of Humility was not my favorite prayer. The seemingly endless repetition of the refrains was monotonous and distracting. I could easily zone out and even snooze while saying it. Also, it seemed too self-deprecating. This led me to never say the prayer. But Jayne had given it to me, and that seemed special. So I read it without the refrains and found a touch of peacefulness. Then I modified it as I have done with many prayers, including the Psalms and even the Nicene Creed. Now I say it daily. Here's how it appears in my daily prayers:

## Oh, Lord, hear me and …

### *deliver me from the desire to be …*

esteemed

loved

extolled

honored

praised

enriched

preferred to others

consulted, or

approved.

*deliver me from the fear of being ...*
humiliated
despised
rebuked
calumniated
forgotten
ridiculed
wronged
impoverished
suspected,
or that others may be loved more than I.

*grant me the grace to desire that, more than I, others may be ...*
esteemed
increased
chosen
praised
noticed
preferred in everything
and holier,

**Provided that I may become as holy as I should.**

For reasons I cannot explain, saying this prayer gives me a deep sense of peace. It is as if a weight has been removed. Indeed, as Matthew Kelly has said, when I am spiritually fit, nothing bothers me. And, as I have heard many times in meetings:

"Humility isn't about thinking less of myself, but about thinking of myself less."

I am coming to understand that the antidote to self-centeredness is an awakening – the start of step 12 working its way into our lives; an awakening to all around me, the people and other wonders of creation and the attention and care they need which I can give them at that moment.

I am not the center of the universe but just one of billions of creatures loved to unbelievable lengths by a God I can never fully comprehend. I have everything I need. God has been more than fair to me.

Every day I try to work to become *entirely* ready to have God remove *all* of my defects. I simply do not want them anymore. Each day I pray for the following:

"Dear God, along with my effort, I humbly ask You to vanquish my pride with humility; my lust through purity; my anger through patience, kindness, and love; my greed through generosity and justice; my gluttony through moderation and restraint; that my envy will give way to gratitude; that my sloth may be dispatched by diligence; that my self-pity may surrender to empathy for others, especially the poor, the dispossessed, the marginalized, the hungry, and the addicted; even as my fear flees before faith; my despair is deposed by hope; and my dishonesty is transcended by truth."

When one defect is proving particularly difficult, I pray about it specifically, but I always keep it in the context of the entire "Seven and Four," because they feed off of each other. To these I will be adding the 5th ugly – self-centeredness -- and its antithesis – a virtue depicting "other-centeredness", attentive consideration.

To start off nearly every A.A. meeting, someone is asked to read from Chapter 5 of *The Big Book*. Entitled "How It Works." As stated earlier, one short sentence impressed me from the beginning:

*"Half measures availed us nothing." (AA, p. 59)*

Very little wiggle room in that statement; little room for interpretation.

At the close of our meeting at FSC, we say in reference to the program, "It works if we work it, sober." But neither the program nor God will impose on us if we are unwilling. At long last, I am learning how to be willing — how to "get ready."

# STEP SEVEN

So there I was at an A.A. meeting on a Sunday night in Cleveland with a guy from work at whose home I was staying shortly after my divorce from Marilyn. It was 1983 and I had about seventeen years of sobriety. We were in town for a conference and decided to take in a meeting that had once been his home group. After the Preamble had been read, we learned that it was a speaker meeting, and the topic was Step 7.

*"Humbly asked Him to remove our shortcomings." (AA, p. 59)*

## THE CLEVELAND KID

The speaker was a kid who couldn't have been more than sixteen years old. Skinny, dark shaggy hair, and the only way you would know he might need a shave was if he had been eating pancakes with lots of syrup on them. That particular meeting celebrated sobriety dates on the first Sunday of each month. The kid was getting his six-months chip.

He started his comments with a statement reflecting the essence of Step 7 — humility.

> *"There's a lot I don't understand, a lot I am not sure of. But one thing I have learned is that either God removes my shortcomings, or they don't get removed. I sure can't do it."*

He went on to say that he had heard people talk about how they were dealing with this defect, or working on that shortcoming, but he didn't understand how that was going to work out for them unless they asked for God's help in removing them. He didn't dispute the value of therapy or individual effort, but he did keep it in the context of the step itself. Forget that he had only six months of sobriety. He knew what he was talking about, what he had learned from his own experience. It left an impression on me.

Like all the steps, 7 is not an event but an ongoing process. That means I must work Step 6 by getting ready every day and start out by identifying the defects that are most likely to cause trouble. In fact, I begin this process the night before in my evening prayers, which start with an expression of gratitude. I need to take Step 7 every day beginning in the morning and humbly ask that God remove them all. I can't just use God as a consultant on tap. Tiny tastes here and there will never adequately feed me with the ongoing peace, humility, integrity, love, forgiveness, generosity, modesty, trust, and faith that provide me with the "joy of living" described in Step 12. I need to ingest Him as completely as I can.

Moreover, selective surrender doesn't work for me. As the Preamble says, we had to "let go absolutely." But then it is up to God. And nowhere in the literature does it say we asked Him, He did it, and we became permanently fixed, free and forever pure.

So, there are big questions: What really are the prospects of our defects being removed? What if we do not even believe in God? Especially an intervening God? And, if we don't believe, what hope is there — especially if what the Cleveland Kid said is true and we cannot remove our own defects? If we do believe in God, can we trust Him to do this? Selfishly, what if I go to all this work — all the self-denial only to fail time and again — and He doesn't remove them? Certainly, that wouldn't be fair. And at some deep level, that may be the biggest question of all. How do I know if God will be fair?

## THE MONSIGNOR

"I've got some good advice for you," the celebrant said as he began his homily.

Msgr. Holmes had been my spiritual advisor for nearly eight years. One may not have thought we would hit it off all that well. For starters, he was small-town Wisconsin bred and one of those ardent, quite-satisfied Packers fans while my Minnesota roots had me growing up in a fairly large city where I became an undying, long-suffering Vikings fan. And then, there was the fact that he was politically unreliable. The only thing he and Barrack Obama have in common is their impressive ears. But all that aside, he is rock solid in the context of being a most kind and humble man with a powerful faith and unwavering love of God. He is also sharp intellectually and an excellent theologian. He is always calm. This particular Sunday, one of the readings at Mass was from the Prophet Ezekiel citing how the Israelites complained that "The Lord's way is not fair." Monsignor's advice:

*"Never pick a fight with God over the issue of fairness."*[15]

Speaking from his own experience, he went on to say:

*"God has been far, far better than fair to me. And, for those
who believe in a hereafter, we do not need to wait
until our final moments for evidence. We need only look
around us at what a train wreck life could be and how very
easily I could have been there if I had not had the
help that was freely given to me countless times and at
critical moments throughout my life."*

As for me, if my Higher Power is objectively fair, when I look at my life and try to determine what I deserve, I cannot claim that He owes me anything at all, whatever my understanding of Him may be. Indeed, Step 7 starts with the word "humbly." If I had received what I deserved, I would never have had the life I have enjoyed. But, as the Psalmist wrote, "The Lord is merciful and gracious … He does not deal with us according to our sins nor repay us according to our iniquities." (Psalm 103:8, 10)[16]

Yet, this still leaves open the question of whether or not He will remove my defects. And, equally important, do I really want Him to. I can only speak from my own experience. Without God, I can't, and without me, He won't.

So let's deal with the second issue first: Do I really want Him to remove my defects. Aside from the personal consideration — the price I pay for the payoff I get — I need only look around me at the large differences that can exist among couples, business colleagues, and even friends, and ask, who is happier.

## WHO WILL BE HAPPIER

My defects had had a utilitarian value and having them removed begged the question of whether I could still get what I wanted without them. Returning to the fear of becoming the hole in the donut without my defects, one of the essential considerations is their overall impact. While they erode the soul and the personal payoff is hardly ever worth the price, they are rarely acted out without affecting others. So let's ask ourselves what we *really* want.

At the most fundamental level, once we pull back the veil of deception created by our defects, we discover that what we *really* want and what we *really* need are basically the same: happiness and peace of mind. While we may be confused as to exactly what that means, it is the essence of what everyone needs and seeks. To get an idea of what we will need to do in order to achieve this state, we can pretty much rely on universal, observable human experiences and weigh the virtues against the shortcomings. In nearly any human interaction — a marriage, a friendship, a business partnership, public service — we can simply ask who will be happier and who will have greater peace:

- Two people who are humble or two who are prideful and ego-centric;

- Two people who are faithful to each other or two people who think there may be a better deal with someone else;

- Two people who are loving or two people who are angry;

- Two people who are generous or two people who are selfish;

- Two people who are self-restrained or two people who are gluttonous for attention, food, sex, or money;

- Two people who are grateful or two people who are dissatisfied, always wanting more;

- Two people who work hard or two people who are lazy;

- Two people who are empathic toward others or two people who are full of self-pity;

- Two people who trust each other or two people who fear each other;

- Two people who can be hopeful or two people in despair;

- Two people who are honest or two people who are deceitful.

The point is clear: Our defects worsen nearly every human encounter and make long-term relationships unhappy and often impossible.

Now to the critical question: Will God really remove these defects for *me*? I can only speak for myself.

Every summer the Cathedral Parish in Madison has a cookout for volunteers in appreciation of their service. It was 2015 and after enjoying the fellowship and the food, Janis and I were crossing the church parking lot on the way to our car, when out of the blue she said to me:

*"You know honey, I am glad you went back to your religion*
*— you have really become a nice guy. You have always been a*
*good guy, but you have become a nice guy."*

It had been five years since I had come back to the church and about two years since I had begun asking God in earnest, on a daily basis, to remove all of my shortcomings framed in the "Seven Deadlies and Four Uglies." It struck me that it had been some time since I had felt the fear, the pride, and the anger that for so many years had driven me. Indeed, all of my relationships with people had become easier, more productive, and less stressful. I had become tolerant even with people who were at the opposite end of the political spectrum from me, some of whom became good friends. And now, here was my wife, my greatest love and at times my strongest critic, giving testimony to the change that comes only when the defects, if not completely removed, have been largely mitigated.

I can, and do, slip backward at times, as those close to me can attest. But overall, God does remove the defects. Daily, I simply need to be ready and humbly ask Him. It helps greatly to be practicing Steps 10 and 11 to secure the blessings of Step 7 on an ongoing basis. But, apart from that, I need a daily routine: first reviewing all the "Seven Deadlies and Four Uglies"; then focusing specifically on those that are most vexing at the moment while citing the specific payoff; and finally offering that payoff up to my Higher Power as an act of love and gratitude.

## GETTING OUT IN FRONT OF THE PROBLEM

When I had bypass surgery, one of the main considerations in the recovery process was pain management. My cardiologist, my A.A. sponsor, my wife, and I all conferred and came up with a plan that worked without jeopardizing my recovery from addiction. Everyone would be aware of exactly what I was doing regarding pain medication, right down to the last pill. This was crucial because the medications for controlling serious pain are highly addictive and fraught with danger for recovering alcoholics and drug addicts. Yet, it was essential to get out in front of the pain so it would not impede the recovery from the surgery, and the only way to do that was with highly addictive meds — morphine and oxycodone. We agreed to try one oxy before I awoke from the surgery; one more afterward and ibuprofen thereafter, and we would play it by ear. The plan worked perfectly. No further meds were needed.

The same is true when it comes to addressing my defects of character in Step 7. In order to get the daily reprieve contingent on the maintenance of my spiritual condition promised in the *12 and 12*, I needed to get out in front of the issues. Therefore, I learned to start the daily process of becoming entirely ready the night before. Taking about ten minutes each night before bedtime, I take an inventory, the details of which are outlined later in Step 10.

The following morning, I have an established meditation and prayer rhythm that consists of some of my favorite Psalms and prayers specifically designed to start the day. It takes about fifteen to twenty minutes and sets the tone for the day. The process begins with an expression of gratitude. The main focus is on the virtues, and I imagine ways that I might practice them. In reviewing my schedule for the day, I identify the things that may be difficult and ask for help with them.

When I start out this way first thing in the morning — before reading emails, paying bills, or diving into work — my entire day is better. I follow up and pray or practice several other spiritual exercises during the day. But, as is evidence of my continuing need for the restoration to sanity promised in Step 2, I do not always do it. Everyone has heard that insanity is doing the same thing over and over and expecting different results. Well, another definition is to discover something that consistently works and *not* do it. Thankfully, as time has passed, I have made progress. But there are still days and some evenings when I neglect to use these spiritual tools. And I always feel the difference.

## SO, HP REMOVES THEM AND THEN WHAT? WHAT IS LEFT?

Returning to the issue of God's fairness, everyone, of course, has their own story. But one look at my life provides a clear, unambiguous answer to that question. He's more than fair. He will remove my defects and, when they come back, He will remove them again. I just need to be humble and willing to ask for His help right in the heat of the action each time they arise. But then what?

The promises of the program materialize. The overall experience, indeed, produces the new freedom and new happiness promised. And, while I do regret parts of my past, I do not beat myself up over it nor wish to shut the door on it.

I consider the circumstances of my birth to a frightened, single young woman during the Depression whose life and future were turned upside-down and who, after caring for me for several months, reluctantly put me up for adoption in hopes of a better life for me. From foster homes to the adoption by Margaret and Stanley and a stable, loving home; trouble all through grade school and into high school; being advised not to attempt college by the guidance counselor, followed by the luck of meeting Father Jim Church who guided me to St. John's where grants secured by Fr. Martin, OSB, enabled me, a "C minus/D plus" student at that point to complete my education there, permanently changing my life; Marilyn's untimely pregnancy leading to the births of five wonderful children and the family life I had yearned for from little on; the heart-rending divorce which opened the path to a fulfilling life with an extraordinary woman, Janis, and her three wonderful daughters; being reunited with my birth mother at age fifty-eight, along with my two birth sisters, Peggy and Patty, and their partners and children, which ultimately led me, at age seventy-seven, to meet John, my birth brother on my father's side, and his lovely wife, Deb, and their children.

And there were other developments over time: essentially being denied boarding in 1964 on a United Airlines flight because I was intoxicated, to becoming the first director of their Employee Assistance Program fourteen years later; wandering into an Al-Anon meeting thinking it was a bar, which turned the key in the prison door leading to my freedom; while still partly drunk answering the Johns Hopkins alcoholism questionnaire in our little apartment in 1965, to consulting with major health care experts at that same great university thirty-seven years later on how to deliver and cost-out addiction and mental health services to the uninsured of Maryland; estranged from the Catholic church in 1969 only to find God in a profoundly deeper and more transformative way more than forty years later in that same Catholic faith; slowly watching a life's dream to become a US Senator evaporate only to have a significant role in making EAP services available to more than two hundred million employees and dependents worldwide, enabling them to have a better, more productive life.

But, had nothing else occurred, I would need only to think of Janis and where I was before we met.

## JANIS

It was 1983 in Minneapolis at the annual ALMACA conference. ALMACA, later renamed EAPA, was the professional association for Employee Assistance Program professionals and a growing, thriving organization. The annual conferences were a big deal, attracting more than two thousand participants from around the country and overseas. The last night of the conference, a group from Chicago, which had one of the most active chapters nationally, decided to go out together and do a little "stepping." The place was crowded, and a dozen or more tables were on the periphery of the dance floor. I arrived after the others had gotten there, and as my eyes adjusted to the dim lighting, I spotted an empty chair next to a woman sitting with some Chicago people. They invited me to sit with them. I took the empty chair.

She was a beauty, dark hair, deep coral lips framing a wonderful smile, and wearing a lovely green silk dress. The others got up to dance, and the two of us chatted for a moment. I thought how much I liked the sound of her voice. Then she asked if I wanted to dance. Unlike me, she was good at it. But my self-consciousness gave way to desire. I wanted her near — I wanted to hold her. We danced one number and then another. Normally I would have been making the rounds in such a setting, talking to as many people as I could, cajoling the guys and dancing with the women. But not this time. I liked her from the very beginning. I asked for her phone number, and her response surprised me.

"What if I give you my number and you don't call me?" she asked.

This was obviously a woman who wasn't into playing games. How often do guys ask a woman for their phone number and never bother to follow up? How many times had I done that?

"Well," I replied, "I'll give you mine and you can call me if you want to."

I wrote it out on a napkin. A few days later, she called, and we went on our first date. It was a Friday night, and we had dinner and danced. I got along with her dog, a Norwegian Elk Hound mixed with a few other breeds. Named Willis, he was sweet, but if any dog ever suffered from borderline personality disorder, Willis was that dog. Barking and snarling as I climbed the stairs to the landing where Janis awaited, she asked, "Are you okay with dogs?" I said I liked dogs and was able to approach Willis and calm him down. In addition to Willis, I was pleased with her choice of Chicago mayoral candidates — Harold Washington. She was surprised at my politics, living as I did in a conservative suburb having nearly zero minorities. Along with having a good management position in a major corporation and dressing the part, it was an easy mistake to make. I was impressed with her. Intelligent, a good sense of humor, not into small talk. It turned out Willis and Harold were two crucial factors in her decision to go out with me again. The following Friday we had dinner and went to a movie. She was great to be with.

Nearly every Friday since, for thirty-six years, we have gone to a movie and dinner. Within a year of that first date, we were married.

I hadn't planned on getting married so soon after my divorce from Marilyn — it had been only two years and the pain of it had been greater than anything I had experienced either before or after. As always, I thought I knew what I needed to do. I had devised a plan: five years or five hundred dates, whichever came last, before I would consider marriage again. Pretty foolish when you think about it. Yet, I was serious. What saved me from myself was that I seriously increased my attendance at A.A. and another twelve-step group, and I went into therapy. The therapist was Phyliss Levy, a truly great clinical social worker. Our EAP at United Airlines had referred several people to her with excellent results. After learning about alcoholism and drug addiction, she went on to become an expert in sexual addiction and helped start the first Sexaholics Anonymous group in the Chicago area. I knew from the experiences of others whose marriages had broken up that the problems are never all on one side, and I didn't want to take the same baggage into a future relationship that had contributed to the demise of my last one. I needed to know where my issues ended and Marilyn's began. Phyliss did a great job helping me sort it out.

When I told my dad that we were getting divorced, the first thing he said was, "Well, that's too bad, but don't hit the bottle and take care of your job." Indeed, my A.A. program, in which I went from a meeting a week to a meeting a day, the therapy with Phyliss, and my career were all I had to hang onto. My two oldest children, Tom and Linda, had finished high school and had gone back to their Minnesota roots. My daughter Carmen had a boyfriend and was on her way out of the house. My youngest, the twins Carrie and Kelly, had been pretty much estranged from me by the pain and anger of their mother. The first year, life was bleak as I tried to find my way forward. A profound sense of failure enveloped me like an invisible leaden shroud. Most difficult was the emptiness. My family, as I had known it, was gone. My marriage had collapsed, and my children were scattered, both physically and emotionally. While not totally at fault, I knew that a large part of the responsibility for this catastrophe lay at my feet.

I did a lot of dating, mainly with women from A.A. and my profession. It was no substitute for what I had lost, but it did give me an idea of the lay of the land should I seriously consider another permanent relationship. Even though many of the women I dated were bright, pretty, and nice, when imagining what life would be like with them nothing appealed to me strongly enough to want to pursue it. There was no spark. I decided to just put it in my Higher Power's hands and let the chips fall where they may. I continued to attend a lot of meetings, and it helped, but I still felt disconnected. At that point I knew it was going to take time — five years, five hundred dates didn't seem unrealistic — and maybe another permanent relationship wasn't in the cards at all.

Then Janis came along, and everything changed. Here she was, a considerate non-observant Russian Jew with a strong, innate sense of what was appropriate and right. And then there was me — a renegade Irish Catholic alcoholic who enjoyed living just a centimeter outside of the boundaries of audacity. And it worked because we shared the same core values in the things most important to us: children and how they should be raised, politics marked by a strong sense of social and economic justice, a love of literature and music, and a good sense of humor. There was also our common background in addiction, she a Certified Addictions Counselor Supervisor and me a recovering alcoholic with a lot of administrative experience in the addiction profession. Then there was our shared EAP experience. While I had received much recognition for my work, she had quietly developed more than forty programs for small companies in the Chicago area. Equally important,

I could learn from her. She had an MPH and a much broader, trained perspective on health care, especially nutrition, areas where I had little knowledge. We both carried the strength of our convictions, worked hard, were insightful, and strived to be ethical. Where our religion was concerned, the great G.K. Chesterton said it best:

> "For religion, all men [and women] are equal as all pennies are equal because the only value of any of them is that they bear the image of the King."

I liked to joke that given our backgrounds, between us we are always right ecclesiastically.

One evening in the loveliness of her embrace, I asked if she thought she could come to love someone like me. She said, "I think I already have." The timid hope that she might be the one — the promised kiss of springtime, as Jerome Kern would say — gave way to the comfort of knowing that she truly was that and far more. And she still is.

Throughout it all, from the beginning of my life until this moment, I have never lost anything that wasn't replaced with something better. Especially my shortcomings. The prayer of St. Francis of Assisi implores, "Lord, make me a channel of your peace." Step 7 unclogs that channel, removing the debris of my shortcomings so I can experience the joy and peace of the promises of the A.A. program, let them flow to others, and have a shot at being the best person I can be.

As Tom D. said many times:

> *"Life isn't fair; thank God."*

As my friend Monsignor Holmes said, God has been far, far more than fair to me. I just need to give Him a chance. I need to humbly ask.

# STEP EIGHT

To be free, we need reconciliation for the harm we have done. This is the essence of Step 9. But just as we had to make a fearless and searching moral inventory in Step 4 before admitting the exact nature of our wrongs in Step 5, and just as we had to become entirely ready in Step 6 before asking God to remove all our shortcomings in Step 7, before doing the 9th Step, we need to prepare ourselves. We need Step 8. Therefore:

> *"We made a list of all persons we had harmed, and became willing to make amends to them all." (AA, p. 59)*

This is where we take our program public. Steps 4 and 5 cover what we did, while Step 8 is seeing clearly who suffered. Up until now, our recovery has been largely low risk and private, developing in a safe cocoon of fellow A.A. members, sponsors, supportive family, friends, and maybe a therapist or clergy. But this just forms the platform from which we need to be launched into the real world. And in the real world, we cannot function very well if we are constantly at odds with the people around us. Unfortunately, many had been harmed by our actions, especially those closest to us.

Simply telling people I was sorry had become an old familiar tune. How many times had I apologized and meant it, only to repeat the same or worse behavior later when the irresistible urge to repeat the experience of getting high had again descended on me? Or worse, how many times had I said "I'm sorry" just to end the conversation and get the monkey off my back? If we were ever to know peace and happiness, we had to break the old cycle of drinking or drugging, acting out, hurting others, apologizing, getting a short reprieve, and then repeating the same behavior. We would go on hurting others, especially those closest to us, and continue the long downward path our lives had taken. As the *12 and 12* says, this is where we try to develop the best possible relationship we can with everyone we know.

Making things right with others — reconciliation — is seldom easy. Nothing illustrates this better to me than the Bible: the first seven pages are about creation and the fall of humanity; the next 1,700 pages are about reconciliation. When faced with such challenges, we have a number of obstacles. Often a deep sense of shame and guilt causes us to recoil from facing those we had harmed. Then there is the ever-present tendency to rationalize: what I did wasn't *that* bad; they were equally to blame; they started it; they disrespected me; and the old reliable, they probably have put it behind them so why raise it again. There is also fear that if I admit I was wrong this time, I will lose leverage in any future conflict with them, and this incident will be thrown back in my face. Such fears are usually triggered by another common pitfall when working Step 8, which is to project forward to Step 9 and imagine the worst. This was especially true for me the first time taking the step.

The A.A. literature stresses the importance of staying in the present.

Indeed, as Joe said many years ago, "If you ever take another drink, it won't be in the future or the past, it will be right here and now — in the present." Aside from that, it's easy to make ourselves miserable imagining the worst. Especially distressing for me was when I was running late for an appointment. That is, until my daughter Carmen put things in perspective when, on one occasion, she said: "Don't worry about it, Dad — you aren't late until you get there."

While it is unlikely that many of the fears about making a direct amend will be grounded in reality, let's just imagine for a moment that they are. After all, as practicing alcoholics and addicts, we didn't always associate with the most stellar, best-adjusted people. Many weren't wrapped all that tight emotionally, having alcohol and drug problems of their own as well as mental health issues. Some came from backgrounds that compromised their chances of being socially well-adjusted, including our own siblings, in some instances, who shared with us a dysfunctional family life growing up. Some had none of these issues but were jealous of us or resentful, and either wanted to sabotage us at work or get even for something we had done to them or someone else. Then, too, there were those who started out fine with few personal issues, got involved with us, and our problems and irresponsible behavior brought out the worst in them. All of this and more may be true, but where Step 8 is concerned, *it doesn't matter*. This step is not about how to change *their* behavior or what their response will be: it is primarily about us and how we are going to find freedom to be the best and happiest person we can be. Plus, *we owe them*. So, without projecting forward, let's just look at what Step 8 says and focus on that alone.

## THE LIST

When I worked Step 8 for the first time, Harry's guidance was crucial. Here's what he said:

- First, focus only on Step 8 and do not worry about 9.

- Second, just make the list to start with, or as a sponsee of mine named Dave said years later, "Just take it to the comma."

- Third, forgive those on the list for anything they may have done to hurt me.

- Fourth, imagine how they felt when I did what I did; it helped to simply imagine how I would have felt had our roles been reversed.

- Finally, focus *only* on my behavior and take full responsibility for it, knowing we are seldom forced to do anything beyond our ability to resist it.

With self-centered fear being such a major part of our makeup as addicts and alcoholics, it is easy to project forward and conjure up the worst conceivable outcome when we think about doing Step 9. And, when these two steps are run together, either in conversation, the literature, or at A.A. meetings, this problem is compounded. Just as with Steps 6 and 7, the process of reconciliation is a big deal, and while 8 and 9 were combined as Step 4 in the original six-step draft of the program — "We made restitution to all those we had harmed by our drinking" — upon further reflection, Bill W. felt that this step and many of the others needed to be broken into smaller chunks. Thus, two separate but related steps were formed in the process of developing the twelve-step program. In the final version, Step 9 tells us what to do but first we need Step 8 to guide us in how to get there.

In just making the list, the immediate question was, "Who should be on it?" First, Harry suggested I include everyone I had had contact with in the previous six months and review what my encounter with them was like, noting any unpleasant experience, argument, or conflict. If there was none, remove the name. This left me with a list of the potential people I had harmed recently and also served as a guide to the kind of behavior I engaged in when hurting others. It was the warmup to making a complete list. Then I went back through my life to recall any others I had harmed, using the 4th Step inventory for guidance. In fact, the wording in Step 4 was aspirational in itself: I had to be "fearless" and "searching" with regard to who went onto my 8th Step list. And borrowing from Step 6, the word "entirely" applied, as well.

## FORGIVENESS

To clear away any distractions or temptations to rationalize, I noted what they had done that hurt me and undertook to forgive them. This part of Step 8 is discussed in the *12 and 12* and in other recovery literature but is easy to overlook. While Step 8 is about the start of freeing ourselves of guilt and shame and making things right with others, forgiving others first is often the most transformative part of the step. Recently I read an inspiring little book written by Allen R. Hunt entitled, *Everybody Needs to Forgive Somebody*. Published first in 2006 under a different title, a new edition published by Beacon Publishing came out in 2016. I wish it had been available fifty years ago. It contains twelve remarkable stories of forgiveness that are hardly imaginable, some for injuries that are almost unspeakable. Hunt writes, and I have found it to be true, that:

> "Forgiveness will unleash a power in your life that is underrated and often ignored … power that is life changing."[17]

When I need to make an amend to someone but forgive them first for their part in the conflict, it no longer matters whether or not they forgive me. I have done my part — totally. Moreover, doing this leaves me with only my part of the conflict, what I am responsible for — that which I can do something about. Harry looked at the list and the specific behavior I had engaged in. In a few instances, it was so minor that the name was removed. Then came the hard part for me. With forgiveness and Harry's guidance, I was now ready to go beyond the comma.

## BECAME WILLING

There is that word again — *became*. From Step 2 on, the program unfolds and implies the passage of time. Nothing happens all at once — not even Step 1, as we become increasingly aware of the powerlessness and unmanageability not only over alcohol and other drugs and addictions, but of our diseased attitudes and thoughts and our lives in general. To re-emphasize: Just as we had to become ready in Step 6 in order to take Step 7, so must we get ready by becoming willing in 8 to prepare ourselves to take Step 9.

I looked at what I had done and tried to imagine how it made those on my list feel, thinking of how I would feel if the same behavior were directed toward me. I prayed that I could own it completely. Without rationalizing, minimizing, or blaming, I prayed for the capacity to admit and accept what I had done and all the ugly consequences of it. The devil hadn't made me do it, nor had the person I had harmed, nor any other outside person or force. This was *my* behavior, and *I was responsible for it*. I wasn't entirely successful at this, but I did the best I could, and it was a good start.

Next, I needed to segment the list into discreet groups, just as the *12 and 12* suggests in Step 9, only Harry had me do it as part of becoming ready in Step 8.

## WHO ARE THESE PEOPLE I HAD HARMED, AND WHAT IS "HARM" ANYWAY?

Naming the specific people is essential, of course, but coming to terms with what "harm" actually means precedes it. The *12 and 12* does a marvelous job of this. It reads:

> *"To define the word 'harm' in a practical way, we might call it the result of instincts in collision, which cause physical, mental, emotional or spiritual damage to people." (12 and 12, pp. 81–82)*

It is interesting to note that it refers to "instincts in collision," which implies a kind of spontaneity as opposed to premeditation. Indeed, without thinking we often automatically respond in ways that can tear apart the fabric of our relationships, whether through anger, cheating, sex conduct, or power-driven impulses. And it points out how we bring out the worst in others through our own often outrageous behavior. But equally important, it cites the more subtle expressions of these behaviors, which can be just as damaging. Being miserly, irresponsible, callous, cold, irritable, critical, impatient, and humorless can make everyone around us miserable. In addition, while not as dramatic, indifference, passive-aggressive behavior, neglect, turning a blind eye either out of fear or laziness, and putting ourselves first all undermine any chance of developing the best possible relations with others, and it hurts them, especially our children.

The first time I took Step 8, I not only ended up with all the usual suspects on my list — wife, parents, close friends — but some I hadn't seen in years. Looking first to see if I thought they had wronged me, I forgave them all. In many instances, their offense was minor or nonexistent. Then, putting myself in their place, I worked to become ready.

In becoming ready, I followed Harry's advice and categorized them according to the suggestion in the *12 and 12* at the beginning of Step 9:

- First there were *"those ... to be dealt with as soon as [Harry and I] were reasonably sure [I could] maintain [my] sobriety."*

- Then there were *"those to whom [I] could make only partial restitution lest complete disclosures [would] do them more harm than good."*

- Next were *"those where action [had best been] deferred."*

- And finally there were *"others where, by the nature of the situation [I would] never be able to make direct personal contact at all."* (*12 and 12*, p. 83)

Most of those on my list fell into the first two groups. For the most part, the plan was for me to affirmatively reach out wherever I could, having a clear idea of what I would say as the right words. Equally important was how I would say it and how much I would say — it is easy for me to over-talk. Not to leave the impression that it was all perfectly scripted, but at least I could envision a way forward and felt some modicum of confidence that if I just did my part, it would work out.

For me, two things were essential in taking this step. I couldn't have done it without Harry, and I couldn't have done it without absorbing the Step 8 reading in the *12 and 12*. This is one step where my approach hasn't varied much over the years. While the way I take most of the other steps has evolved with the passage of time, I have never felt that the length of my sobriety waived either the need to have my sponsor involved or a serious review of the *12 and 12* narrative when taking Step 8.

# STEP NINE

Clearing out the wreckage of the past is one of the principal objectives of the program, and it is not a new idea. Thousands of years ago, the Psalmist pleaded for God to "have mercy on me in your kindness, *blot out my offense*" (Psalm 51:1). Indeed, some religions teach that when God forgives, it is as if the sin had never even existed — the slate is truly wiped clean. However, humans are seldom as capable of such largesse, so in our expectations, we need to focus on our part of the deal and what the step actually says:

> *"Made direct amends to such people wherever possible, except when to do so would injure them or others." (AA, p. 59)*

In my case and that of my sponsees, the preponderance of those to whom we made amends were gracious, and the amend led the way to reconciliation, although in various degrees. With some it took time for the person to trust us and then only after we had a period of continuous sobriety marked by improvement in our ability to take responsibility for ourselves. In other cases, the relationship vastly improved but never quite returned to its original form. In still others, it became better than it had ever been. But, sadly in a few instances, our amend did little or nothing to improve the relationship.

Then there are those that just take time — lots of time. A guy named Ron at the FSC tells the story of how he had hurt his best friend and made an amend. The friend's response was:

"The best thing you can do is just leave me alone."

Over the years, Ron reached out in various ways to no avail. After sixteen years, he received a message:

"Call me and give it your best shot."

Today they are again best friends; the relationship has been restored

There is no qualifier in Step 9 that implies that it needs to be done only if we think we will get a good reception. A positive response from those we have harmed is encouraging, of course, but it isn't essential, and sometimes the person simply cannot be gracious. We need to keep in mind that many of those close to us were not wrapped all that tightly themselves — they have their own problems quite apart from us, and with some, our behavior made things worse. In a few cases, their biggest problem may have been us, especially where parents, children, and spouses were concerned.

Occasionally we may have a situation where the person is so bitter that they use our amend as a weapon to try to hurt us. Perhaps they tell us that our amend is too little too late, or that we can do nothing to make things right, or that they aren't going to let us off the hook *that* easy. We hurt them, and now they sense an opportunity to hurt us back. The more we try to reconcile, the more they resist, sometimes passively, sometimes in cruel or aggressive ways. This can become a trap from which there is no escape. Especially when taking this step for the first time, our own insecurity and low self-esteem combined with their resentment can wrap us around the axle and keep us there as long as we continue rolling in the same direction. Unless we stop and reverse course, we can continue with endless apologies, hoping to evoke a response that will never come.

A dear friend in the program, Grant B., once described this situation:

> *"An alcoholic is a person who has a pathological need to seek acceptance from someone who has a pathological need to withhold it."*

A practical alternative was expressed by a retired Chicago cop named Joe, who used to say every time our Mustard Seed meeting came to Step 9:

"My ex-wife doesn't like me drunk *or* sober, so I just leave her alone."

In some instances, they just may not want to hear it because doing so can cause them to relive the trauma our act caused them.

So, while Step 9 is about others insofar as justice requires us to clear up any doubt about who was responsible for what *we* did, it is essentially about admitting our transgressions and making things right to the extent to which we are able. Often the full result of our effort needs time to evolve.

The *12 and 12* starts out on Step 9 by saying:

> *"Good judgment, a careful sense of timing, courage and prudence — these are the qualities we shall need when we take Step Nine."*
> *(12 and 12, p. 83)*

It concludes with:

*"Above all, we should try to be absolutely sure that we are not delaying because we are afraid."* (12 *and 12*, p. 87)

In between it says we cannot buy our own peace of mind at the expense of others, and it does not lighten our burden when we recklessly make the crosses of others heavier. But at the same time, recognizing the ability of alcoholics to rationalize, it cautions:

*"Let's not talk prudence while practicing evasion."* (12 *and 12*, p. 85)

Harry helped me navigate these waters with a plan for each person on my list. With some it was specific, with others pretty general. Some on the list would be easy to approach, in other cases, not so much. With some, I just needed to wait until they crossed my path and rely on the promise that I would intuitively know how to handle situations that once baffled me. In still others, fortunately a few, I would, in fact, just botch it. But I had completed Step 8 and had become ready. I was going to make amends. I would try to mend the tear I had caused with each of the people I had harmed.

At the top of my 8th Step list were my wife, my parents, and a dear friend who had become a surrogate father to me. As much as anyone, he had helped me stay on a generally straight path at critical times during my teen years. His name was Louie.

## LOUIE

I was about nine years old when I walked into the most popular corner grocery store in our neighborhood. "Lou's Cash Food Market" was typical of small, independently owned grocery stores at the time, before big, self-serve supermarket chains hit the scene. Entering the store through the angled corner doorway, fruits and vegetables were laid out in a window display on the left. On the far wall was a counter with a National cash register out of the 1930s and a scale to weigh cold cuts, cheese, and bulk cookies. The counter was flanked by a bread rack on the left, and a lunchmeat counter on the right was set at a right angle, which was next to a candy counter at yet another right angle. Together they formed a "U," which could only be accessed through a narrow opening alongside the counter. At least half of the goods were behind this configuration on wall shelves reaching nine feet from the floor. The clerk would fetch whatever the customer wanted. Lou Sr., the owner, was my father's age, not good with people and tight with money. He had three sons, the eldest of which was Lou Jr., whom most people called Louie. Louie was behind the counter that day, having just been discharged from the military where he had served as a Navy pilot. Before enlisting, he had been an all-state football star and one of the most popular students at Cretin High School.

With wavy chestnut hair, a broad face, a stocky build, a great tan, and a smile that could raise the candle power in any room, he was talking to some of the locals. To this day, I haven't met anyone who was more engaging than Louie. To top it off, he drove a brand-new '47 Ford convertible and had begun dating the most beautiful young woman in the neighborhood, Beth. She lived right across the street from me along with her two pretty sisters. I would see Louie tooling up Orange Avenue in the shiny maroon convertible with the top down and then driving off with Beth. Within a year, they were married.

That day I approached the counter with a nickel for an ice cream bar. Louie looked directly at me with a big smile, asked me my name, and made a little small talk. It's telling how that event sticks in my mind. Here was this obviously important guy paying attention to me. It was a big deal. He made a point of knowing everyone's name and a lot about their lives. Over the years, people grew to love him. He was funny, kind, smart, and generous. He let some customers charge groceries and take care of the tab on payday. Others fell on hard times, but they were never without food. Taking orders over the phone if he didn't have an item, he sent me off to a competitor to buy it so he could fill the order without sending the customer elsewhere. He survived three big supermarkets less than a mile down the road, and years later, when a 7-Eleven chain store came in across the street, neighborhood mothers and their daughters circulated a petition supporting Louie and urging a boycott of the intruder. The 7-Eleven ultimately went out of business. It was a great source of pride in the neighborhood how *our* Louie was "the only small grocer in *recorded history*" to put a 7-Eleven out of business."

My parents didn't believe in giving me an allowance, so I had to find ways to make money. At about age fourteen, I came up with an ingenious plan to solve this problem, and it involved Louie. He stacked soda bottles in wooden cases against the outer wall at the back of the store, awaiting the delivery truck. When I needed a little money, I would liberate some of the bottles, take them home, rinse them out, and bring them back to Louie to get a refund. One day he said:

"Jimmy, these bottles look familiar. Where did you get them?"

"Of course, they look familiar," I replied. "They are Coke and Pepsi bottles!"

He asked again, with a trace of a grin, "Yeah, so where did you get them?"

"Home," I replied.

"Okay, if I call your mother, will she tell me you brought them from home?"

Shit-damn! Caught! Finally, I admitted that they were his bottles and that I had been scamming him for some time. He said I had to pay him back. I told him I didn't have any money and little way to get any, which was a lie because I had been caddying since age nine. That didn't back Louie down.

I was going to have to make things right. I had to make an amend. He didn't call my mother; he didn't call the cops. He didn't embarrass me by telling anyone else, including his father. He didn't shame me or try to make me feel guilty.

He just said, "Okay then, you are going to have to do some work."

We had Catholics, Lutherans, and Baptists in our neighborhood, and many of us boys caddied at a Jewish golf club where professionals and businessmen imparted values supplementing those of our dads. But the primary shared theology for all of us was work, and getting paid for it by someone other than our parents was a rite of passage for my buddies and me. The first job Louie gave me was sweeping the floor. From there, I helped stock shelves. Pretty soon he said we were even on the bottles, but I could continue helping him — for pay.

As a Catholic teenage boy who loved God but had trouble handling one particular "instinct," Bill W. referred to so eloquently in the *12 and 12*, I went to confession regularly. And, over the years, I made a number of 9th and 10th Steps in A.A. But having to admit the wrongdoing and making that amend to Louie by sweeping the floor and stocking shelves stands out as one of the most important I ever made in my life. It turned out to be the beginning of a lifelong friendship that gave me living skills and a sense of self I may not have ever developed otherwise.

Eventually, I had the best job in the store, behind the counter waiting on customers, the envy of other neighborhood kids. Following Louie's lead, I got really good at it. Through my junior and senior years in high school, two years in vocational school, and part time while in college during breaks and holidays, I worked in Louie's store. By then, Louie and Beth had practically adopted me. The best meals and some of the best advice I got were from them. After I got married, I still worked there part time and, in addition to the money, he gave us groceries to help us get through.

I emulated Louie, his sense of humor, his honest business practices, and how he treated customers by often going above and beyond. I developed a work ethic that lasted a lifetime. As much as anything, working with him was fun. His encouragement was crucial during those years. Mostly, it was honest praise for honest work — there were no "participation trophies"; no overly enthusiastic "great job!" remarks for doing something trivial like taking out the trash or washing my hands before slicing cold cuts. Because the praise was honest and appropriate to the effort, my self-esteem soared. The quiet criticism when I made a mistake was equally honest and important. And, whether praise or correction, it wasn't thrown at me every five minutes. Coming from Louie and Beth, it meant something. We became big fans of each other. It was love. My parents were the oldest of all my friends' parents; they were solid people, and I loved them, too, and was loyal to them. But my dad was not at all expressive while my mother was overly so. I didn't think either was an accurate barometer by which to gauge how I was doing. So, Louie and Beth's advice, encouragement, and criticism was critical. They had a clearer understanding of me and my generation.

By the time I was twenty-six, my drinking was already taking a toll. Of necessity, I still worked part time at Louie's in addition to a full-time job. By then we had three kids, and I was working sixty hours a week, but we just couldn't get ahead. I often showed up at the store to work evenings having had a few drinks en route from my regular job. On two occasions, noticeably under the influence, Louie sent me home. He had to stay to work my shift. So, when it came time to make amends, he was at the top of the list.

The amend was made in a sauna in the back of a barber shop in North St. Paul. A few months earlier, when I told Louie I had stopped drinking and was in A.A., he was genuinely happy and relieved. That night I told him about the amends part of the program. I apologized for the embarrassment and inconvenience I had caused him and Beth, who by that time had become as close to me as Louie. I didn't embellish or go into much detail. We both knew what I was talking about. I still remember his response:

"Well, Jimmy, I didn't know you were an alcoholic, but I knew you drank too damn much."

When I asked him what I needed to do to make things right, he told me that by quitting drinking and taking this step, I had already done it. My parents and wife responded the same way.

Sometime later, Louie remarked how he and Beth always knew when I had been drinking late in the evening because I would walk up Orange Avenue from the bus stop at eleven or twelve o'clock at night, singing loud and out of tune. I didn't recall any of that.

In the years that followed, Louie sent people my way who he thought could benefit from "going on the wagon." Some of them made it, some didn't. Our friendship remained until I received a call while at a national conference in Seattle in 1995. Louie had died — he was sixty-seven. A piece of me went with him. Several years later, Beth also passed, along with another piece of me. I still think about Louie and Beth and what those pieces meant.

I still love them. Always will.

## MARVIN

The 10:00 a.m. Sunday meeting at the Mustard Seed in Chicago had become an important part of my recovery. In 1993, I was elected to lead the meeting and then reelected every six months for another six years. It was a step meeting, and as many as fifty people would file in, representing virtually every culture, religion, and race, from homeless to millionaires. After one meeting sometime in the late '90s, a powerfully built Black guy came up to me and asked if I would be his sponsor. I gave him my stock response — I would be his temporary sponsor until we were sure it was a good fit. His name was Marvin.

I didn't know it at the time, but Marvin had been a widely known gangbanger on Chicago's West Side. Unlike many of that group, he still had an intact family — mother, father, siblings, wife, and children. He wanted to stay sober and was at the beginning of his recovery. His lifestyle lent itself to a full catalogue of material for his 4th Step inventory and later for his amends list. The "old timers" in A.A. broke the program down to three issues: "Find God or die; clean house; help another alcoholic." Up to that time, no one in my experience had done a more thorough, courageous job of cleaning house than Marvin, starting with Step 4 right on through 9.

In addition to other transgressions, he had stolen from friend and foe alike, so his list was long. There were a few people on it to whom a direct amend was out of the question: people he had cheated on drug deals who carried weapons and weren't afraid to use them. And there were others where most people might have shied away not only from admitting what they had done, but from making it right. Some had known full well that they had been ripped-off, but they had no idea who had done it. He made the list, and we went over it, what he would say and the possible amend.

To determine exactly what the amend would consist of required a leap of faith on his part. After admitting what he did, he simply asked the person, "What do I need to do to make this right with you?" In short, he resolved to treat everyone he had mistreated with greater respect, and he repaid everyone he had stolen from, including one exceptional case.

During his using period, Marvin had bought a car and completely totaled it long before it was paid off. He could barely make payments on a car that functioned; paying off a loan on a total wreck was out of the question. The bank wrote it off. We decided he would contact the bank and arrange to pay back the $3,000 they had written off by taking out a personal loan, giving the bank the proceeds, and making monthly payments. It was a small bank, and the manager was less than cooperative, owing partly to the unusual nature of the transaction. After some wrangling, in which the bank actually made Marvin's credit score worse for the effort, he got the loan but only on the condition that I co-signed it. He paid it off without missing a payment or even being late. At the end, his credit rating improved significantly. Since he and his wife both had reasonably good-paying jobs, they were eventually able to move out of a small apartment in one of the most dilapidated, crime-infested neighborhoods in Chicago and buy their own home. A big step up for any minority family, especially one where a main breadwinner had Marvin's history. For a time, his self-esteem, productivity, and life overall proved the promises of the program. Then Janis and I moved from Chicago to Madison and, while keeping in contact, Marvin had to get a new sponsor. Circumstances and the rhythm of his recovery changed.

To my knowledge, Marvin stayed sober and clean for about three years. Unfortunately, relationship problems with family members, some with their own substance histories, persisted in nipping away at the edges of his serenity. And he had other health problems, both physical and mental, which doctors treated with addictive medications leading to a series of relapses marked by years of struggle. He was in and out of treatment programs, trying to reconcile the dilemma of the abstinence essential to addiction recovery with the need for medical treatment that countermanded it. Also, in retrospect, he wasn't always forthcoming with me, so my capacity to be a helpful sponsor was limited, especially after I moved from Chicago. One could view those years simply as a seemingly miraculous ascent followed by a heart-breaking, tragic fall. But there is more to the story than that.

We normally see success as an outcome, and indeed it may well be the truest, most meaningful marker. Yet, I have learned that credit must also be given for the effort, especially when it is heroic. Everyone close to Marvin benefited from his effort to achieve sobriety, especially his children. Like all of us, none have perfect lives. But all of us, including me, are better for Marvin's struggle. His effort on Step 9 became the gold standard for me in working with other sponsees.

## DAVE

Recently a woman named Johanna showed up at our Sunday morning FSC meeting. Not having seen her in many years, I was overjoyed. Seventeen years ago, she approached me. A close friend of hers — a young guy — had overdosed and died the previous week. She had another friend, Dave, who she feared was heading in the same direction. She asked if I would be willing to talk with him.

We got together to see if there was a good fit, and after a few meetings, Dave and I developed a solid connection and went through the steps. I became aware of the high-risk behavior in which he had been engaging and came to realize the gravity of Johanna's concerns. I had the benefit of seeing the results of Marvin's work and laid out virtually the same approach for Dave: a written Step 1, weighing the severity of the instances of powerlessness and unmanageability; tracking the trajectory of this severity over time to establish evidence of the unfolding restoration of sanity in Step 2; using this evidence as an indication that it was safe to turn his will and life over to the care of God in Step 3; and then taking Steps 4 through 8 pretty much following the approach outlined here. By then, Dave had a clear idea of whom and what to include in his 9th Step. We reviewed each name on his 8th Step list, assessed the seriousness of what he had done, and developed the strategy for carrying out the amend. He was determined to clear away the wreckage of the past while avoiding doing harm to anyone, including himself. Along with Marvin, he did the most complete job of anyone I had ever sponsored.

Some on his list simply were not available for a direct amend. To those, he wrote heartfelt, unsent letters, clearly admitting what he had done, pledging not to repeat it with others, and asserting that he would have done whatever was requested to make it right, had direct contact been possible. For those with whom he could make direct amends, he followed the same approach Marvin had used.

It was transformative, not only for him but for me as well. In a short period of time, virtually all areas of his life improved markedly, including living arrangements, finances, relationships and, above all, freedom from the bondage of the disease.

Like many of us when we begin our recovery journey, Dave was uncertain about what profession he might follow. He loved cars and, for a while, was a successful salesman at a leading dealership. But his true calling was to be a teacher, which he has done in a brilliant, creative fashion for fifteen years and is now the principal at a middle school. In the meantime, he married a wonderful, talented woman, moved to a section of the country that felt more like home to him, and had a child who has given him tremendous joy. Through his recovery, family, and profession, he is reaching people in ways that otherwise would not have been possible, and the ripple effect is incalculable.

## JUSTICE AND FAIRNESS

While we alcoholics can be pretty sensitive about whether or not *we* are being treated fairly, Step 9 enables us to earnestly start cleaning up our side of the street regarding what is fair and just where others are concerned. Many to whom we make amends have their own self-doubts, their own insecurities, their own problems. If they are co-dependent, they may well have wondered what they did wrong to cause us to treat them so badly. If they suffer from low self-esteem, they may even think they somehow deserved such treatment while pondering the why and how of it. When we finally do the 9th Step, we are telling them that they were not responsible for what we did — we were. That we know and now are acknowledging that it wasn't their fault, and they weren't crazy — we were. At long last, we are starting to treat others with some sense of the fairness with which we want to be treated. Through honesty, contrition, and as much love as we are capable of giving, we are starting to be fair and just.

## FREEDOM

The 3rd Step prayer asks for freedom from the bondage of self. In my personal experience, my self-bondage is closely tied to the people I have wronged. Until I freed myself from those wrongs in Step 9, I couldn't be completely free. At this point, the question was how to remain free.

# STEP TEN

What a journey! At Step 10 — perhaps long before now — many of us in recovery have felt, thought, and done things we never would have dreamed possible when we started out. We had gotten sober and, indeed, our lives were better. The big issue now was how to *stay* sober — how to sustain and increase the gains we had made to date; how to "continue" the journey of recovery from alcohol and drugs uninterrupted *and* without acquiring new disorders, particularly other addictions. And finally, how to experience peace and joy in the process. The *12 and 12* says that we ...

> *"Continued to take inventory and when we were wrong promptly admitted it." (AA, p. 59)*

These were questions the founders of A.A. pondered, as well. Many are the sound recommendations they could have made: read *The Big Book*; go to meetings; call your sponsor every day; pray, pray, pray; forgive; avoid the old haunts. They could have suggested a daily review of the first nine steps. Instead, they gave us a special step specifically designed to meet the challenge of staying sober and, equally important, growing in the program. Step 10 expresses the one action that took precedence over all others: we continued to take inventory.

A topical index of *The Big Book* shows that more space is devoted to inventory than any other subject. And the *12 and 12* provides insight gained through the ages, harvesting what many great individuals and religions have had to offer while going into the minds — the thinking — of alcoholics and addicts.

Each step has but one fundamental purpose — to keep me away from that first drink — just like Harry said more than fifty years ago. To do that, I need to avoid engaging in self-defeating, self-destructive, shameful, guilt-ridden behavior that will cause me to want to drink as Mike C. observed more than thirty years ago. We learn that if we do not practice the steps, we can be abstinent from alcohol and drugs for years while struggling with other issues, including other addictions and compulsions, which are inevitably fed by our shortcomings. Inventory is not a "one and done" event ending with Step 4. We needed a specific way to cope with the daily entanglements of life. Step 10 leads the way.

When we finally put our addiction in the caring hands of God as we understand Him in Step 3, we are not required to expend as much effort on the multitude of issues that can drag us back into the quagmire of relapse. The belief we were gifted with in Step 2 begins to unfold, and we are able to take Steps 4 through 9. But, if we are going to enjoy this state of relative peace and joy, we need to keep the channel unclogged, the slate clean. Getting out of our own way is one of the main tenants of Step 10, and we have many options for how to do this. But first, I needed an understanding of what the word "continued" entailed.

## CONTINUED

Step 10 is perhaps the greatest evidence the program offers that we are human and therefore fallible. We are never really cured from our addiction, nor are we ever without some challenge that can threaten our recovery. While circumstances and other people can contribute, by far the biggest and most frequent of these challenges come from our basic nature, which some theologians say is a fallen nature. Whatever it is, it can be miserable, but we do not need to stay there. Moving forward takes work and the kind of fearless and searching look at ourselves called for in Step 4 only on a daily basis. This work can be relatively simple or very difficult, depending on our personal commitment and how we go about it. The *12 and 12* suggests three types of inventories:

1. The "spot check" inventory to be taken anytime we are getting tangled up.

2. The daily inventory, usually done at bedtime.

3. The periodic "housekeeping," done every six to twelve months, reflecting on our progress since the last time we did it.

In addition, I have found a "pre-spot check" process that can also help greatly.

In setting the tone and attitude for Step 10, the *12 and 12* says:

*"For the wise have always known that no one can make much of his life until self-searching becomes a regular habit, until he is able to admit and accept what he finds, and until he patiently and persistently tries to correct what is wrong." (12 and 12, p. 88)*

In my experience, the wise who have always known come from virtually every religious faith, as well as those professing no particular faith, "the nones," as they are often referred to. In addition, agnostics and atheists have also been among the wise, starting with Harry when my recovery life began.

## SEEING

Steps 1 through 9 go a long way toward enabling us to develop the capacity to "see" when we come to Step 10. Unfortunately, without having committed to Step 3 for so many years, this was largely out of reach for me. I came to a point where the years of sobriety had been mounting but my defects just didn't seem to be diminishing, ranging from relatively minor to serious. One of the most annoying to people around me was fear, which manifested itself as hubris and arrogance. But I couldn't see it.

Later we quote Rabbi Ismar Schorsch, who stresses the need to sharpen our vision when examining ourselves, and that requires work. Of equal importance, I must sharpen my vision when viewing others.

First, I must see my brother and sister as deserving of love and respect. Then I must head off potential offenses to them by not rising to the bait when they do something annoying or provocative.

My frame of mind is the key, and I found something quite by accident that has been helpful. It came from a faith I had not looked into but had only heard about and often not in a favorable light. It helped me form a prequel to the continuing inventory process.

## THE PRE-SPOT CHECK: THE PRACTICE OF RESPECT

On "Ali Islam," the official website for the Ahmadiyya Muslim Community, "Codes for Social and Moral Behavior" based on the Quran and the Tradition of the Prophet Muhammad exemplify the profound respect toward each other that Muslims are asked to practice in their daily lives.

One of the more impressive practices for doing this was what I learned on the Ali Islam website in the section on "Islamic Manners and Etiquettes," which starts with:

> "When two Muslims meet, they greet each other by saying *Assalamo alaikum*, meaning "peace be upon you," and *wa alaikum assalem*, "upon you be peace."

A number of other examples are set forth depicting everyday interactions between Muslims and the practices that should accompany them, nearly all of which refer to Allah — God. This may not seem practical for those of us who live in a pluralistic, secular society, especially if we are a "none," an atheist or an agnostic. But these practices offer something meritorious and practical in the maintenance of our spiritual condition. If not saying them aloud, we can express these sentiments inwardly, silently blessing the other person, as it were, thereby setting the stage for a respectful engagement with others, no matter who they may be. From the very beginning, it puts our Higher Power in the midst of every interaction we have with others and can reduce the likelihood of our committing a wrong for which we will later need to make an amend. Equally important, it can reduce the likelihood of taking their inventory instead of our own.

## THE SPOT CHECK INVENTORY

The *12 and 12* includes a spot check inventory "taken any time of the day when we find ourselves getting tangled up." Anytime I am getting pushback or even passive resistance from someone, especially if I am upset, it is likely a cue that I need a spot check inventory. Likewise, anytime someone says or does something that hurts me, and I want to strike back with a gesture or a snide, negative comment, I need to exercise restraint. The *12 and 12* warns against rising to the bait:

*"Our first job is to sidestep the traps."* (*12 and 12, p. 91*)

The bait in the trap can be almost anything that triggers a negative emotion. In my case, this seems to always occur when I am not attending to some task I need to do, and my wife repeatedly reminds me, maybe even offers helpful little hints, about how I might do it. But just stuffing the negative response isn't likely to provide a lasting solution. That can be like lifting a heavy weight overhead that saps the strength to the point where we are forced to let it come crashing down. At an FSC meeting, a guy named Alex suggested an approach that helps me when I do it, which is not often enough. It entails three brief but related actions:

*Pause*

*Pray*

*Proceed*

This is especially helpful when tempted to make a knee-jerk reaction using email or any other electronic communication device.

We can all think of times when the actions of others are a trigger for us to react badly. The adage "restraint of tongue and pen" comes to mind, and along with it *NO* email or other electronic response. But equally important, there are times when we are solely at fault and others react to us. We may even know we are wrong, but we do not have a clue how to correct the problem. I found myself in such a situation a few years back.

Earlier we discussed pride but did not make some important distinctions. Nothing is wrong with taking satisfaction — pride as it were — in a solid achievement. That's authentic pride and is enjoyed most when attended by humility and gratitude. Hubristic pride is another matter, largely characterized by overplaying my hand. Then there is arrogance — being so self-righteous that I do not believe I even need to play my hand; everyone else should just fold their cards.

During the long years that I was struggling with Step 3, repeatedly turning my life over — but not my will — only to take it back, I had a difficult time admitting that I was wrong about anything. The flip side, of course, was that I thought I was always right, that my ideas and perceptions were superior. I would never say it outright, but in large measure it was my subconscious belief. Janis recognized the problem early in our marriage and pointed it out on a number of occasions through the years:

> "You always think you are right — you don't want to listen once you've made up your mind; you even get annoyed when someone stands their ground and doesn't agree with you."

and,

> "You talk too much — you interrupt. Relax a little, you'll get your chance to speak."

Always needing to be right put me on a collision course with those close to me. Instead of increasing my credibility, which was what I wanted, I was slowly eroding it. People realize that everyone makes mistakes. We all have misconceptions, and none of us have a corner on the truth. But when the facts become obvious, or even when they are not and another expresses an alternate opinion, and I refuse to accept them, instead of securing the esteem of friends by demonstrating an ability to admit error and learn from it, I undermine any respect I might enjoy. Moreover, an absolute insistence on one viewpoint doesn't leave room for the fact that we are often only partially right, even when the facts appear to be on our side.

This came to a head while I was serving on the board of directors of an important organization. I had spent years giving keynote addresses, lectures to large audiences, and consultations one-on-one or in small groups. And, I had served on several boards, usually with twelve or fewer members, often chairing them. In these scenarios, I was in control and often the acknowledged expert or leader. Now I was on a thirty-plus member board. If anything was going to get accomplished, it was imperative to the flow of discussion to have mutual consideration and share airtime equally without a lot of crosstalk. That proved to be a problem for me.

Frequently over-talking, interrupting, trying to talk first to make sure I would get my point in and get credit for it in case someone else wanted to make the same point, I was becoming a disruptive, irritating annoyance instead of the solid contributor I wanted to be. My closest colleagues on the board approached me to point out that I was undermining my own effectiveness. The chair even confronted me in private, telling me how disruptive and disrespectful it was. When I thanked him for the "feedback," he said, "This *isn't* feedback, Jim. Just don't do it."

It was obvious that I needed to retool. I turned to Janis. Echoing the others, she started by saying I had a lot to offer, although at that moment it didn't feel that way. One of the mysteries that emerges when trying to improve is that assets and defects can be so closely inter-twined. While I was knowledgeable, my self-esteem was brittle, and I felt the need to constantly prove myself. She also said that other people recognized that I had something to offer, but so did they. She re-em-phasized that whether in a group setting or in a one-to-one encounter, I would always get my turn. I understood this, yet I was anxious.

When having trouble being a part of a group, whether dominat-ing or hiding beneath it, fear is often the driving force. So, what was I afraid of? It turned out that my deepest fear, the one that drove this particular process, was that I would not remember the point I wanted to make if I didn't express it the instant it came into my mind and the moment would be lost. Unfortunately, I have a noisy head. So many thoughts go through my mind when I am taking something in that I can't always keep track of them. When someone said something that triggered a point that I thought could add value, anxiety would strike and grow until I could interject. So, what was I going to do?

Well, as often happens, an infusion of humility helps. The first step was to recognize that if I couldn't remember the point I wanted to make, maybe the world could survive without the benefit of my opin-ion on every subject, however important I thought it might be. Even this small practice of humility relieved some of the anxiety. Second, maybe someone else around the table had the same opinion and, if I gave them a chance, the point would be made. The main thing was that it would still be expressed by someone, not necessarily me. Therefore, at the next board meeting, I decided to try to do the following:

1.  During the meeting, make a note. If necessary, write down the point I wanted to make in response to someone else.

2.  Go last: wait until everyone else had commented and then, if

my point hadn't been made, express it; if it had been made, add anything of value provided it wasn't redundant.

3. If someone else wanted to talk at the same time I did, *always* let them go first.

This turned out to be a game-changer for me. My fear was unfounded. Others were often more eloquent or incisive in making the point I thought was important. By going last, I found that my contribution could be even greater, more incisive, often integrating it with other ideas board members offered after the time I would have jumped in. Miraculously, the anxiety evaporated. Some of the other board members noted the difference and privately complimented me. Getting to this point involved a process that became clear only in retrospect and can apply to many types of interpersonal problems:

1. Confer with someone you trust, especially someone who has commented on the annoying behavior you have engaged in.

2. Realize that it may not be easy for them to offer criticism, so be grateful they are willing to do so.

3. Resolve to follow any suggestions.

4. Develop a practical, specific plan with specific actions, and check it out with them.

5. Put the plan into effect, and tweak it where necessary.

6. Check back to see how you are doing.

Listening is a gift I can give others. Everyone wants to be respected, and that starts with knowing they are being heard. Those who want this most from me are my loved ones, followed by friends and team members. The less I listen, the less I learn; the less I learn, the less I can give. Most importantly, the less respect I am showing. Sometimes the best thing I can give is my silent presence and an open ear and heart.

## THE DAILY INVENTORY

For me, the heart of the inventory process began with intentional, ongoing daily effort, so we will take that first. One of the best analogies I ever heard regarding how this works came early in my recovery.

## JAN

Jan was one of three women at my first meeting at the old Uptown Group. One night she shared a household experience common to many of us at the time: a leaky bathroom faucet. In the old days, faucets had rubber washers seated between the base of the handle and the pipe feeding water through the spigot. In time, the washers would wear, and the faucet would drip. The iron content in the dripping water would leave a yellow stain on the white porcelain sink. If not attended to, the ever-deepening stain could eventually turn orange and then brown while permeating the porcelain surface and becoming permanent. Jan told us how every day, she wiped the slight trace of a stain away with a washcloth until she could eventually replace the washer. The wipe with the washcloth was her daily Step 10 inventory, the washer replacement a periodic housecleaning.

An important part of this analogy is that it speaks to the fact that, like the leaky faucet, we are not perfect. Even after wiping away the wrong by promptly admitting it, we will still make mistakes, sometimes the same one, and we will need to repeat the reconciliation process.

If we fail to do this, our defects will accumulate until they do damage that we may not be able to undo.

## MATTHEW

Notwithstanding the many ways to continue to take inventory, it was a struggle for me. I either didn't do it at all, or I made half-hearted, haphazard attempts which yielded little. Then I alighted on a formal approach from a non-A.A. source. One of the wise turned out to be Matthew Kelly, who happens to be a prolific Catholic writer. I had never heard of him until my pastor mentioned him in a homily one Sunday. He referenced a way to do a daily examination of conscience outlined in a book by Kelly entitled *The Four Signs of a Dynamic Catholic*. Kelly describes a prayer process as part of a daily routine that goes like this:[18]

1. **Gratitude:** Begin by thanking God in a personal way for whatever you are most grateful for today.

2. **Awareness:** Revisit the times during the past twenty-four hours when you were and were not the best version of yourself. Talk to God about these situations and what you learned from them.

3. **Significant moments:** Identify something you experienced today and explore what God might be trying to say to you through that event (or person).

4. **Peace:** Ask God to forgive you for any wrong you have committed (against yourself, another person, or God) and to fill you with a deep and abiding peace.

5. **Freedom**: Speak with God about how He is inviting you to change your life, so you can experience the freedom to be the best version of yourself.

6. **Others**: Lift up to God anyone you feel called to pray for today, asking God to bless and guide them.

7. **Finish** by praying the Lord's Prayer.

This gave me the start I needed to "continue" to take inventory. Later, my inventory migrated into a format that combined Kelly's suggestion with a more traditional approach and a primary focus on the "Seven Deadlies and Four Uglies," thus creating a continuity that had started with Step 4.

Here's how it works for me:

- I place myself in the presence of my Higher Power and express my gratitude for the day.

- I ask to be made "clean." I need a mind that is clean of all the debris and rubble of the day, so I can see and think clearly.

- I ask for help in acknowledging my defects and virtues: What have I done wrong? What have I done right? What could I have done better?

- I take a brief inventory reviewing the "Seven Deadlies and Four Uglies" and their corresponding virtues.

- Then I ask myself: This day, did I stay conscious of my Higher Power? Did I make good use of my time? Did I try to make life pleasant for others? Did I criticize anyone? Was I forgiving? Did I ask God to help those around me?

- I ask forgiveness for the wrongs I did, forgive anyone who injured me, offer thanks both for any good I may have done and for blessings received.

- I think of how I may have done better overall, especially if I had a problem with someone.

- Then I make specific resolutions for the next day to:
  - **Stay away from certain temptations** and, if possible, the circumstances in which they can arise. If the circumstances are unavoidable, I ask for guidance in how to navigate them at the moment they confront me.

  - **Avoid specific faults,** such as letting in a little bit of anger, lust, self-pity, or a fantasy about drinking, overspending, or overeating.

  - **Exert special effort to practice a virtue**, usually acts of humility, love, forgiveness, and self-restraint.

  - **Take advantage of opportunities for improvement** by declaring my powerlessness and asking for help when tempted to engage in some thought, word, or deed that can be offensive to others, self-defeating, or self-destructive, and then resolving to turn it over, offering it up to my Higher Power, surrendering it.

- **Conclude by asking for help** with the specific defects that are most difficult for me.

I continually tinker with this format to try to make it more relevant as I navigate through life, day by day. I expect that by the time this memoir is in print, I will have changed it. I do not want any major part of my recovery to become stale.

## THE PERIODIC HOUSECLEANING

Over the years, I have taken several 4th Step inventories, but they were largely a catalogue of my wrongs. They lacked the second and equally important part of Step 10, which is to promptly admit the wrong to the person I had harmed — to atone. I undertook to find a process whereby I could combine the essence of Step 4 with Steps 8 and 9 into a coherent Step 10 periodic housecleaning. Again, "the wise who had long known" often were not within my immediate sphere of living.

## THE RABBIS

Janis's Jewish faith has brought me into casual, intermittent contact with other Jews in the community. Moreover, while devoutly practicing my own faith, I participate with Janis in some of the Jewish holidays and have been struck by the messages. More recently, I discovered the profound place personal inventory has in the lives of observant Jews, especially during the High Holy Days.

Rabbi Janet Marder in *A Teshuvah Inventory: Step by Step* describes Teshuvah as "The spiritual work of the High Holy season — the literal meaning of which is "turning" or "returning." She says further:

*"Implied in this word is a powerful idea: no matter how destructive our actions have been, our core, our essence, remains pure, precious and sacred. [Teshuvah] offers the opportunity to turn away from unhealthy paths, reorient ourselves, and return to the essentially good people we are."[19]*

It requires a step-by-step process of assessment, briefly summarized here:

***Turning inward: In what ways have I done harm to self and others:***

- In what harmful ways has my aggressive, egoistic drive manifested itself?

- In what ways have I fallen short in caring for my body and physical self, in developing my mind and remaining intellectually alive, and in caring for my own emotional needs?

- In what ways have I fallen short in relating to family members, friends, and colleagues?

***Turning to God: Renewing my spiritual connection.***

- In what ways have I become disconnected from my source?

- Am I grateful? Do I appreciate the beauty of creation?

- Do I pray regularly, meditate, study, observe, identify entrapments such as addiction, ponder my purpose in life, live in God's presence, and ask His help?

*Turning to others: Repairing relationships.*

- What relationships are strained or broken and to what degree am I responsible?

- Who did I harm and what did I do that was wrong?

- From whom must I seek forgiveness, and how can I make reparations?

*What progress have I made in these areas this past year?*

- In taking care of myself

- In relating to family members, friends, and colleagues

- In developing my spiritual life

- In repairing problems in relationships

- Note significant accomplishments

In the Jewish faith, the High Holy Days link the Jewish New Year — Rosh Hashanah — and the Day of Atonement — Yom Kippur. Elul is the month leading up to them during which Teshuvah is undertaken.

As recovering people, notwithstanding our own faith journey, our "New Year" can begin any time. But if it is to be truly new and not just another date on the calendar, we cannot simply *look* at what we have done wrong. We must also *atone,* and that requires work.

Atonement isn't just an apology nor is it just forgiveness. Breaking the word down, it can be seen as "at-one-ment." We take the pieces of broken relationships and our broken lives and put them back together.

This process cannot be done in a day or two. But neither does it need to be dragged out forever. A lot of progress can be made in a month if we commit ourselves to it.

### Sharpening our vision

In another essay entitled "Taking a Spiritual Inventory," posted on September 21, 1998/5759, Rabbi Schorsch writes:

> "Whatever else our High Holy Days might be, they are surely about helping us sharpen our vision. If I had to reduce the drama and choreography, the prayer and music of this protracted season to a single encompassing goal, it would be to enable us to catch a glimpse of what has grown dim or discover an insight beyond our ken."[20]

Similarly, Rabbi Paul Kipnes, in an article entitled "Do Your Spiritual Homework for the High Holidays" (originally published in *Calabasas Style Magazine*), writes:

> "At its root, these days are about introspection, self-evaluation, and change."[21]

Rabbi Kipnes urges us to look deeply into ourselves, engaging in serious introspection to evaluate our lives. The principal purpose of *Teshuvah* is to help us turn (and re-turn) to the person we *should* be. He could be talking about me when he writes, "Too often, we fall off our path because we lose focus, we mess up relationships, and we forget about our dreams. We get lost."

The objective is to reflect upon who you are, who you could be, and who you should be. Open yourself to self-reflection. Review your relationships and begin the process of cleaning them up. Consider how you can make things right. Words alone won't get the job done: they need to be followed up with actions. In "Do your Homework," Rabbi Kipnes offers an outline based on a process referred to as *Teshuvah*. It consists of four major steps during Elul.

- **Step 1: Count your Blessings**

  The Hebrew word "to bless" (*l'varech*" contains two other words: *lev* (heart) and *rach* (softened). To bless someone, to feel blessed, you must soften your heart to feel the blessings within your life. Think about your family, work, love life, social life, community, and spiritual/religious life. In what ways are you blessed? Make a list.

- **Step 2: Ask the Big Questions**

  The Hebrew word *chet* (usually translated as "sin") might be best understood as "missing the mark." When an archer aims and shoots, but the arrow misses the target, he refocuses and aims better. In our lives, we, too, must refocus. Ask yourself: How am I not living up to the image of who I could be?

- **Step 3: Do a Spiritual Self-Inventory**

  We cannot transform our lives until we first clean up our messes. Judaism teaches, *"For the chet (harm) between a person and God, Yom Kippur atones. But for the chet (harm) between one person and another, Yom Kippur does not atone until the two people make peace with each other."*

  Think about:
  - *Your relationships*: Who have I slighted? Nor paid enough

attention to? Have I really invested enough in my spouse, my partner, my loved ones?

- *Your workplace*: Was I too harsh with my coworkers, employees, or boss?
- *Your community*: Did I share or spread gossip? Complain instead of helping improve? Engaged enough in *Tikun Olam* (fixing the world)?

- **Step 4: Teshuvah: Return to the Right Path**
  Now return yourself to the right path by looking over your inventory, committing to approach people you have harmed, apologizing sincerely, and asking how you can fix the brokenness.

In conclusion, Rabbi Kipnes recommends finding a place to celebrate and reflect with community. For us, it could be with our recovering friends. As recovering people, we can review our lists and actions with our sponsors or spiritual advisors. At issue is: Are we taking the necessary steps to transform our lives? The object is to point our new selves toward the vision of who we should be. A "New Year," whatever its start date, filled with blessings can be ours if we just clean up our past.

One of the biggest payoffs of taking Step 10 is that it brings to light the things I do, large and small, that make life difficult, and it gives me a chance to do something about them. I do not need to resign myself, as I once did, to the notion that I will be forever plagued by my shortcomings and simply need to slog through life doing what I can in spite of them. While some may never go away completely, I can still significantly reduce their frequency and impact in my daily life. But, waiting to take action when I am wrong is rarely helpful.

## PROMPTLY ADMITTED "I WAS WRONG"

Admitting my wrongs promptly is crucial, and that means all of them, large and small, whether they are known to many people or to just a single person. It is one thing to be literally forced to change behavior when it becomes an embarrassment undermining one's personal credibility and effectiveness, but doing it in private affairs can be another seemingly less-compelling matter. Yet, this is the context in which most of our challenges occur, and the longer a wrong act is left without atonement, the more damage it can do. There were my friends and acquaintances, my family, and most important, my wife who also were affected, not only by this specific defect — procrastination — but by others as well.

Often, especially early in recovery, we simply are not aware when we are wrong. The more we had turned in on ourselves in the throes of addiction, the less aware we became of others and their needs, much less the effect we had in their lives. And for those who grew up in a household fraught with addiction, the craziness became the standard by which their relationships in general were measured. And then there is the life we evolve into after leaving our childhood home. Whether before or afterward, many of the people we associated with had their own issues. As we continued in some of these relationships after stopping alcohol or drug use, when problems arose, it was often difficult to determine where their issues ended and ours began. Ever the great rationalizers, even after getting sober, the old habits often hung on. We had become so adept at blaming others for our problems that when the opportunity arose, it was easy to pin the responsibility on someone who had obvious shortcomings themselves. Deflecting responsibility for our behavior had become second nature to us.

So, notwithstanding the role of other parties, how would I know I was wrong so I could either promptly admit it or, better yet, head off a problem before it materialized?

Again, the program has an answer. The *12 and 12* states:

*"It is a spiritual axiom that every time we are disturbed, no matter what the cause, there is something wrong **with us.**"* (*12 and 12, p. 90*)

My own disturbance with any situation was the key to knowing whether or not I was wrong. The other party may have been wrong, too, but it didn't matter. It was my recovery and my life that was at stake here. It was my well-being that these steps were all about.

The next question emanated from that word "promptly." When I began to take Step 10 seriously and was willing to admit I was wrong, it took far too long for me to admit it to the other party. Sometimes weeks would pass. It was only later, after practicing the prompt admission of my wrongs, that I experienced one of its greatest and most immediate benefits: The sooner I was able to admit I was wrong, the sooner the burden of carrying it around with me evaporated. The hang-up for me was that I wasn't sure how to do it — what to say, exactly. Then I heard something that was a clear indication of how *not* to go about it.

In a major election, one candidate had obliquely referred to a competitor who happened to be of Italian descent as a mafioso. When called on it, he apologized, sort of. He started by saying, "If I have offended anyone ..." and I thought, *Good Lord, if he had offended anyone*?! He just referred to a specific public figure of Italian descent as a mafioso and, without even referring directly to the offended party, there is question in his mind about whether or not his vile characterization was offensive.

I concluded that keeping it simple with no qualifications was the cleanest, most honest way to wipe the slate clean and keep it that way. I started with Janis:

"Honey, when I got angry earlier and insisted that [something was black instead of dark grey], I was wrong."

*I was wrong.* Clean, clear, unambiguous, no excuses, no qualifications, no explanations. Lo and behold, the first time I did this, what was Janis's response?

"Well, I was wrong, too, honey."

As often as not, this has been her response. A bonus unearned and unexpected, but greatly appreciated. Yet, her response wasn't the point — my prompt admission was. This not only worked with Janis, but with others as well. I was wrong — three of the most important words in any recovering alcoholic's vocabulary.

## BEYOND

Sometimes a step can take us far beyond the place we expected it to, to places not covered in the *12 and 12* or *The Big Book*. I hadn't been working Step 10 with any real intentionality, but at my FSC meeting we came around to it every three months or so. Slowly it dawned on me that the "wrongs" I shared with the group were stubbornly chomping into the walls of my soul and hanging on. I was talking about the same stuff every time we came to Step 10, and often when we discussed the other inventory steps. I had forty-three years of sobriety at the time, but it didn't seem to matter — I was stuck. A shroud of dysthymia enveloped me and, like my shortcomings, it wasn't going away.

## THERAPY

A friend suggested I find a therapist that specialized in EMDR — Eye Movement Desensitization and Reprocessing. I had been in therapy from time to time over many years. Except for the sessions years earlier with Phyliss Levy following the divorce from Marilyn, therapy had had limited results.

EMDR was different than any therapy I had experienced. It is an integrative psychotherapy approach that has proven effective for treating trauma. It incorporates protocols that integrate elements from many different types of treatment, and silence is as important as talk. Included is a special process in which the patient begins by focusing on a traumatic experience. The therapist then employs a bi-lateral eye movement technique, and the patient lets his mind go wherever it will. There is no attempt to direct the thoughts and no talk during this phase of treatment. My therapist used a combination of earphones that softly beeped and handheld electrodes that softly pulsated in cadence with the beeps — alternating between left and right.

Complete treatment covers past memories, present disturbance, and future actions. The goal is to completely process the experiences that are causing or contributing to problems and to include new ones that are needed for full health. "Processing" does not mean talking about it. It means setting up a learning state that will allow experiences that are causing problems to be "digested" and stored appropriately in the brain. Anything useful from the experience is learned and stored with the related emotions and can guide the patient to positive pathways in the future. The inappropriate emotions, beliefs, and body sensations are discarded. Amazingly, the brain virtually alone does the work that needs to be done. There is no formal action plan — it just happens. This was followed by talk therapy employing various approaches.

I was in my seventies when I went back into therapy, deciding to try EMDR. I scarcely knew what trauma had been in my life. It turned out there were events I had buried deep into my subconscious and, while exhibiting their manifestations in my behavior, I had no sense of their connection to each other. There were other experiences so painful that for decades, I couldn't think about them without reliving the pain of the moment when they had occurred. One by one, with the guidance of an excellent therapist, I reprocessed them using EMDR, and afterward when they came to mind, they no longer troubled me. It has been more than ten years since the treatment, and the trauma is still in remission. EMDR worked. I do not know the mechanics of how, but it worked.

The reason I share this is not because the idea of professional help is new, but because it is old and largely overlooked. It is a belief that Bill Wilson, Dr. Bob, and Bill R. from my early days in recovery all shared: there are issues that cannot be reached by the twelve steps for which alcoholics will need professional help. Moreover, sometimes this help may sound unusual and not fall in the mainstream of common therapeutic practice, which was certainly the case of EMDR when it first came on the scene. The two most important issues with any treatment are always: First, is there a risk of harm? And second, does it work at least for some people? In the case of EMDR, I am not aware of any risk of harm, and it works for many people. However, it is a supplement to the twelve steps, not a substitute.

## A ROLE MODEL AND A RETURN TO FAITH

God as I understand Him does not force Himself on us. He doesn't interfere with our lives or the laws of nature. Respecting the freedom of His creatures and thereby maintaining His own credibility, He does not reserve to Himself all exercise of power. So, if in the final seconds of the Super Bowl, the kicker's foot doesn't collide near-perfectly with the football from fifty yards out, I do not believe God will breathe heavily on the ball, changing its errant flight into a game-winning field goal.

Yet, there are times when the sun, the stars, and the moon all seem to align, not necessarily in a single moment but certainly during a given time frame. And I do believe God helps me when I pray for knowledge of His will for me and the power to carry that out, my personal willingness being implicit in the request.

So around 2010, joining forces with the EMDR therapy and the awareness that my defects weren't going away or even improving, was Ted Kennedy's death after a valiant battle with the same brain cancer that took the life of Senator John McCain a few years later. In *True Compass*, written during the last two years of his life, he acknowledged his many imperfections and the mistakes he had made both politically and in his personal life, some of which were dreadful and, in the minds of some people, unforgiveable. His shortcomings aside, he authored more social service legislation helping the poor and middle class than any other senator in history — even surpassing that of another of my heroes, Hubert Humphrey. While his shortcomings are detailed, other qualities shine through in the book: his deep resolve, his commitment, and his loyalty. He never gave up on an issue he believed in, *and* he never stopped practicing his faith. He went to confession regularly and received communion. When he screwed up, he went back to confession, was absolved, and received communion again. And again. When I finished reading it, I said to myself, "What a fool I have been."

I hadn't practiced my faith in years. Yet I held to some of its most essential teachings, including the belief in the true presence of God in the Eucharist. I wanted that union, and the only way I could get it was to come back to the church. But the church was fraught with scandal: sexual abuse of minors and, worse, the cover-up; financial improprieties; virtually no leadership roles for women; and a public perception that it was badly out of touch on major social issues. I had to discern between its undeniable human failings apparent to nearly any level of human reason and its undiminished divinity that could only be explained by faith. I turned to my Higher Power and simply said, "If you want me to come back to the church, I will, but You are going to have to show me how." Within a few days, I found myself in the Adoration Chapel at Holy Redeemer Church. I had never been in an adoration chapel before and wasn't sure what to do. But, after checking out a number of area Catholic churches, that was the only one where a door was unlocked. I couldn't get into the main chapels of any of the other four or five I tried. It was the first small step that eventually brought me back into a full practice of my faith and led me to St. Paul's on the UW campus where I heard Father Eric's homily. It has changed my life.

## GIVING THE POWER GREATER THAN OURSELVES A CHANCE TO WORK

I cannot remember where I first heard it, but this is one of the best axioms I have heard regarding my relationship with my Higher Power:

"Without God, I can't, and without me, God won't."

I believe my Higher Power is everywhere and in virtually everything and everyone, and blesses me with everything I need. After years of struggle while sober, I finally arrived at a place where I was using the resources my Higher Power had provided: my twelve-step program, effective therapy, my religious faith, my wife, my sponsor, family and friends, and the teachings and thoughts of thinkers great and small. Some of the blessings came from people, places, and things where one would expect them to be, others from unlikely sources. Some I had to search for while others had been hiding in plain sight. But they came. Following Rabbi Schorsch's belief about the effect of the High Holidays, Step 10 helped me to sharpen my vision. It enabled me to see myself, then others, and finally my Higher Power's will for me.

# STEP ELEVEN

We cannot survive as happy, productive human beings if we are little more than an empty vessel. While Father Eric's advice to the young man to "first get the sin out" is crucial, if that is all we do, our lives are but a faint shadow of what they were intended to be. Fortunately, that isn't where the recovery process ends. So, all the while being powerless and unmanageable by ourselves, in Steps 1 through 9, we search our souls to root out the negative, right the wrongs we have done, and get our lives headed on a new path. In Step 10, we actively work to keep the contamination out and stay the course on this new path. And in Step 11, we plug into the positive power we need in order to "trudge the road of happy destiny" and live an authentic life with true purpose. And so, we …

*"Sought through prayer and meditation to improve our conscious contact with God as we understood Him, praying only for knowledge of His will for us and the power to carry that out." (AA, p. 59)*

I am grateful for all of the twelve steps. Each has made an indispensable contribution to my sobriety and enhanced my life. And each step helps to sustain and more deeply disclose the richness of the others. But, if there could be just one step, and one step only, for me it would be Step 11. It not only enables me to reclaim the power my addiction robbed me of, but it tells me what I need to do and how to do it in order to achieve that goal. By aligning what I choose to think, say, and do with God's will, I have a shot at attaining the best possible life. As a great friend of more than forty-five years, Fran C. from St. Paul, Minnesota, once told me:

"Step 11 is really the whole ball game. But we need all of the others to get to it."

In praying "*only* for knowledge of His will for us," we reach back to Step 3 in the *12 and 12*:

> *"when we try to make our will conform with God's that we use it rightly." (12 and 12, p. 40)*

When we discard our diseased attitudes, beliefs, and behavior, we discover our true selves, other people, and God. I no longer believe God is just a force outside of us to be brought inside: He is inside waiting to be discovered as we clear away the debris.

I believe God's will for me is to be the best possible version of myself sustained by peace and joy, which can only be secured through virtue. This is the ultimate goal, and we each need to discover what that is for ourselves. Step 11 helps us come to this knowledge through prayer and meditation.

## PRAYER

Over the years, I have developed a robust prayer regimen. But most people do not have the time such a practice requires. However, there is a prayer that has such value that it is singled out in the *12 and 12,* and securing its benefits does not require a great investment of time. Each individual line taken separately can serve as inspiration and the focus of contemplation.

The prayer of St. Francis of Assisi, sometimes referred to as the 11th Step prayer, on page 99 of the *12 and 12,* is offered as a model, and a very good one it has been for me and others.

It starts by asking God to make me a "channel of His peace." In order for a channel to function properly, it must be clear of debris, and that is what the first ten steps of the program do for us: they clear away the wreckage of the past and open the channel of our lives so our Higher Power's peace can flow through. Some versions of this prayer use the term "instrument" instead of channel. Using this metaphor, the program steps are equally appropriate. As with a musical instrument, they fine-tune it. And as an instrument of repair, they sharpen it, all so we can function as we were intended to.

The near tragedy of taking so long to completely take Step 3 while giving Steps 6 and 7 such short shrift was that for years, the channel of my life was clogged up by the debris of the "Seven Deadlies and Four Uglies." As an instrument, my life had been worn dull and out of tune, even though I had not taken a drink. As a channel, it became increasingly clogged like an artery of my heart, blocked with plaque.

This isn't to say that the sobriety I had achieved did not matter: it certainly did. Each day sober, however imperfect, gave me the opportunity to fight another day. But the fullness of the program and my Higher Power's grace were not being realized. Yet, that often seems to be how recovery works: we do not rush to heaven with open arms so much as we grudgingly back away from our hell one faltering step at a time. Sometimes all we can do is just hang on while the calamities of life, replete with comorbid mental and medical disorders, profound disappointment in our institutions, and a world seemingly full of hatred and dysfunction, all churn away. But there is a way to rise above it all, and that is through knowledge of God's will for us and the power to carry it out. For me, this is the ONLY thing I need to ask for, and I get it through prayer and meditation.

So, once the channel is open and the instrument has been tuned, the first thing St. Francis asks for is peace. *Peace.* And that requires action. As Rabbi Kipnes says, we first need to "see," and once we see — the hatred, the wrong, the despair — St. Francis tells us to do something about it. Far from putting our heads in the sand or resorting to the comfort of an insular existence surrounded by like-thinking family, religious persons, recovering friends, professional or political associates, we pray to be able to squarely face the problems of our lives and the world without shrinking from them. Just as we do what comes "unnaturally" when facing the "Seven Deadlies and Four Uglies" uncovered in our personal inventories, St. Francis asks us to do what comes unnaturally in facing the challenges of life outside of the cocoon of our personal existence. Let's examine what he calls us to do.

> **Lord, make me a channel of thy peace;**
> that where there is hatred, I may bring love; that where there is wrong, I may bring the spirit of forgiveness;
> that where there is discord, I may bring harmony;
> that where there is error, I may bring truth;
> that where there is doubt, I may bring faith;
> that where there is despair, I may bring hope;
> that where there are shadows, I may bring light;
> that where there is sadness, I may bring joy.

**Lord, grant that I may seek rather**

to comfort, than to be comforted;

to understand, than to be understood;

to love, than to be loved.

For it is by self-forgetting that one finds.

It is by forgiving that one is forgiven.

It is by dying that one awakens to eternal life.

Amen.

There is a treasure trove of lessons to be learned in looking at both the challenges and the responses in this prayer. It reminds one of the Preamble from *The Big Book*: "What an order. I can't go through with it." And yet, we must at least try if we are going to improve our conscious contact with God as we understand Him. As *The Big Book* goes on to say, we should not be discouraged — none of us works the program perfectly.

Beginning with hatred, St. Francis cites some of the most vexing problems we face in life and offers a response to each. The question is, how do I bring these solutions about, starting with love? Poets, mystics, and religious have provided an abundance of exquisite descriptions of love and its power. They edify and inspire. The soaring language of Shakespeare's 29th Sonnet tells what love can do. And one of the most quoted is from St. Paul in I Corinthians (13:4–8), who, like many other authors, describes *what* love is — its attributes — and they can surely improve any relationship. But, for a simple yet practical principle for *how to do it*, a guy named Alex at my Fitchburg group best summed up the practice of love for me when he said:

"If I can help you, I will; if I can hurt you, I won't."

In short, I will exercise my will in your best interest.

Next St. Francis cites wrong, and the response is forgiveness. Love and forgiveness are each at the essence of the other — it is impossible to have one without the other. The objective of Step 11 — "knowledge of His will for us and the power to carry that out," — is what theologians refer to as grace. When witnessing wrong, it is tempting to want to set things straight, and this can involve a strong inclination to engage in some kind of retaliation. Along with many other faiths, the Catechism of the Catholic Church speaks to this:

> "Without the help of grace, [people] would not know how to discern the often narrow path between the cowardness which gives in to evil, and the violence which under the illusion of fighting evil only makes it worse. This is the path of charity, that is, the love of God and of neighbor. Charity is the greatest social commandment. It respects others and their rights. It requires the practice of justice and it alone makes us capable of it. Charity inspires a life of self-giving." (CCC 1889)

On a personal level, I have found a practical advantage in forgiveness. It lifts the burdens of resentment and self-pity from my shoulders; it gives me a shot at peace.

Next, St. Francis cites discord, and harmony is the response. Harmony is a form of peace, and to have peace in the heat of the action, more than anything, I need to remain calm. Using the Serenity Prayer as a mantra helps. When the adrenaline is rising, and I want to bring peace by jumping into the fray, usually with a lot of self-will or criticism, I only make matters worse. Wisely, Step 10 in the "*12 and 12*" cautions us against rising to the bait. It doesn't matter what my intentions are or even if I have a good idea of what the outcome should be. I need to respectfully model peace by getting my ego out of the mix and gently trying to be a calming influence in order to bring harmony to such a situation. And, I must admit that after all these years in recovery, I am still not very good at it.

Next in line is error and the solution is truth. If ever there was a tricky solution, this is it. Our natural tendency when we think there is error is not to seek truth but to impose our version of correction, hoping we can change the other person's mind. There are two problems with this. First, we may not entirely understand what the other person means by what they are saying. Second, how do we know if what we are proposing is really the truth? If a child asserts that 2 plus 2 equals 5, the task is easy, but on an adult level, things are rarely that simple. Again, humility is the key. I need to get my ego out of the way, refer to facts not opinions and, most importantly, if I am not sure, simply say so and open my mind so it can be discussed with love.

Then there is doubt, and Francis implores us to respond to it with faith. Doubt can be a subtle expression of fear: A belief that things either aren't as we had once believed them to be, or that something in the future will not materialize the way we want it to and, either way, we will somehow get hurt. The effect can isolate us from our Higher Power.

Doubt and faith, as well as fear, have an important commonality. All three are *beliefs* without having all the facts to back them up. And we are free to believe pretty much what we want. Faith believes things will turn out well, doubt not so much, and fear not at all. Each may have a perceived coherence of facts or events from which we draw a conclusion. But rarely are these proofs, and often they are little more than opinion. I lived in doubt for many years, focusing on a series of facts and events that caused me to lose hope in myself. And underlying this was fear, largely self-centered. A good therapist helped me to see events that had occurred in my life, including some things I had done that he considered to be admirable, which helped me to develop faith, however weak at first.

Despair is a close sibling of doubt, and hope is the response Francis proposes. Again, we are talking about beliefs where tangible evidence is not perceived to be present. With both doubt and despair, we can help those afflicted to reframe the issues that are vexing them. Whether dealing with our own despair or someone else's, pat answers or pep talks usually fall short. The reframing must come from our own experience, strength, and hope, flowing from the reservoir of our own recovery and that of others. In addition, therapy — in my case, EMDR — can be a great tool.

Then there are the shadows. Certainly, the hatred, the wrongs, the discord, error, doubt, and despair can cast one into the dark shadows of life. Even a single calamity can do this. Francis says we should bring light to the situation. But what is this light? In my own life, it has been truth spoken with love. It has come from my wife, Janis; Arden, my therapist; my A.A. sponsors Harry, Tom D.-I, Tom D-II, and Mac; my spiritual advisors, Monsignor Holmes, Father Eric, Father Abbot Rooney, and other clergy; my children and other family; and my many friends. They have all brought light to my life with patience and kindness. Cursing the darkness never worked because it is rooted in the past and often fueled by either anger or self-pity. When I have been in the shadows, I needed to move forward. There were many years when I never expected it could happen. I must say that moving into the light would have been impossible for me without the twelve steps, and it has been much, much easier since I returned to my religious faith. I needed other people and a relationship with them that was based on love and forgiveness so they would be willing to help me. The twelve-step program and my religious faith helped me to form those loving relationships.

Along with all the ills cited by St. Francis can come a profound sadness. We need only look around to see it. Our family members, friends, fellow A.A. members as well as the actively addicted, class-mates, work associates, the poor and underserved, and anyone suffering a loss. Francis implores us to bring joy. But we cannot give away something we haven't got, and this depends on where we are in our own lives. Unfortunately, the opportunities do not always present themselves when we are in a good place. Sometimes we just need to reach deep, penetrating through our own sorrows to find a kind word, a gesture, a favor to pass on to another. Sometimes just a smile. Seldom is anything momentous required.

St. Francis leaves the toughest part for last: the part where we put the interests of others ahead of our own.

Lord, grant that I may seek rather to comfort than to be comforted. We are addicts, often chained to more than one addiction. Our lives even after recovery are frequently fraught with challenges. The times when we are completely without discomfort will be rare, and if we wait for one of those fleeting moments before we seek to comfort others, we may never do it. Indeed, Bill Wilson found that when he was most uncomfortable, the craving for a drink so strong that he could taste it, it seemed like the only effective way of getting past it was to find and try to help another alcoholic.

Next, Francis asks that God help him to understand, rather than to be understood. How important it has been for me to be understood! So often, I believed that if only the other party *understood me,* they would most certainly agree with me. So I would attempt to persuade them with multiple explanations and arguments. Once again, hubristic pride and sometimes flat-out arrogance were the true motives. In the meantime, I failed to understand what they were saying. That meant I passed up an opportunity that is absolutely essential to improving my life: I failed to learn from the occasion. I left the encounter knowing only what I knew when I entered into it. I didn't listen, and so as Rabbi

Kipnes implored, I was unable to *see* any clearer afterward than I could before. The fact is: everyone yearns to be understood. Their need is as important as mine. When I put my own needs first, I not only fail to learn but, worse, I fail to connect, and the anxious apartness referenced in the *12 and 12* takes over and separates me from the other person. With my noisy head and eagerness to be understood, I often need help with this and find myself asking God to help me be patient and calm so I can understand. Otherwise it becomes nearly impossible to follow St. Francis's final request:

"Lord, that I may seek rather to love than to be loved."

If I can help you, I will, and if I can hurt you, I won't.

He concludes with the rewards we receive from following these suggestions.

"For it is by self-forgetting that one finds."

Without always realizing it, I am continually seeking, but if I am primarily thinking about myself and my needs, I am not likely to find what I need.

"It is by forgiving that one is forgiven."

I carry a burden when I do not forgive, and forgiving often means first admitting my part in the wrong.

"It is by dying that one awakens to eternal life."

Daily, sometimes moment to moment surrender is the key for me: "I am powerless — please help me — thy will not mine be done. Amen."

Again, looking at the world and its problems — global warming, poverty, children starving, sex trafficking, racism, addiction, perpetual war and its millions of refugees, and many, many more — a reasonable person could seriously ask what keeps it from falling completely apart. I like to think that each day it is held together, however tenuously, by billions of small acts of kindness between one person and another.

This prayer of St. Francis constitutes a lifetime practice — it doesn't all come at once. Again, willingness is the key: if I can help you, I will, if I can hurt you, I won't. Regardless of what I might be feeling at the moment. You, before me.

## MEDITATION

Meditation is the means by which we deepen our understanding, and it takes a great deal of commitment and practice to learn to do it well. In Step 11, we are trying to improve our conscious contact with God, and the call to action in the prayer we choose is the objective. But enmeshing ourselves in the deeper meaning of it requires meditation.

Meditation is hard for me with my noisy head and ADHD tendencies. Minimally, it is not daydreaming, fantasy, euphoric recall, or even contemplation. It is a calm, single-purpose focus on what is going on inside of me. I want to go deep into the sacred silence of my soul where there is no one or nothing but my Higher Power. To do it entails both the proper setting and a mental process most of us seldom use. Having a quiet setting without noise or any other distractions is the first essential. For me, the Adoration chapel is perfect, but there are places in my home that also work well. I pray for the gift of calm and freedom from any of my daily concerns without drifting off. But what is occurring outside of my mind is seldom the biggest distraction; it is what is going on inside of it that is the most stubborn challenge to achieving the peace and calm I need. My mind has a mind of its own, and I need to quiet it. I am powerless to do this by myself, so I pray that God will remove all my best, most ingenious, creative ideas; all my most pressing, urgent concerns; all my biases; all the wonderful arguments, explanations, and rationale I love to indulge as I conduct imaginary encounters with those whom I am convinced need the benefit of what I know, especially if they are not in agreement with me. At this moment, I simply want to be in God's presence, unencumbered and fully alert. In EMDR, I learned what this state can be like. But on a daily basis, I do not have my therapist and the apparatus he uses, so I need to try to replicate that state on my own with the help of my Higher Power.

In addition to settling down my noisy head, I ask God to remove all "noise" in my chest, my stomach, and throughout my body. I try to consciously breath through my diaphragm rather than my chest. I want my mind to rest in a specific focus that leads me to the depths of my soul and into the mind of God — the source of my consciousness. Yoga techniques have long been recognized for their effectiveness in setting the stage for meditation.

The purpose of prayer and meditation is to improve our conscious contact with God *as we understand Him.* As the conscious contact improves, so does my understanding. It's an ongoing challenge.

## KNOWLEDGE OF HIS WILL FOR ME

Acquiring knowledge of His will for me, and the power to carry that out on a day-to-day, moment-by-moment basis, is the ultimate result, not only of this step but of the entire program of recovery. What else could I possibly want? What more could I possibly need? Nothing! This is it. As Fran said, this is the whole ballgame.

Yet, I am human. At any given moment, I can delude myself into thinking that the payoff from acting out my defects is what I want, what I desperately need. Sometimes my whole being seems to be screaming for it, even telling me I'll die without it. Old habits die hard and concupiscence will never go away in this life. But in recovery it has long been clear to me that when I allow the truth in, I see that the payoff from acting out any of my defects is just never worth the price. On the other hand, doing God's will is *always* worth the price, although it may not seem that way in the heat of the moment, which is exactly when I need to declare that I am powerless and ask for His help. Beyond that,

I ask that even the faintest trace of the urge be completely removed. If it doesn't relent upon the first request, I repeat it over and over until it evaporates. And, of course, I don't die.

Above all, the quiet peace and joy I get from doing God's will makes it the best bargain ever. The promises of the program do materialize. Indeed, I do get a daily reprieve contingent on the maintenance of my spiritual condition. And when my spiritual condition is in a state of peace and joy, nothing bothers me.

## GRATITUDE

Of paramount importance before going on is an indispensable comment about what holds all of my recovery together as a single coherent endeavor.

The world is full of wondrous edifices reflecting the beauty of the human spirit. I have been privileged to see many of them personally, from the magnificence of our nation's capitol, to the breathtaking view of a castle in Ireland's countryside, to the astonishing beauty of the Sistine Chapel. But, however stunning their external beauty, whatever the complexity of their form, however inspirational their presence, what gives them strength and sustains them through the ages is their infrastructure. Perhaps the most profound and tragic example of this is seen in the aftermath of the 2019 fire in the spire at the Cathedral of Notre Dame, which imperiled the entire structure. Confounding matters was that the delicate process of removing fused scaffolding in order to begin the restoration could, itself, cause the ceiling vaults to fall apart, destroying the entire structure.

So it is with recovery. However beautiful it may look on the outside, and however solid the foundation may be, without a strong infrastructure that can last a lifetime it can ultimately fail, especially when a calamity occurs. The foundation for me has been total and complete abstinence; the infrastructure has been the virtues, and the main load-bearing beam has been gratitude.

I have heard many expressions of gratitude over the years, but those of recovering people have touched my soul most deeply. Among the very best is the following from my friend Tom D.-II.

> *"I have found that the greatest and most singularly powerful gift from all the steps, but perhaps culminating in Step 11, is gratitude. It is an antidote to envy, self-pity, anxiety, wanting [more], and all the other defects of character. It keeps me in today. It is thanks and willingness wrapped into one. And it leads me, not just out of duty, but spiritually to try to carry the message that was so freely given to me. Because by all rights, I could have awakened this morning on a heating grate or fighting off someone in a crowded shelter while wondering how quickly I could get my next drink."*

Desire gets us on the path of recovery, but gratitude keeps us there.

# STEP TWELVE

W ell, here we are from Harry's Step 12 that led me into recovery more than fifty-four years ago to the unfolding saga of my own Step 12.

> *"Having had a spiritual awakening as the result of these steps, we tried to carry the message to alcoholics, and to practice these principles in all our affairs." (AA, p. 60)*

In the *12 and 12,* the Step 12 narrative begins and ends with "the joy of living" as the main theme. But, to experience this, we must be awakened, first from the physical effects of our disease and the chronic search for chemical exhilaration with its never-ending desire for "more" — more physical gratification, be it alcohol, drugs, sex, food, or anything else; awakened from the mental effects of our disease and the futility of our insistence that our wrongs are justified because of what others have done to us or failed to do for us; and finally awakened from the spiritual emptiness of the dogmatic slumber into which we had descended as we held onto our "old ideas."

The manner in which we become awakened can start in as many ways as there are recovering people. Mine was about as uneventful as one could imagine, yet at the time I knew what it was, and it was significant.

## ROBERT STREET

It was spring of 1966. Every morning for nearly four years, I had taken the bus from St. Paul's East Side downtown, getting off at Robert Street and walking the four blocks south to work. I knew the storefronts of dozens of shops and businesses along the way and had practically memorized the cracks in the sidewalk. But this bright early morning, a new experience awaited. For the first time, I noticed what the buildings looked like above the first level. Some new at the time, their glass and steel shimmering as they reflected the rising morning sun; some old and worn or rendered drab in the shadows of taller neighbors; some ornate, some plain; all different heights, window styles, and exterior materials. I was no longer walking hunched over or hungover. My head was clear, recently having been given a yellow, three-month button at the Uptown meeting — this was before medallions were awarded for sobriety dates. And I was looking up instead of down. Somehow this moment has stood out over the years as the first tangible evidence of a spiritual awakening. I was becoming aware.

## THE SPIRITUAL AWAKENING

The first and foundational element of Step 12 is the spiritual awakening. Importantly, the step reads that this is "*the* result" not "*a* result" of the steps. Aside from the absence of pain and danger that accompany intoxication, without a spiritual awakening, that hole in my soul never would have been stitched up to keep the good stuff of life from seeping out, if recovery had only been mere abstinence or even sobriety with its staid, somber moods. Without question, both abstinence and sobriety are absolutely essential to recovery, and with life's ups and downs, sometimes they are all we recovering alcoholics have to hold onto. They are life preservers that give us a chance to fight another day — a day we might never see without them. But, if these are all we have, the promises of the program, which constitute much of the essence of the spiritual awakening and the foundation for a new life, are largely out of reach.

Offered in the context of Step 9, where we take serious action to right our wrongs, the promises began to be realized in my life and even earlier in Harry's recovery. While virtually all medical professionals and therapists try to offer hope for a better life, few, if any, will seriously make concrete promises, and appropriately so. The endless variables which can change the circumstances of one's existence militates against unequivocal predictions. But not so with the A.A. program. Set forth on pages 83 and 84 of *The Big Book* are unambiguous promises. Because of their power and the hope they offer, they are presented here:

*"If we are painstaking about this phase of our development, we will be amazed before we are halfway through.*

*We are going to know a new freedom and a new happiness.*

*We will not regret the past nor wish to shut the door on it.*

*We will comprehend the word serenity and we will know peace.*

*No matter how far down the scale we have gone, we will see how our experience can benefit others.*

*That feeling of uselessness and self-pity will disappear.*

*We will lose interest in selfish things and gain interest in our fellows.*

*Self-seeking will slip away.*

*Our whole attitude and outlook upon life will change.*

*Fear of people and of economic insecurity will leave us.*

*We will intuitively know how to handle situations which used to baffle us.*

*We will suddenly realize that God is doing for us what we could not do for ourselves."*

Then it asks and answers a key question:

*"Are these extravagant promises? We think not. They are being fulfilled among us—sometimes quickly, sometimes slowly. They will always materialize if we work for them."*

The experience walking down Robert Street in the spring of 1966 was just the beginning of these promises being kept in my life. Far more awaited and, while some took much longer than others to materialize, all of them have ultimately been fulfilled.

So, if the promises are evidence of the spiritual awakening, then the overarching question is how they are brought to fulfillment. The answer is in taking the first eleven steps to the best of our ability, not as a series of episodes but as an integrated ongoing daily effort. And we take these steps with others who are also taking them. We couldn't make much progress in isolation. At each stage, we found that we had to surrender something we had previously considered to be "our right," starting with our embrace of a false believe system and "our right" to act out the "Seven Deadlies and Four Uglies." In Step 1, this was the belief that we either could or should be able to have the power to manage our own lives. Therefore, what need was there for a power greater than ourselves in Step 2, and what point would there be in turning our will and our lives over to such a Higher Power in Step 3? As for admitting complete defeat? Forget it!

By the time Harry had reached the two-and-a-half month point in his recovery, he had been painstakingly working those first nine steps and had immersed himself in Steps 10 and 11. He had something to offer me he would not have had if he had only been abstinent. He had the beginning, at least, of a spiritual awakening in which he intuitively knew how to handle a situation that would have baffled him three short months earlier. And it saved my life.

Among other things, as the result of these steps, we become aware that we are …

> *"… able to do, feel and believe that which [we] were unable to do before on [our] own unaided strength and resources alone. [We] had been granted a gift which amount[ed] to a new state of consciousness and being." (12 and 12," pp. 106–107)*

Like the river of recovery itself into which we had meandered, slowly, sometimes imperceptibly, we changed. Just as the river is always somewhat the same but somewhat different than it had been, to the extent that it makes sense, we were at once the same human being but a different person.

## TRIED TO CARRY THE MESSAGE – DON

Early in recovery, Harry had volunteered with the local A.A. Intergroup to be available for 12th Step calls. Someone had called in asking if A.A. could call on a guy named Don whose address was passed on to Harry. At the time, Harry had about five months of sobriety. Following the program's recommendation not to go on twelve-step calls alone, he enlisted me, sober less than three months, to go with him.

On the way over, I asked Harry what we should say. He told me to first ask my Higher Power for help, and the words would come, and then simply tell my own story about what it was like, what happened, and what it was like now.

Don was in his mid-thirties and not in good shape. He was holed up in a dingy third-floor attic in one of the old deteriorating mansions in the Summit Avenue area. To get to it, we climbed a long, separate staircase that did not go through the main living quarters. A single bare light bulb lit the small room which had one chair, a beat-up old couch, and cigarette butts along with a couple of empty whiskey bottles on the floor. Don sat on the edge of an unmade bed. Harry started it off by asking him how he was feeling. Don had been fired from his job, recently divorced, and had prevailed on a friend to use the attic on a temporary basis. He hadn't eaten much that day because he was feeling sick. Then Harry told his story, and I followed with mine. That part of the call seemed to go well. We offered to take him to a meeting. Don would have been a prime candidate for public detox, but there was no such service at that time, just hospital psych wards where they often strapped down alcoholics, driving them into DTs, which too often led to death. Don thanked us for coming and said he would think it over. Harry left his telephone number.

Not having convinced Don to get his coat and join us to attend a meeting, I thought we had failed, but not Harry. First, just a few months earlier, *we* were Don. But for the grace of God, we both could have ended up like him or worse. That reality came through loud and clear to both of us as we sat with Don that evening. Next, there's something about the very act of sharing a belief that reinforces one's own faith in it. In fact, I did feel stronger in my conviction about my own powerlessness and the need to be restored to sanity. Finally, both Harry and I came away sober and, while we couldn't carry the man, we did carry the message. As Harry always said, we drive stakes and plant seeds. The more encounters an alcoholic or addict has with someone who carries the message, the greater the chance that they will eventually get on the road to recovery. We could only hope it would reach that point for Don. That evening turned out to be the only time either Harry or I ever saw him.

Over the years, there have been many other twelve-step calls, and in my EAP career, literally thousands of interventions in the programs with which I have worked. One thing that continues to astonish me is the persistence of a near-universal condition that, while correctable, nevertheless continues even with all the knowledge we have gained about addiction. That is, how far down the road to destruction the preponderance of addicts must travel before those around them take action. Even health professionals including EAP staff, through lack of knowledge or willingness, wait far too long. Yet, experience shows that the earlier the seeds are planted and stakes are driven with someone suffering from addiction, the greater the chance of full recovery and the less suffering they and those around them must bear.

Looking back, I see that the highest point of my professional career was when I was the director of the Employee Assistance Program at United Airlines. In addition to family and dependents, our annual first-time unduplicated employee utilization rate was nearly 4 percent overall and more than 5 percent for officers and directors. Of that number, about 40 percent were diagnosed with a Substance Use Disorder, and nearly 90 percent of them accepted our referral for the level of care we recommended. The first-time recovery rates for those accepting the recommendation was 73 percent for ground employees; 84 percent for flight attendants; 92 percent for pilots; and 94 percent for senior managers. We defined recovery as one year of continuous abstinence from all mood-altering chemicals and marked improvement in lifestyle and life functioning. While an accurate initial assessment is imperative, equally important in achieving these rates was the total EAP support system involving the manager (and where appropriate, the union representative), the family, the company medical doctors, and the structured aftercare/follow-up effort coordinated by the EAP professional which ranged from one to two years, all with the participant's written authorization. Thirty-two years later, the manager of that EAP reported at a national meeting that the recovery rate for pilots was still 86 percent.

I still think about Don, as well as Bob and Rich and all the millions of others like them who have had only a small fraction of the effort expended on their behalf that we invested in our EAP referrals at United. When one adds up the total US death toll from addiction to substances, including those related to tobacco use, it is more than 600,000 per year. Indeed, it seems that all of us — the general population, family members, health care professionals, and even EAP practitioners — are hard to train, and it doesn't last long. Virtually no one can recover if the identification of the problem is not clearly stated, or if they are left to struggle in isolation and without extensive support.

## PRACTICE THESE PRINCIPLES IN ALL OUR AFFAIRS

And so, as we ponder these final words in the final step of the A.A. program, once again the exclamation from the Preamble of A.A. meetings taken from Chapter 5 of *The Big Book* comes to mind:

*"What an order, I can't go through with it." (AA, p. 60)*

But as always, close attention to the wording is important. We "practiced these principles in all our affairs." We *practice* the principles because we can never perfect them.

## TED

On September 28, 1941, the Boston Red Sox's Ted Williams played in a double-header against the Philadelphia Athletics on the last day of the regular season. Entering the game, he was batting exactly .400, a near-unattainable feat as evidenced by the fact that no one has done it since. His manager offered to bench him so as not to jeopardize the achievement. Instead, Williams chose to play. He collected six hits in eight trips to the plate, raised his average to .406, and become the last player to hit .400. In his final game exactly nineteen years later at Boston's Fenway Park, he hit a home run in his very last time at bat. He has long been considered the best hitter of all time.

Sports reporters have loved speculating about various circumstantial matters that may have contributed to Williams's success. In one instance, he responded by quoting back what many people had said on the subject: his quick wrists, great eye, the short right field fence in Fenway Park, no night baseball in 1941, and far fewer relief pitchers during his career. He agreed with many of these points. But, never having attended charm school, he dismissed others with a few potty-mouth phrases and observed that no one ever mentioned the single most important factor in his success: how much he practiced. That throughout his career, he practiced his swing for hours on end in front of a mirror with a broomstick or hairbrush and took extra batting practice after games and whenever else he could. "Practice, practice, practice. You gotta practice!"

And so it is with us. Like Ben Hogan or Tiger Woods who hit hundreds of golf balls a day, we need to practice if we are ever going to get good at recovery. And some of it seems pretty mundane, especially in the beginning. But it prepares us to face life on life's terms without fear. Just as Ted Williams knew he was prepared to hit in that last game in 1941 and chose to play rather than sit out, if we practice the principles in all our affairs, we will not fear what may await us because we will know we are prepared. And, as practice produces results, we can grow to enjoy it because the byproduct — a useful, productive life of service to others — will bring us the joy and peace so crucial to our happiness. Like Williams, we won't want to sit out either.

## PRACTICE, PRACTICE, PRACTICE.

So how do we practice?

Start small. No one is expected to shrug off serious problems with our children, spouses, work, or money. We are not expected to ignore the conditions of the world as they press in on us. But, in recovery we do not need to take on the biggest, most momentous challenges first. As a practical matter, much of what we get exercised over is trivial in the total scheme of things. Chances that we even will be thinking about them next week or next year are slim to none. Yet, they can upset us, and since the trivial recur in some form or another every day, we can find ourselves in a near-constant state of anger, depression, fear, or distress without a sure, quick way of addressing them. What's even more vexing, these events can be real or imagined. Fantasy and projection of something unpleasant — especially images of someone doing us wrong — can be just as upsetting as the real thing. And if, in our job or personal life, we truly are facing large challenges, we will be less capable of dealing with them if our time and energy are sapped by the trivial.

Speaking for myself, the reality is that most of my fears never materialize, and most of the things that upset me are either largely inconsequential or beyond my ability to do anything about in the here and now. So, I need to surrender them each and every time they come up *and as quickly as possible.*

It was necessary for me to take to heart the quote from the *12 and 12* in the Step 10 narrative that whenever I am upset, there is something wrong with *me.* This applies regardless of what the other party has done or might do. Also, there's Matthew Kelly's quotation from *The Four Signs of a Dynamic Catholic* — "When we are spiritually healthy, nothing bothers us."

## ON THE TRACK

But what about the big things? I had to start small there, too. While my bypass was a big interventive action achieved by a skilled doctor, in order to maintain and increase the gains, it represented I had to start small.

To keep my heart disease in remission, I try to get over to the health club five days a week. I spend time in the sauna each day and do some weightlifting three of the five days. But the most important thing I do is walk — forty-five minutes between 2.4 and 2.6 miles — five days a week. Two years ago when I started this regimen, I could only go for ten minutes and half a mile. But increasing it a little at a time, I've reached a point where presently, I'm not even out of breath when I finish. Having practiced by starting small has proven to be crucial in persisting in a regular routine. Many times on the way into the health club, the thought of not walking that day crosses my mind. I am tempted to head directly to the sauna and see my buddies. If I entertain this notion and argue with myself over it, the temptation to skip the walk will win out. But, if I start small in my thinking, committing to just walking for five or ten minutes — "just to see how it feels" — I always end up taking the full walk. Life gives us many opportunities to practice on the small stuff, so we can get started on the bigger issues.

I am focused while walking, noting my lap times while praying as I circle the track. More than anything, I consider the track to be *my* workout space, existing only for me and my fellow walkers and joggers. The track is one-tenth of a mile around and borders a large workout area crammed with equipment. At peak times, more than a hundred people can be in the place, the preponderance of which are careful not to go onto the track and get off of it when walkers and joggers approach. But every now and then, someone, usually a young guy transfixed on his cell phone, which in itself I find annoying, will stand on the track, oblivious to his surroundings. A little grunt or close brush when walking past usually awakens them, and they are off by the time I come around again. But sometimes not. They just stand there, and I have to walk around them two, three, sometimes four times, adding precious seconds to my all-important "world-class" lap time. With resentment and self-righteousness building each time I pass them, conjured-up images dance in my head that range from lecturing them to having them thrown out of the club, right up through punching them out to the cheers of the masses, while being oblivious to that absurdity given my dwindling strength and advanced age. I end up squandering all the cool I've got while they continue to block my lane on the road of happy destiny, poring over the latest text or image from a would-be girlfriend or their own fantasy-world goddess. They are in a state of reverie, and I'm silently seething.

Days later, I can't think about the episode without playing it over again and again in my mind. Ironically, at the same time, out of habit I pray every day for a loving and forgiving heart! Finally, it occurs to me when praying the Act of Charity — the part about "I forgive all that injured me," I connect the dots: my prayer applies to the smarmy little peckerheads standing idly on the track as much as it does to anyone else. So, I start praying for them. I don't want to. They haven't earned it. They'll never even know what a great guy I am for doing it! Yet, I have no choice if I'm going to be relieved of the bondage of self. But in order for the prayer to work, I need to commit to something more: immediacy, brevity, and persistence.

## THE FIVE-WORD DECLARATION OF INDEPENDENCE: "I'M POWERLESS, PLEASE HELP ME"

I'm not only powerless over alcohol, but it turns out I am powerless over each of the "Seven Deadlies and Four Uglies" as well. Whenever the anger arises, right in the heat of the action, I need to say, "I'm powerless, please help me." I need to repeat it until the anger, or the call to pride, sloth, lust, or any of the remaining deadlies and uglies, subsides. And I always feel peace. This small act has been indispensable in gaining victory over my defects, especially lust, anger, pride, self-pity, and it has become an integral key to the maintenance of my spiritual condition.

Because the declaration of powerlessness and the plea for help itself is very small — only five words — it works better for me. It immediately gets my head going in the right direction. In a longer, more formal prayer, with my noisy head and the difficulty I have focusing, I'm easily distracted and can get right back into recalling the incident and feeding the anger before I even get to the end of the prayer, by which time I am merely mouthing the words. Depending on the day and the extent to which I feed my defects, I may need to say, "I'm powerless, please help me, Lord" ten, twenty, fifty times. But that doesn't matter. I don't care how many times I need to say it. I don't want the weight of the defect, the frustration, and the cascading synergy of sin on my shoulders. I don't want this defect to run amuck in my brain and migrate into others, creating a maelstrom that can be nearly impossible to escape. I want freedom from the bondage of self. I want the peace and joy of the promises.

## CUTTING PEOPLE A LITTLE SLACK

Patience, self-control, and a prayer asking for the ability to forgive are essential everyday tools. As simple as this is and as easy as it sounds, doing it didn't come naturally to me. For one thing, the old payoffs are still very much alive and inviting. Many had been ingrained into my psyche and had become an almost automatic default response. But, having broken through a few times in the heat of the action with the five-word declaration and plea, followed by the peace it rendered, doing it gradually became more natural — more natural than feeding the temptation.

Eventually, I was able to reframe the various issues. An annoyance could be reframed by acknowledging that I, too, had on many occasions been inconsiderate of others, or that I, too, had been lacking in generosity, refusing to cut someone a little slack. Most telling was that I, too, had often been guilty of the same thing that angered me in others. I was slowly becoming more patient, kinder. With lust, I was able to stop objectifying women and reframe the situation by looking away and acknowledging that they were not there to be lusted after any more than I was. That should be common sense considering most are in their thirties to fifties, and I am eighty-two! But what can I say? The restoration to sanity promised in Step 2 does not happen spontaneously by merely wishing for it or even praying for it. I need to practice the virtues as a way of life, moment by moment. I do not always do it — I often fall short. But when I do the practice, it works.

More than anything, a loving and forgiving heart can save the day in any situation.

## THE JOY OF LIVING

Some things bear repeating. So, at this point a redundancy is intentional when mentioning that in the *Twelve Steps and Twelve Traditions*, Step 12 begins and ends with a most powerful theme: the joy of living. The text held back on this until the last step. Had we started with this notion straight from the beginning, many of us despairing of our circumstances in the throes of addiction may well have dismissed it out of hand, and not without reason.

A look at the world in which we live, or our own country, sometimes our own neighborhood, too often our own families, and surely ourselves personally, and we see distress, pain, fear, despair, dishonesty, and above all, the injustice. Racism, poverty, hunger, global warming, war, refugees — the issues seem endless, the solutions barely in sight.

So, what keeps it all from falling apart? I believe it is the tens of billions of little acts of kindness we show each other every day, not because of our circumstances, but in spite of them. The spiritual awakening that feeds the dream inflames the hope for something better that we all need in order to live, the practice of the principles that gives us joy brings that same joy to others, and sharing the rewards of the practice with others disposes them to love and appreciate us.

One day on that same walking track where I encountered the smarmy little peckerhead who rudely insisted on his right to block my path, I had a mishap. I was really booking around a corner and foolishly cut it too close. An untethered cable hand grip was lying on the floor. I stepped on it, lost my balance, and fell, scraping my knee in the process. Within seconds, a young guy rushed over to me, pretty much scooped me up off the track, and made sure I was all right. It was sweet.

He was among the billions that day worldwide who, gratuitously and spontaneously, extended themselves for someone else — someone he didn't even know. And he had looked up from his cell phone to do it.

"If they can help, they will; if they can hurt, they won't."

I want to be that way, too. That is the joy of living; that is what it looks like at its most basic level.

I do not need to come up with a world-changing invention or scientific breakthrough. I do not need to design a magnificent edifice, compose a great symphony, or write a great book. I do not need applause. I do need to get over myself. Whenever I see someone lying on the track of life, I simply need to stop what I am doing, help them up, make sure they are all right, and then go back to what I was doing; perhaps even looking at my own cell phone.

# PURPOSE

As I have grown old, one of my biggest preoccupations concerns how I can be relevant, what is my purpose. While I am engaged in my community, my church, my recovery program, and my family, all of it can be just a lot of frenetic activity to keep me from getting bored. It can be a way to satisfy a somewhat A-type personality or, worse, a disguise to avoid doing something truly essential to my calling.

I find myself being directed by two great guideposts for living. First is the final sentence of Step 12, "we carried the message." The second is from my namesake James in 2:14–26: "faith without works is dead." But, inspiring as these and other sources are, for me their wisdom is all rolled into one statement made by a cultural icon when it comes to summing up what I see as my purpose.

When Johnny Cash died in 2003, Bob Dylan remarked, "Johnny was and is The North Star; you could guide your ship by him."

Indeed, each of us is called to be The North Star by which those around us can safely guide their ships through the turbulent seas of reality. I have been blessed to have many whose personal glow lit the pathways of my life, both within and outside of my recovery circle.

## THE GALAXY

During the daytime, whether blinded by the garish brightness of the sun or obscured by rain, sleet, and snow, it can be hard to recognize or even see the beauty of the lights illuminating our path. But, as the darkening sacred purple twilight of my life slowly approaches, the stars in my galaxy gradually shine more radiantly into view.

Harry, Tom D.-I, and Tom D.-II were my A.A. sponsors, and for forty-eight years, led me through the steps, guiding me through some of my most serious difficulties. Mike C., Fran C., and a host of others supported and prayed for me over many years, along with many clergy. And, then there is Mac, my current sponsor with whom I meet weekly and call almost daily — more about him later.

There were my career mentors: Leonard Boche at the State of Minnesota, whose unique insight into addiction recovery formed the public continuum of care that helped Minnesota become a model of public policy for addiction nationally; Dan Anderson at Hazelden, who, when looking at an alcoholic, didn't just see a patient with a fatal disease but a person he loved while conceiving the range of services — addiction, psychological, spiritual, and family — specifically tailored for a full recovery, thereby creating the nucleus of what would become the Minnesota Model; Governor Wendell Anderson and Wheelock Whitney, a lifelong Democrat and a lifelong Republican, who married the public and private sectors into a statewide chemical dependency initiative that has never been matched, serving both underserved and employed populations and then honoring me to implement and operate it; and at United Airlines, Dr. Dick Harper, whose unwavering support and guidance in a contentious work environment gave me an opportunity to build an exemplary internal EAP that still stands after more than forty years, and in the process, solidify my career in the EAP field.

Louie and Beth, best friends and surrogate parents, helped me to develop confidence and a sense of humor while providing guideposts by which to stay on a safe path at a critical time in my life; Father Jim Church, without whom I would never have gotten a college education, much less the social justice values I learned from the Benedictines at St. John's; the neighbors as I was growing up, through whose vigilance my mother nearly always knew what I was up to, instilling in me a belief that we never really get away with anything.

Catherine, my birth mother, a seventeen-year-old girl, unmarried and pregnant at a time and place more given to shame than to kindness, younger than all but one of my granddaughters today. I think of her dirt-poor Depression-era family so loving and supportive, but more than anything, how incredibly brave and selfless she was. I have often heard how difficult it is for a woman to decide to have an abortion, and I believe it. But I wonder how difficult it must have been for Catherine to decide to carry a baby to term and then love and care for it for several months, only to surrender it in the hope that it would have a better life. Then she lived most of her life without knowing if that hope had ever materialized.

My parents, Margaret and Stanley, uneducated but with unshakeable values and a strong work ethic, taught me the difference between right and wrong, how to pray, and the need to be dependable and honest. Most important was to be fair and considerate, best expressed by my dad, a union man, whose daily living mantra was …

*"You have got to watch out for the next guy."*

Of greatest importance, while we didn't always understand each other, we always knew we loved each other. I never had to wonder where they were — they were always present. And once I was on my own, they always answered the telephone, hoping it would be me.

Of course there are my children, Tom, Linda, Carmen, Caroline, and Kelda, and Janis's daughters, Cherie, Lisa, and Zoe. At least a chapter could be written on each without doing them justice. The best way to describe our children as a group is that they each have great hearts. Each has had their challenges, and they are a diverse group. But their loving hearts form the common bond describing who they are. One of the joys of growing old is to see how your children mature and flourish and how you can learn from their wisdom. Beyond that is the knowledge that no matter what happens, you will never be alone.

The star shining brightest is Janis, the love of my life. If not for her, I'm pretty sure I wouldn't have lived long enough to write this memoir. In addition to longevity, the quality of my life these past thirty-five years has been better than I ever would have imagined, especially these later years. It starts with being kind to each other and doing things for each other. Little things, often gratuitously. We have our patterns and codes of living, large and small. One small thing is that whoever gets up last in the morning makes the bed. But occasionally, especially if the late riser is in a hurry or hadn't had a good night's sleep and can barely drag the body from the bed into the bathroom, we'll make the bed for each other when it isn't our turn. In the total scheme of things — world peace, eradicating racism, saving the environment, achieving economic justice — this seems pretty small. But, when I am racing through my shower, running late, preoccupied with a day jammed full of stuff to do, and come out of the bathroom primed to make the bed but annoyed at the thought of the task, and I find that its already made, a lovely feeling comes over me. She was thinking about me. She did me a favor I hadn't asked for. There are countless other examples, and they go both ways. We also have quirks, our shortcomings, our arguments, and distressful moments, but Step 10 is a reliable rescuer. As important as anything, we always express our gratitude for each other and all of our blessings. We do not take anything for granted. From that first moment I held her on that dimly lit dancefloor all those years ago, she's been dancing me, as Leonard Cohen would say. Dancing me to the end of love.

## DIS-EASE: THE GATEWAY TO GROWTH

Celebrating sobriety dates is an important part of A.A. life. It happens regularly throughout the year and is always a time of joy, gratitude, and hope. Shortly after moving to Madison from Chicago, I celebrated my thirty-fifth A.A. anniversary. While there were a number of people both in St. Paul and Chicago with longer periods of sobriety, I hadn't met anyone in the groups I attended in Madison who was close to the length of time I enjoyed. Just as a certain deference is afforded those who reach an advanced age, the same is true for those with long-term sobriety. And while it certainly feels good, it can also be a trap testing one's humility.

After a few years, I found myself beginning to feel like an elder statesman, and it was uncomfortable. It was inconsistent with how I viewed myself. For one thing, I still hadn't completely come to terms with Step 3 and believing the axiom that you cannot give away something you haven't got, I felt like I was somehow flying under false colors. Another saying also bothered me, one that dwelled half-hidden in the crevices of my mind:

"In A.A., there are students and there are teachers, and the teachers all get drunk!"

I wished that someone who had more sobriety than I would show up. I was concerned that the deference might be due more to the length of my sobriety than the quality; that there was an automatic assumption I had to be doing something right to have been sober so long, and that the "something" was reflected in virtually everything I said. Considering my struggles at the time, my outside wasn't matching what was going on inside of me. My conscience told me that I should want to just be a member among members, as the *12 and 12* says, but my ego so much enjoyed the special attention. I had a very good sponsor in Tom D.-II. But we were each struggling with an issue that was seemingly intractable to both of us at the time. And with twenty years less sobriety than I had, I didn't think he was experiencing the kind of ego inflation issue I was encountering.

## MAC

Then one day at a local chapter meeting of the Employee Assistance Professionals Association, Janis met a recovering guy who was preparing to move to Madison. He was looking for an A.A. meeting. He recognized her last name and asked if she was related to me. She passed his name and number on to me, and we met for a cup of coffee. His name was David Macmaster. Everyone called him Mac.

Mac was born the year A.A. was founded, 1935, and grew up in Welland, Ontario, Canada. He had his first drink at age sixteen and almost immediately became a drunk. In his own words, the next five years were marked with violence, misadventure, terrible judgment, and a loss of all values. He had been in jail for drinking-related behavior in Australia, Canada, and the United States before he was legally old enough to lift a glass. He had the rare distinction of getting kicked out of the Canadian Navy because of his alcoholism, which was indicated as a psychiatric problem on his discharge papers. Going AWOL during wartime was not considered cool by the Canadian government.

After returning home, among several drunken episodes was one where he directed his wrath at the windows of a dance hall on Valentine's Day 1956, escaped into a nearby woods and was discovered unconscious in a water-filled ditch with his head barely above the water line. Wrapped in a sheet, he woke up naked in a funeral home with flowers around him and young women sobbing. More than sixty years later, recalling this event, Mac remarked: "There had been many things I had been able to talk my way out of, but this wasn't one of them."

A few months later, he was delinquent on the rent in his five-dollars-a-week apartment. Having downed a fifth of 150-proof rum the evening before, he arose one morning, searched his apartment for alcohol, and drank a half-empty bottle of beer flavored with cigarette butts. Some sixty years later, he would remark:

"I knew I had a problem with alcohol when I was taking drinks between my drinks."

Staggering into the bathroom, he looked in the mirror and had a spiritual experience. He didn't see a robust, twenty-one-year-old man reflected back at him. Instead it was the image of an aged, decrepit, down-and-outer whom he could barely recognize. With the image came the stark realization that he was doomed.

He reached out to his minister who wasn't available. He considered drowning himself in the Welland Canal but was deterred by the thought that he would not die immediately and would suffer greatly in the ice cold water. He called his mother for help. She had been an Al-Anon member for years and his father an active member of A.A. They arranged for him to go to an A.A. meeting on October 8, 1956, Canadian Thanksgiving Day. A family friend showed up in a car that Mac had damaged in a hit-and-run collision a few days earlier and took him to his first A.A. meeting. He hasn't had a drink since.

Over the years, Mac had six children from three marriages, which he refers to as times of "relationship distress." The times in between marriages weren't that much better, with one love interest trading him in for a Canadian Mounty. Traveling all throughout Canada, his work took him into three factories, a tavern waiting tables, a radio station where he became a star disk jockey, a uranium mine several hundred feet down in the Lake Athabasca basin, various sales and services jobs including one as a Playtex bra salesman, and a partner in a literary marketing company that featured books on paranormal UFO activity.

Practicing alcoholics are often referred to as "train wrecks." Mac had the distinction of actually being in a train wreck — a real one — after he was seven years sober! He was working in New London, Ontario, on a tobacco farm. Riding in the passenger seat after work with a friend driving, the car suddenly stalled on a railroad track. Neither Mac nor his friend was able to escape before a Canadian Pacific locomotive pulling a mile-long freight train crashed into them at fifty miles per hour. Both Mac and his friend were seriously hurt but survived. Sometime after at an A.A. gathering, a friend spotted him accompanied by a young woman, who was in the late stages of pregnancy and dubbed him "Disaster Macmaster." It stuck.

Nineteen-seventy-four found him in Decorah, Iowa, with eighteen years of sobriety. It was the beginning of the heyday for chemical dependency treatment, and he heard that the government was paying to train people — especially recovering alcoholics — to become addiction counselors. He was a natural. Mac boarded a career train that journeyed him forward on the track of addiction services for the remainder of his life. In 1981, he started an outpatient program that is still operating, and he held numerus key positions in the field over many decades. For the past several years, he has been a recognized national expert on tobacco-related illnesses, leading a battle to persuade substance abuse and mental health treatment programs to include nicotine addiction as an integral part of their treatment offerings.

## RECOVERY CAPITAL

With the kind of personal background Mac has had — just the wildly diverse ways in which he earned a living — it isn't surprising that his picture of recovery would be painted in broad strokes. Not only did he have more sobriety than I, but he could help me expand my view of recovery and how people achieved it. I was an A.A. classist while Mac was more of an iconoclast. My background included the comfort of orthodoxy starting with my Catholic upbringing and later reinforced by my professional life as I became steeped in federal procurement regulations, helped set forth EAP practices and standards, promulgated regulations on addiction treatment, and helped write laws on public health issues. All the while, I lived for forty years in one place and twenty years each in two others, all located within four hundred miles of each other. Mac, on the other hand, was laissez-faire, mining uranium, selling bras, and waiting tables across the vast expanse of Canada after having sailed the ocean blue to a different continent in a different hemisphere. Even the events triggering our entries into recovery reflect the difference. When I walked into an Al-Anon meeting thinking it was a bar and met with Harry shortly afterward, there was some measure of order and predictability for what followed. When Mac was carried into a funeral home and woke up naked without a clue about how he got there, an A.A. meeting was unlikely to have been on anyone's list of top ten nominees for a future destination.

The accumulation of all these experiences, positive and negative, form what William White and William Cloud refer to as *personal recovery capital*.[22] They are the reservoir from which our world view emerges to form the context within which each of us, in our own way, will interpret and take the steps of recovery informed by the multitude of successes and failures stored in the right side of our brains. Keeping what will work and discarding the malformed, they are the superstructure of the bridge we must build between where we are and where we hope to go, with substructure components added by others as they share elements of their recovery capital and reinforce our own.

In addition to the benefits of his vast experience and views, there have been special bonuses as my friendship with Mac has evolved over the years. As much as anything, he is a wonderful, pleasant, optimistic, funny, humble, and kind man, filled with gratitude.

Indeed, everything I have ever learned came from someone who saw things differently than I did. Especially Mac.

## NO SINGLE PATH TO RECOVERY

Ironically, Mac's view was more consistent with Bill Wilson's than mine when it came to one very important issue: the multiplicity of recovery paths. Described so well in their paper "A Message of Tolerance and Celebration: The Portrayal of Multiple Pathways to Recovery in the Writings of Alcoholics Anonymous Co-Founder Bill Wilson," Bill White and Ernie Kurtz cite many times when Wilson made emphatic statements on the subject. Moreover, a critical prerequisite to recognizing that there are various recovery paths is to first acknowledge that the path any of us has followed isn't the *only* one. Once again, we must go to the top of the list of "Seven Deadlies and Four Uglies" and set aside our pride because underscoring Wilson's statements is a profound spirit of humility.

Wilson also encouraged specific alternatives to A.A. Of those cited by White and Kurtz, the following one stood out for me:

"Bill Wilson was asked whether the principles of Recovery, Inc. — a self-help mental health recovery program founded in 1937 by

Dr. Abraham A. Low — might be used to help alcoholics. Wilson's response illustrates A.A.'s values of modesty and tolerance even in judging ideas, people, and programs counter to A.A. central tenets.

"I have always looked with great sympathy upon Recovery, Inc. The founder of that movement was a psychiatrist. In actuality, Recovery, Inc. is very much of a heresy to A.A. But it's the kind of heresy that often seems to work. Those good people operate on the basis that through a program of discipline and constant exertion of the will, their several compulsions and hexes can be directly attacked and eliminated … In many cases their results have been extraordinary. … Altogether I have the highest opinion of that outfit." (Wilson, B. 1960. Address to the National Clergy Conference on Alcoholism, New York, April 21, in *The Blue Book,* volume 12, pp. 179–210)[23]

While A.A. does not have dogma, it does have core values, and they are reflected throughout the literature. The most frequently mentioned are honesty, modesty, humility, humor, tolerance, patience, unselfishness, kindliness, love, and service. And, in *The Big Book* more than any other is inventory.

Regarding what A.A. is, Wilson humbly emphasized that its core philosophy is not new:

"At the very outset it should be made ever so clear that A.A. is a synthetic concept … Drawing upon the resources of medicine, psychiatry, religion and our own experience of recovery. You will search in vain for a single new fundamental." (Wilson, B., 1944, Basic Concepts of Alcoholics Anonymous, *New York State Journal of Medicine, 44 (16)*, pp. 1805–1808)[24]

As to different paths within the twelve-step framework, I return to my initial contact with a twelve-step program, the night I wandered into that Al-Anon meeting thinking it was a bar. Those sayings on the wall that I dismissed as trite and rarely gave much thought to during the course of my own recovery — "Let go and let God," "First things first," "Think, think, think," "One day at a time," — proved to be pivotal forty years later in the recovery of someone I love deeply and greatly admire: my daughter Caroline.

So, while this memoir reflects the path I took to reach a level of joy and peace I never imagined possible, and while I wish with every fiber of my being that all addicted people, regardless of the form of their addiction, could experience what I have, I realize each will follow their own path. It may resemble mine, or it may be significantly different. It may use the twelve steps, or it may not. In the end, it's the destination that counts. And, while benefiting from the experience, strength, and hope of others, we each need to do what works for us.

But critically, after years of research on the subject, my friend Norm Hoffman, PhD, has found a striking commonality in the various approaches to recovery: few can do it alone. "Women in Recovery," SMART, and other approaches he has studied all involve one addicted person helping another addicted person — whether one-on-one or in a group.

## THE BACKLASH AGAINST A.A.

Having said all that, it must also be said that tolerance and appreciation for multiple pathways to recovery do not justify what has become a "backlash movement" against A.A., A.A.-oriented addiction treatment, and the disease concept of addiction. Often characterizing A.A. as practicing coercive, cult-like indoctrination and a one-size-fits-all anti-professional, anti-scientific approach to recovery, its proponents pretend to accurately present A.A., how it works, and its results. While they correctly state, just as A.A. literature has for decades, that there are alternatives to twelve-step recovery, they seem unable to leave it at that. Particularly distressing is that while the leaders of this movement are long on criticism, they are woefully short on experience, and the intensive research by White and Kurtz underscores this sad reality: here's what they say in "A Message of Tolerance and Celebration":

"Defining what A.A. does and does not practice is difficult in light of the variability across Twelve Step programs, the lack of central leadership within such programs, and the variety of local practices that can be found under the Twelve Step umbrella. We have been struck by the number of people we have encountered who have talked with a few A.A. members or have attended an Open A.A. Meeting where they talked with a few willing informants and left such experiences feeling as if they understood A.A. As long-time researchers it is our experience that the person most willing to speak first on behalf of A.A. is by definition, the least qualified to do so."

That is largely because, as they write:

"Most advocates with Twelve Step recovery experience, in keeping with The Twelve Traditions, maintain anonymity at the level of press regarding their past or present affiliation with Twelve Step groups. When they speak in their advocacy roles, they do so as *persons in recovery*, not as members of A.A., NA or any other Twelve Step fellowships."

Catholic priests are bound by the Seal of Confession in which it is their absolute duty to not disclose anything they learn during the course of the Sacrament of Penance (confession), even if the sin confessed is not of a serious nature. Moreover, therapists and attorneys are bound by confidentiality regulations and codes of ethics to not disclose client information except in rare instances specifically prescribed by law. So, if someone were to inaccurately quote or falsely accuse any of these professionals, the priest, the therapist, or the attorney would have little recourse but to remain silent — they couldn't defend themselves. There is no law or sacred doctrine that applies to A.A., but there is a code of honor that is widely observed. So even the A.A. members most experienced in what the Fellowship offers cannot defend it on level footing in the media with the critics who pose as experts.

Particularly distressing to me is how dishonest some of this backlash can be. In reading any of the basic literature or even one synopsis of A.A.'s core beliefs, such as the White and Kurtz piece, it is immediately apparent that the most virulent criticism of A.A. is flatly contradicted by its actual core values.

Therefore, no one speaks for A.A. or other twelve-step programs, and that certainly includes those with scant knowledge who want to proclaim a personal viewpoint as being fresh when it has been known and written about in the core A.A. literature since the founding of the organization. And, worse, at times they misrepresent the Fellowship in the process.

## RECONCILING MY BELIEFS

The two most important organizations in my life have been Alcoholics Anonymous and the Catholic Church. One is saving my life, and I believe the other is saving my soul. One seriously questions orthodoxy, the other venerates it. So, where am I with this apparent dilemma? Simple: I believe both. As a professor at St. John's emphasized, to become educated one must recognize and accept that life is filled with paradox and ambiguity.

To begin, I do not subscribe to the relativistic notion that there is "my truth" and "your truth" and therefore nothing is absolute, everything is relative. At the same time, humility and realism are imperative when considering what the truth is. So, while I believe there is but one truth, damned if I have ever had a handle on the entirety of it. Nor do I know anyone else who has in an empirical sense. But, as for nothing being absolute and everything being relative, the statement itself is a contradiction: *Everything* necessarily includes our thoughts, deeds, and words. To say "nothing is absolute" is to make an absolute statement. Therefore, the statement itself contradicts its own assertion.

So, I had to ask myself what absolute do I see where recovery is concerned? It is simply this: Even while following certain basic principles, everyone ends up doing it their own way, whether in a twelve-step program or some other way. Failure to acknowledge and embrace this truth is to fall into an orthodoxy that can seriously impede the need in our society for more than twenty million desperate addicted people to get on the road to recovery. I can attest to my own personal experience and about my perception of how I believe a majority of people stay sober in A.A. But I cannot speak for others or for A.A. as a whole. Nor can I speak for other paths of recovery, only that they exist and are not the same as mine.

Yet, orthodoxy can be comforting in a world wracked with uncertainty. Having a life ravished by the vagaries of addiction, when finally getting on the road to recovery it can be tempting to believe that our personal journey is the "one true way." This is especially early on when the contrast between active addiction and the freedom we experience from recovery can be so stark. Having been locked in failure behind the door of addiction for years, we may feel the joy of a new and generous heart beating within us. Upon finally seeing all around us the misery addiction is causing others, we will want to share what we have found with those still suffering. In the process of trying to help others, it is only human to want to reinforce our beliefs when sharing our recovery and the way we attained it. This especially holds true when confronted with the addiction of someone we love. Having had such a tenuous relationship with the truth when we were drinking or drugging, we feel that, at last, we have found the real thing. Yet, authentic truth (not that there is any other kind) is never simple. Certainly, the truth handed down by political and religious leaders is often incomplete and frequently suspect. Too often the powerful reveal truth only to the extent that it suits them. Without humility, the manner in which we express our newfound freedom may be seen in the same light.

The brilliance of A.A.'s founders is displayed in their insight into this danger and the threat orthodoxy posed to the Fellowship. Consequently, there are no authorities in A.A. Tradition 2 clearly states:

> *"For our group purpose there is but one ultimate authority — a loving God as He may express Himself in our group conscience. Our leaders are but trusted servants, they do not govern." (12 and 12, p. 132)*

And, Tradition 3 (The Long Form):

> *"Nor ought A.A ever depend on ... conformity." (12 and 12, p. 189)*

Emphasized throughout A.A. literature is the admonition that no one speaks for A.A. And, in the *12 and 12*, page 26:

*"First, Alcoholics Anonymous doesn't demand that you believe anything at all. All of its twelve steps are but suggestions."*

So, what is my role? How should I see myself given my experience? On one hand, people are dying every moment from addiction to alcohol and other substances, not to mention the havoc wreaked by addictions to food, lust, and gambling. I am constitutionally unable to just stand by and watch it happen before my eyes without at least trying to do something. I can invite them to try the program that has saved my own life. In doing so, I cannot predict the outcome. While nearly anything may work for someone, nothing will work for everyone, not A.A. and certainly not this memoir.

At the same time, do I believe that if all twenty million addicted people in the US attended A.A. for a year, got a sponsor, took the steps, shared their experience, strength, and hope, that there would be a profound improvement in the health and well-being of the group as a whole? Absolutely! With sixty-seven thousand A.A. groups worldwide and 1.9 million members in the US alone, it is far and away the path most accessible, most trod, and most tested. But it is a path based on total abstinence.

Therefore, do I also believe, from my own experience and personal observation, that an alcoholic must stop drinking in order to recover? Yes! Mathematically it may well be that of the several hundred million alcoholics in the world, somewhere, somehow, some continued to drink and yet avoided the harmful consequences of the disease, but in fifty-four years of recovery, I haven't yet met any of them. And critically important, while some such alcoholics may exist, no one has been able to come up with a reliable diagnosis to differentiate them from those who cannot drink without harmful consequences. Moreover, as some suggest, will abstinence mean the deprivation of some essential social or cultural necessity that will seriously impede one's happiness or retard their success as a human being? It could depend on the culture, but it hardly holds true in the United States with one-third of the population already abstaining. Given that alcoholism is primary, progressive, and fatal if not arrested, and leaves a wake of misery for others to contend with, in my opinion the stakes are too high to take chances. Yet, I know from personal experience that some alcoholics apparently are just unable to abstain, and the most we can hope for is a reduction in the harm they will cause themselves and others. Again, it is virtually impossible to differentiate between them and the people I have met who went through treatment a dozen times before finding recovery in total abstinence.

So, if I am truly called to be The North Star, it simply means this: my role isn't to prescribe exactly what the route should be for those ships that may be gazing at my light because they all start from a different point and each is configured differently with different capacities to stay afloat. My job is to light the way of whatever route they ultimately take, however misdirected it may seem to be at any given time; to offer suggestions but demand nothing. To do that, I must be humbly and continuously present and aglow, simply stating what it was like for me and others I have known, what happened, and what it has been like since. While the paths may be different, common skills are necessary in navigating nearly any ship in order to keep it afloat.

## MY HOPE FOR YOU

Well, here we are, finally at the conclusion. Based on my own experience and that of many others I have personally known, I have hope. The flame of hope lit at my first A.A. meeting has seen what seemed like maelstroms and tornados of life, but it has never been extinguished. No matter what your connection may be to addiction — your own or someone else's, whether in the throes of the disease or in recovery — I can honestly say that better days lie ahead for you. I have witnessed this in myself and in countless others over these many years. If you are struggling, no matter how hopeless, no matter how helpless, no matter how powerless your life may seem, there is hope and there is help. And, most of all, there is a power greater than you. Whatever your addiction may be — alcohol or drugs, food, gambling, lust, or something else — you do not have to do the things that are making your life so miserable, things that are hurting you and those you love and who still love you, inexplicable as that may seem. And you do not need to do it alone — in fact, you probably can't do it alone.

So, my suggestion is to start small. Simply ask yourself if your life *as it is right now* was to never change, would it be good enough. If you have a desire that it change for the better, then just pick a path. Your desire will be indispensable in the success you will have, regardless of the path you follow. If you cannot pick a "good" path, pick a "lousy" one and try it. Being as honest as you can in trying to stay on that path, if you and those closest to you do not see tangible improvement within the first month to six weeks, pick a different one. If you want to avoid endless starts, failures, and regroupings, choose one with a reputation for helping people with your specific addiction. Pick up the phone and call, and then go where that call leads you.

Regardless of how your recovery comes to you, it is a gift. Like any gift, it will not benefit you if all you do is merely look at the beautifully wrapped package. You need to untie the bow, remove the wrapping, take the gift out of the box, read the instructions, and use it with whatever practice is necessary. Putting it another way, you have a river to swim across and you won't get to the other side if you just dip your toe in the water. So dive in with others who have done it themselves swimming beside you.

And, for those already in recovery, I have never subscribed to the term "recovered" because the "…ed" means it is past, completed. This is good news, because no matter how far along you are, it can get better, or more precisely, *you* can get better. Our circumstances and the "world" may get worse, but *we* get better. By better, I mean more joy and peace in our lives; more ability to feel, think and do the things that make life worthwhile. Recovery is lifelong, and whether we are doing it with the help of the twelve steps or another way, it is not a destination but a journey. Over the course of my life, I have learned that when I was drinking, no matter how good life seemed, time was an enemy; but when I got sober, no matter how difficult life may have seemed, time was a friend.

More than anything, I hope this memoir convinces you that nothing you undertake needs to be done perfectly in order to get onto the path of recovery or improve the journey once you are there. It is obvious that I am a flawed man with a plethora of challenges. Nevertheless, I have a life I would never have thought possible and it is because of the gift of my recovery — a gift for which I can never be sufficiently grateful.

Perhaps we will meet face to face some day as we trudge the road of happy destiny. At a minimum, we will be together in the fellowship of the spirit — the spirit of recovery. My grandest hope, most fervent prayer, and fondest wish are with you — that you may find peace and joy.

# ACKNOWLEDGMENTS

There are three groups of people who made this work possible: those who helped create the story of my recovery, the organizations charged with safeguarding the legacy and written material of Alcoholics Anonymous and its co-founder Bill Wilson, and the professionals who helped produce the book.

I do not believe but a rare few can attain meaningful recovery all by themselves. We all need help. In my case, there are too many to mention individually so I will try to acknowledge them as follows:

First are the thousands of recovering alcoholics who have gone before and have freely given of themselves in carrying A.A.'s message of hope.

Then there are the people, both in and out of the program, who directly impacted my life – many of whom are mentioned in this story.

Then, I have had four sponsors over the past fifty-five years: Harry, Tom D-I, Tom D-II, and Mac. Each has been indispensable to my sobriety in their guidance and love. I can never be sufficiently grateful for their generosity and wisdom.

There is my wife, Janis. Every day she makes recovery all the more worthwhile as she increases my experience, strength, hope, and joy with her love, honesty, and patience.

Darlene Smith, Senior Intellectual Property Administrator at Alcoholics Anonymous World Services, and Sally Corbett-Turco, Executive Director at Stepping Stones – Historic Home of Bill and Lois Wilson, Co-founders of AA and Al-Anon Family Groups, went above and beyond while short-staffed during the COVID-19 pandemic to secure permission to include quotations and excerpts from A.A. literature and Bill Wilson's writings.

Finally there are the book publishing folks. Self-publishing sounds a lot easier than it is. After a couple of false starts, I was fortunate to alight upon a superb team of professionals. Rich Wolf of My Word Publishing coordinated the overall production process, handling a myriad of details across more than a dozen major tasks in bringing the work to market. Victoria Wolf of Wolf Design and Marketing applied her wonderful skills to design the cover, format the text into a real book, and help develop the marketing plan. Jennifer Jas of Words With Jas LLC did a great job copy editing and proofing the material. All are top-notch professionals and wonderful to work with.

Then, there's my Higher Power, everlastingly and lovingly present. Nothing more to say.

# ABOUT THE AUTHOR

Out of respect for A.A.'s Tradition of Anonymity, the author chooses not to include autobiographical material. He simply wants to be known as Jim W., a grateful recovering alcoholic—a man who got lucky.

# NOTES

1    *The Big Book*, Alcoholics Anonymous will be referred to as "AA" when referenced hereafter.

2    D.G. Walters, "Spontaneous remission from alcohol, and other /drug abuse seeking qualitative answers to qualitative questions." American Journal of Alcohol and Drug Abuse 3 (Aug. 26, 2000): 443–460, https://pubmed. ncbinih.gov/10976668/. Comment by Norman G. Hoffman: "'Remission' ranged from around 26% to 18% depending on definition of remission. In this area of research there is sometimes an unclear diagnostic determination due to mixing abuse and dependence. I have estimates from around 20% to 60% when they include abuse."

3    The Twelve Steps and Twelve Traditions will be referred to as the 12 and 12 when referenced throughout the remainder of this book.

4    W. White and J. Kelly, "Alcohol/Drug/Substance 'Abuse': The History and (Hopeful) Demise of a Pernicious Label," Alcoholism Treatment Quarterly 29 (2011): 317–323.

5    "Epidemiology of DSM-5 Alcohol Use Disorder," JAMA Psychiatry 72(8) (Aug. 2015): 757–766, https://www.ncbi.nlm.nih.gov/pmc/articles/ PMC5240584/. Comment by Norman G. Hoffman: "This is confounded by the diagnostic criteria used. With the DSM-IV the estimate for dependence is about 6%. That said, it is estimated that 25% of Americans over the age of 18 have 'binged' in consuming 5 or more drinks in a day or 4 for women. One way to interpret this is that they have consumed to the point of being intoxicated. This study is based on the DSM-5 which will include mild alcohol use disorder: 12-month prevalence of any Alcohol Use Disorder (AUD) = 14%. Lifetime prevalence = 29%. This probably includes some who would

be considered abusers but not dependent. This report also cites 8.5% for 12-month prevalence."

6   Don Cahalan and Robin Room, "Problem Drinking Among American Men Aged 21–59," American Journal of Public Health Vol. 62, No. 11 (Nov. 1972), https://pubmed.ncbi.nlm.nih.gov/5085512/.

7   Kessler, et al, "Lifetime and 12-month Prevalence of DSM-III-R Psychiatric Disorders in the United States," Table 2, www.researchgate.net.

8   National Epidemiologic Survey on Alcohol and Related Conditions-III (NESARC-III), National Institute on Health, 2017.

9   Behavioral Health Trends in the United States: Results from the 2014 National Survey on Drug Use and Health," Substance Abuse and Mental Health Services Administration (SAMHSA), https://www.samhsa.gov/data/sites/default/files/NSDUH-FRR1-2014/NSDUH-FRR1-2014.pdf. Comment by Norman G. Hoffman: "Page 33 of this SAMHSA report has co-occurring conditions in terms of number of people. Of the 20.2 million who have a Substance Use Disorder (SUD), 7.9 million have both SUD and Mental Health Disorder (MHD )or 39%."

10  "Psychopathology in Offspring from Families of Alcohol Dependent Female Probands: A Prospective Study," Journal of Psychiatric Research 45(3) (March 2011): 285–294, https://www.ncbi.nlm.nih.gov/pmc/articles/PMC3272270/. Also, "Impact of the Number of Parents with Alcohol Use Disorder on Alcohol Use Disorder in Offspring: A Population-Based Study," The Journal of Clinical Psychiatry 74(8) (Aug. 2013): 795–801, https://www.researchgate.net/publication/256489637_Impact_of_the_Number_of_Parents_With_Alcohol_Use_Disorder_on_Alcohol_Use_Disorder_in_Offspring_A_Population-Based_Study. Comment by Norman G. Hoffman: "Given an alcohol-dependent mother, offspring have a 3.6 greater risk of alcohol use disorder." 1 parent => 2.5 fold increase in risk to kids of being alcohol dependent. 2 parents who had alcohol dependence indicated a 4.4 fold increase in risk to kids."

11  "Early Drinking Linked to Higher Lifetime Alcoholism Risk," National Institute on Alcohol Abuse and Alcoholism, July 3, 2006, https://www.niaaa.nih.gov/news-events/news-releases/early-drinking-linked-higher-lifetime-alcoholism-risk. Comment by Norman G. Hoffman: "Those who started drinking before age 14 had 47% risk of alcohol use disorder vs. 9% if drinking started at age 21."

12  In Step Six, I describe a later addition of a 5th Ugly, self-centeredness.

13  See notes 5 and 6.

14  All excerpts and quotations from Father Eric Nielsen's homilies are included with his permission.

15  All excerpts and quotations from Monsignor Kevin Holmes's homilies are included with his permission.

16  Psalm 103:8–10, Revised Standard Version of the Bible, Ignatius Edition, Copyright 2006. Division of Christian Education of the National Council of Churches of Christ in the United States of America.

17  Excerpts from Allen R. Hunt, "Everybody Needs to Forgive Somebody," Prologue, p x; included with permission of DynamicCatholic.com.

18  Excerpts from Matthew Kelly, "Four Signs of a Dynamic Catholic," Chapter Two, "Are you spiritually healthy?"p. 71, included with the permission of DynamicCatholic.com.

19  All excerpts and quotations from Rabbi Janet Marder's writings are included with her permission.

20  All excerpts and quotations from Rabbi Ismar Schorsch's writings are included with his permission.

21  All excerpts and quotations from Rabbi Paul Kipnes's writings are included with his permission.

22  All excerpts and quotations from William White's writings are included with his permission.

23  Reprinted with permission of Steppingstones. "Speech by Bill Wilson, Blue Book of the National Clergy Conference on Alcoholism is from Stepping Stones Foundation Archives' A.A. Coll., Box 10, Folder 5 of Stepping Stones, the historic home of Bill and Lois Wilson, Katonah, NY, steppingstones. org. Permission is required for further reproduction or distribution. Use of archival material does not mean that this publication's contents have been reviewed or endorsed by Stepping Stones.

24  Reprinted with permission of Steppingstones. Remarks by Bill Wilson, New York State Journal of Medicine is from Stepping Stones Archives' William Griffith Wilsons Coll., Box 41, Folder 6 of Stepping Stones, the historic home of Bill and Lois Wilson, Katonah, NY, steppingstones.org. Permission is required for further reproduction or distribution. Use of archival material does not mean that this publication's contents have been reviewed or endorsed by Stepping Stones.

The Author gratefully acknowledges the cooperation of all parties cited in these endnotes in granting permission to include excerpts from their written and spoken material.

"Access to Stepping Stones, the historic home of Bill and Lois Wilson, Katonah, NY, (steppingstones.org), and its archival materials does not necessarily imply that the author's views or conclusions in this publication have been reviewed or are endorsed by Stepping Stones. The conclusions expressed herein, and the research on which they are based, are the sole responsibility of the author."